To Eileen McNeal
Enjoy your Leed's home!

Gail Appel
Oct. 22, 2014
"pray without ceasing"
(1 Thess. 5:17)

PRAYER
Warrior

Praying According to God's Will

GAIL APPEL

CROSSBOOKS
PUBLISHING

CrossBooks™
A Division of LifeWay
1663 Liberty Drive
Bloomington, IN 47403
www.crossbooks.com
Phone: 1-866-879-0502

Edited by R. Craig McGarvey, Ed.D.

Unless otherwise noted Scripture quotations taken from the New American Standard Bible®, Copyright © 1960, 1962, 1963, 1968, 1971, 1972, 1973, 1975, 1977, 1995 by The Lockman Foundation. Used by permission. (www.Lockman.org)

Author's Note: Parentheses used in the Scripture were added by the author to clarify the subject.

First published by CrossBooks 03/26/2014

ISBN: 978-1-4627-3556-3 (sc)
ISBN: 978-1-4627-3557-0 (e)

Library of Congress Control Number: 2014904410

Printed in the United States of America.

This book is printed on acid-free paper.

Any people depicted in stock imagery provided by Thinkstock are models, and such images are being used for illustrative purposes only. Certain stock imagery © Thinkstock.

CONTENTS

ACKNOWLEDGMENTS

There are four special people I wish to thank for their support in this project.

I wish to thank R. Craig McGarvey, Ed.D., my brother in Christ, classmate, and editor for challenging me to undertake this book in the first place. He saw the book in its raw form, in a plastic box with hundreds and hundreds of 3 by 5 Prayer Cards and said that if I did not make it available to the public, all the insights which the Lord had given me over many years would perish with me and God would not get the glory He deserved. How can you argue with that kind of wisdom? Thank you Craig for all your hard work.

A special thank you to Buddy Lee Appel, my wonderful husband of 38 years who still thinks I can achieve anything I put my mind to. However, without his love and support, I would not have had the perseverance to finish the course. Thank you for being one of my readers and for the valuable suggestions you provided along the way.

To my special saint and excited reader, Jeanette Williams, whose love, prayer, encouragement, as well as her faith in my ability to stay the course and hear the voice of the Lord, a heartfelt thank you. You are such a blessing and an example to me.

To my dear friend, dedicated reader, fellow classmate and wonderful travel companion, Ann Jacobs. We have laughed together and prayed together through all of life's challenges. You will never know how much I value your friendship and support. Thank you for your excitement and cheerleading especially when you can see God's hand in a ministry before I do. Above all, thank you for your spiritual honesty!

Thank you one and all for your contribution to this book. I love you all.

Gail

PREFACE

My spiritual journey into an investigation of biblical prayer started shortly after my conversion in 1978. I was in my late twenties when the Lord called me and I have discovered since then that my testimony is unique in several aspects. While I had a personal history of Protestant church attendance as a child, I had formed neither a coherent concept of a personal God or any foundation of faith upon which to guide my adult walk.

Through the kind lifestyle witness of a coworker and the testimony of Joni Eareckson Tada in her first biography, *Joni (1976)*[1] the Lord awakened in me a sense of my own inadequacy and sinfulness. I offered up my first tentative prayer since childhood, which was something poetical such as, "Okay, if there's anyone up there, I'm listening". The Lord, in His infinite grace (and perhaps a touch of humor?) answered my prayer in dramatic fashion.

The very next morning, He arranged for me to be housebound on a workday, stuck in bed (and bathroom) with a book for company. Now, let me explain that I have always been a prolific reader, and I cannot remain inactive for any length of time without a book in my hand. Sick as I was, I reached for a book at random from my bookshelf. I will never understand how the book I grabbed was a King James copy of the *New York Bible Society Bible* with a dust jacket which included topical suggestions to look up, such as what does the Bible say about depression, or fear or finances? You get the picture. What I couldn't understand was how that Bible came to be in my home without my knowledge.

By the end of a very long day, my husband returned home to a newly born-again Christian who had read her way through much of the New

Testament. I knew beyond a shadow of a doubt, that the words were completely true and; therefore, completely trustworthy and warranted my complete obedience.

Now, you might wonder, why that little detour was necessary in describing my journey into biblical prayer? Feeding my newfound love for the Word of God, I soon stumbled upon two extraordinary verses. When I read that we are to "pray without ceasing" (1 Thessalonians 5:17), and that "… if we ask anything according to His will, He hears us" (1 John 5:14), I knew without hesitation that God expects me to pray without ceasing. I finally understood that there was such a thing as praying according to His will. Since Jesus modeled prayer frequently in His walk here on earth, clearly I needed to find out how to pray and make it a cornerstone of my walk.

That very first day of my entrance into the kingdom of heaven, the Lord impressed upon me that my life would be transforming rapidly and that I would need to keep a journal to record all the mighty miracles He had begun in my life. Later on, as I explored my spiritual gifts, one of which happens to be teaching; He told me that if He taught me something new from the Word, or applied it to my current circumstance, it would be wasted or lost unless I could retrieve it when I needed to do so. He taught me that these insights would be used either to edify myself again or to pass on His wisdom to someone else (which is, after all the purpose of all spiritual gifts, to edify the Church). Over many years, He has given me new insights into the power, purpose and privilege of prayer. This work is the result of that journey.

May God richly bless you as you explore this rich world of prayer with me.

Gail Appel

2014

CHAPTER 1

PRAYING WITHOUT CEASING

Okay, let me start by admitting that I am a dinosaur. A quick calculation of the biographical data presented in the Preface will confirm that I was raised in an era before smart phones, ipods, PC's or Facebook. I interacted socially face-to-face, on long walks, lingering over cups of coffee, and heart-to-hearts with loved ones long after the sun set. I am telling you this because I was taught that love is spelled T-I-M-E.

We do not need to be told how to communicate effectively when we are passionately discussing an upcoming Presidential election, or the Head Coach's decision to put the second string quarterback in the game last night for the last three minutes, or where you and your date should go out on Saturday night or answering the question, "How did you meet Mommy (or Daddy)? We can converse easily and animatedly with those whom we are comfortable on topics of mutual interest. However, when it comes to prayer, it feels differently and at times perhaps unnatural.

Yet, 1 Thessalonians 5:17 tells us we are to, "pray without ceasing." The verse before it says to, "Rejoice always." Why is it so hard to communicate naturally and passionately with our Heavenly Father, our Creator and Savior? We are born with a carnal nature. We respond to what our five senses can perceive and are ruled by our physical needs and desires. We are social creatures who crave companionship but God is Spirit. He loves us beyond what we can comprehend. We are His blood-bought children created for fellowship with Him. We must be spiritually awakened in order to comprehend the magnitude of His grace and His desire to have an eternal, passionate love relationship with us.

Our earthly friendships and love relationships are filled with passion and are spontaneous. We do not have trouble staying awake or having our mind stray when we are in the middle of a conversation. Can we say the same about our prayer life? Do we watch the clock when we are laughing with a friend? When our Lord is as real to us in our spiritual life as our human relations are here, we will not be self-conscious or stilted in our prayers. We will realize that we can spiritually crawl up into Abba Father's lap and tell Him our deepest secrets, our innermost hopes and desires and lean in real close to hear His answer. He is our most trustworthy friend, our strongest ally and our most loving parent. We can be totally transparent with Him and He will always protect us with His grace and mercy.

I think of prayer as my spiritual conversation with my Creator/Savior/Friend. He is always available, always forgiving, always delights in talking with me and always ready to guide me. He deserves my praise, my joy and my love. My enthusiasm for prayer should always exceed my excitement in spending the day with my best friend.

Praying without ceasing involves practicing the presence of the Lord. Practicing the presence of the Lord affects our response to our circumstances, our dependence on Him to meet our every need and our gratitude for the beauty of this world. He provides us with our five senses to interact with our world and provides many opportunities to deepen our relationship with Him. Even our fears, our frustrations and our confusion can drive us to our knees in surrender to His paternal love. In Philippians 4, God again directs us to rejoice and pray. Our prayer life transforms our thought life: "Finally, brethren, whatever is true, whatever is honorable, whatever is right, whatever is pure, whatever is lovely, whatever is of good repute, if there is any excellence and if anything worthy of praise, let your mind dwell on these things" (Philippians 4:8).

God has designed the Church to be His agent here on earth: "God shapes the world by prayer. Prayers are deathless. The lips that uttered them may be closed in death, the heart that felt them may have ceased to beat, but the prayers live before God and God's heart is set on them and prayers outlive the lives of those who uttered them" (E. M. Bounds).[2]

CHAPTER 2

GOD'S WILL

Once I established the inescapable fact that God's Word is true and that I now belonged to Him by virtue of my repentance and belief that God's Son died in my place to pay for my sins, I recognized that along with His many blessings came obligations. If I am committed to following Jesus as my Lord, there are certain expectations that come along with that relationship.

Prayer is the chief means by which we access God's throne of grace. He prepares our hearts and minds for our eternal citizenship in His kingdom. As I have shared in the Prayer Card section of this book, the kingdom of heaven is the reign of God in a person's life. This kingdom life has already started in the heart of every believer. We have immediate and continual access to God's heart and ear, to both receive His incredible wisdom and love, as well as the privilege to bow before Abba Father and pour out our hearts and needs before Him.

But there are very distinct guidelines regarding this prayer life, just as there are for nearly every other aspect of our walk with Him. In 1 John 5:14 we read, "And this is the confidence which we have before Him, that, if we ask anything according to His will, He hears us." Did you catch that? What in the world does "according to His will" mean? If God's Word is His love letter to us, and it is true; and it is our obligation before Him to "pray without ceasing" (1 Thessalonians 5:17), then apparently our Dad is trying to teach us something important here. Prayer has rules and He gets to set them!

How, I wondered, do I know whether my prayers are according to His will? Here is where this journey gets exciting. God is pleased to give us all the wisdom necessary to follow Him in obedience. So if I wanted to know how to pray according to His will, I needed to ask Him! This may sound silly or even hyper-spiritual, but over the course of three plus decades, I have learned to hear God's still quiet voice in my spirit. Usually, it is confirmed by His Word. This is crucial because the sad truth is that we are seriously flawed. "The heart is more deceitful than all else and is desperately sick; who can understand it" (Jeremiah 17:9)? Why would I trust my own heart to determine God's will?

He directed my attention to Jesus' strange interaction with Satan as described in Matthew 4. Jesus had been baptized by His cousin John and was directed by the Holy Spirit into the wilderness to be tempted by the devil. That particular event could take a whole year to study all by itself. However, what God directed me to notice was Jesus' strategy in resisting the temptation. Satan is a deceiver and the father of lies, so it is no surprise that he tried to misuse Scripture to cause Jesus to commit presumptuous sin. Presumptuous sin is committed deliberately, willfully and is born of pride and self-confidence. Satan even promised Jesus the world if He would worship him. Jesus could have called down angels, He could have petitioned His heavenly Father but He did something even more startling. He quoted Scripture to Satan! God's wisdom for victory over the devil's lies is found in the living Word. It sounds so simple, but what was the result?

"Then Jesus said to him, "Begone, Satan! For it is written, 'You shall worship the Lord your God, and serve Him only.'" Then the devil left Him; and behold, angels came and began to minister to Him" (Matthew 4:10-11).

There it is! The foolproof strategy for determining the will of God is to find the relevant Scripture and pray it back to our Heavenly Father. Whether the issue is spiritual warfare, confusion over important decisions, a health crisis, or a relationship that is about to implode, the answer is to follow Jesus' model. Why is this so necessary? It is absolutely necessary because we are too flawed to have God's perspective on our circumstances.

As you read through this book, I will discuss the balance between praying Scripture back to God and praying as David did, a man after God's own heart (Acts 13:22). My experience is that researching and using these Prayer Cards on a regular basis brings God's perspective to my worship as well as my prayer time and gives me peace in the storms of life.

CHAPTER 3

EFFECTIVE PRAYER

I was very excited about this new method of prayer. However, it turned out that it involved many lessons to be learned in the "School of Prayer." Andrew Murray, a nineteenth century pastor and writer, coined that phrase in the title of his classical work on prayer called, *With Christ in the School of Prayer*,[3] and I find it very apt.

When I started this "course," I would typically begin with a time of praise and worship, followed by personal confession and lifting up my needs, and then interceding for my husband, family members, coworkers, Bible Class members, pastors and on down my mental list. It was fascinating to research each topic, defining the term and finding appropriate Scripture. In the early days, I used my extensive Christian library to create each Prayer Card and added almost daily to the box of index cards over many years. I found my understanding of each subject expanding as time went on. When I revisited a subject at a later date to pray for someone, I frequently needed to add a Scripture or a definition to address that particular situation.

My prayers had a new urgency to them and I felt empowered as I petitioned my Father on my own behalf and those around me in my little corner of the world. But God had only just begun. Prayer has this uncanny way of changing you. I began to realize that prayer is an incredible privilege and I needed to see the world from His point of view in order to pray effectively. God drew my attention to the second part of one Scripture verse. "... The effective prayer of a righteous man can accomplish much" (James 5:16). I was intrigued by the term, "effective prayer." We will return to James' teaching about prayer in Chapter 5, The Prayer of Faith. However, I want to explore this concept of praying effectively first.

Surely, if my prayers mattered, if they are part of my responsibility as a committed Christian, then it is vital that they be effective. But, how in the world do I determine whether they are or not? One of the definitions of righteousness from my Prayer Card is, "whatever conforms to the revealed will of God" (p. 241). Coupling my prayer with Scripture seemed to me a good way to conform to His will. However, it still did not address the issue of effectiveness.

Did I mention that we serve a powerful and creative awesome God? I discovered a wonderful truth along the way. If I am willing to put in the time, He will direct my path and teach me the next step... not steps. What is the old adage? We make time for what is important to us. I was getting more excited by the day but He had a huge surprise in store for me.

At that time, I belonged to a medium sized rural southern church which had a heart for short term missions. This church sent small groups out from the congregation to serve both in Africa and Mexico on a regular basis. I had the privilege of serving on one of those mission teams. One particular Sunday, a team was presented at the altar which was going to Kenya, I believe, to minister to a church and orphanage. The pastor asked for volunteers to come forward in a show of support as he prayed over the team. I noticed that my Bible Study Teacher was among those kneeling up front, and with many others, went forward to lay hands on him as the pastor prayed. When the prayer was over Jerry looked up, saw me among the crowd and specifically asked me to pray for him while he was in the field. I was a little surprised at the urgency of his request, since clearly, we had all committed to support them in prayer but I readily agreed.

The next day, as I came before the Lord in prayer, He directed me to record the topics I prayed for during Jerry's missionary trip. I had no idea what was happening on the ground and I was totally dependent on God to direct my prayers. I understood that this was an incredible opportunity to see if I was hearing from the Lord or superimposing my thoughts rather than being guided by the Holy Spirit. On the Wednesday of the Mission Team's return, I arrived at the church for Choir Rehearsal and went to find Jerry who led an Awana group (a children's faith ministry) in another building. I handed him the list of topics I prayed for him along with the dates and asked him to take a look at it when he had free time and let me know whether they made sense to him.

I had been very confused as I prayed in his absence. I was given two specific prayers; one for safety and the other for a doctrinal topic such as judgment. The prayer for safety was offered after they had already arrived in Africa (I thought) and the second prayer was offered later on in the week. The prayer about "judgment" did not make any sense to me. In truth, I thought I had "heard wrong."

The next Sunday, I missed the service for the first time I could remember. I became ill suddenly and had no choice but to remain home. My best friend was sitting in the Choir loft and gave me the following account later. As was the custom after such mission trips, various members were given the opportunity to share their experiences with the congregation. When Jerry rose to speak, he had my list in his hand and was pale and shaken. He turned to see if I was behind him in the choir loft but the Lord had carefully removed me from the picture. This was not about me. This was a God-moment. He explained about our agreement to be prayer partners throughout this trip and explained about the list in his hand.

On the day that I prayed for his and the team's safety, they had already arrived in Africa overnight but had not yet been picked up from the airport. The host pastor and his son, the worship leader, drove two vans to pick up our group. On the trip back to their village, the van driven by the worship leader overturned and pinned his arm which was resting on the window ledge under the vehicle. Sadly, his arm had to be amputated later. Thankfully, our entire mission team escaped any serious injury. Later that week, in spite of the fact that there were three ministers among them, much to his surprise, Jerry was asked to speak extemporaneously on the very subject I had been directed to pray about. Jerry clearly was overwhelmed by the hand of the Lord's protection on him through the miracle of directed prayer!*

I had my confirmation from my Father. If I would be diligent in my commitment to pray regularly and faithfully, He would make sure my prayers were effective. Since I was praying Scripture back to the Lord, I had this additional promise, "So shall my word be which goes forth from My mouth; it shall not return to Me empty, without accomplishing what I desire, and without succeeding in the matter for which I sent it" (Isaiah 55:11).

I believe with all my heart that if we make ourselves available to the Holy Spirit for the ministry of intercession, He will honor that commitment and use our prayers to effect all of eternity, one prayer at a time! Someday, I am equally sure that we will be able to witness the results of our prayers from the perspective of Heaven!

*Note:
Isaac, the Worship Leader was able to lead worship a week later, before the mission team returned home. I had the good fortune to play volleyball with him later that summer when he was visiting the United States to have a prosthetic arm fitted. He is an excellent athlete. Our church sponsored his trip and the medical expenses, and he is a delightful Spirit-filled joyous brother in the Lord.

CHAPTER 4

TWO-WAY COMMUNICATION

One of the hardest concepts for me to grasp has been that prayer must be two-way communication. As I struggle to understand why this is so difficult, it occurs to me that it is because the Church does not have a balanced understanding of the purpose and nature of prayer and; therefore, does not model prayer accurately.

One of my pet peeves is when pastors ask the congregation to bow their heads and join them in silent prayer and then never once stop talking about what they should be praying for. When they finally run out of gas, they pray a thirty second prayer, and ta-dah, corporate prayer is over! I believe the Lord may have somewhat the same reaction when we come before Him with our list of requests, finishing with in Jesus' name, and then we are on our way.

Prayer is much more than that. Prayer is the meshing of human and divine will in accomplishing God's eternal purpose. Prayer is a dialog between God and His children. Prayer is meant to soften our hearts and give us eyes and ears which are open to His spiritual guidance. Proverbs 20:12 says, "The hearing ear and the seeing eye, the Lord has made both of them." But He is not talking about our senses here.

Jesus elaborates further when He admonishes His disciples in Mark 8:17-18. "And Jesus, aware of this, said to them, "Why do you discuss the fact that you have no bread? Do you not yet see or understand? Do you have a hardened heart? "Having eyes, do you not see? And having ears, do you not hear?" Without spiritual discernment, we are not equipped to act as God's agents here on earth. One of prayer's chief purposes is to realize that we are completely powerless to pray or act without His transforming power working in us.

Isaiah is a good example of a man whose character was permanently changed by his encounter with God. In Isaiah 6 we read, "… I saw the Lord sitting on a throne, lofty and exalted, with the train of His robe filling the temple… And one (Seraphim) called out to another and said, "Holy, Holy, Holy, is the Lord of hosts, the whole earth is full of His glory." And the foundations of the thresholds trembled at the voice of him who called out, while the temple was filling with smoke. Then I said, "Woe is me, for I am ruined! Because I am a man of unclean lips, and I live among a people of unclean lips; for my eyes have seen the King, the Lord of hosts" (Isaiah 6: 1, 3-5). We learn about our spiritual condition as we bow before the Throne of God. Isaiah learned to reflect the God he represented while on his knees before Him.

God understands the fact that we do not come by our desire to pray naturally. That is why He provides us with intercessors: "And in the same way the Spirit also helps our weakness; for we do not know how to pray as we should, but the Spirit Himself intercedes for us with groanings too deep for words" and "who is the one who condemns? Christ Jesus is He who died, yes, rather who was raised, who is at the right hand of God, who also intercedes for us" (Romans 8: 26, 34). This does not absolve us of the responsibility of prayer, but with time and sanctification, it changes us into reflections of Him. Our prayers change as we are changed.

I have come to believe that the primary purpose of prayer is to seek Him, not His blessings. They are the by-product of a loving Father. "But from there you will seek the Lord your God, and you will find Him if you search for Him with all your heart and all your soul" (Deuteronomy 4:29). We intercede for ourselves and others out of an earnest desire to fulfill His will. "Thy kingdom come. Thy will be done in earth, as it is in heaven" (Matthew 6:10 KJV).

Developing an attitude of listening for God's still quiet voice requires two things; taking your hands off the steering wheel of your life, and having an attitude of prayer which is, I believe, what praying without ceasing is all about. I ask for God's wisdom about how to proceed in a matter or to edify me on a topic, so I can understand it from His perspective. I have learned that I can leave that request at the altar. When my will is submitted to His, He will answer in His time. I enjoy His creativity in responding to me. It has come in the form of a Bible verse, a praise song lyric, a magazine article, a book, a trusted friend, or just a confirmation in my spirit that I know that I know that I know. He is as creative as He is awesome. He always answers and always on time.

Whether He is placing names of people in my heart to pray over, whispering a prayer need into my soul or finding an unending army of lost objects, He always comes through. Through this labor of love, I have come to realize that no prayer goes unheard or unanswered. Each time I have confirmation of His love and His endless desire to give good gifts to His children. I have also been taught, by my Father, that each blessing deserves a heartfelt thank you! It has become automatic and joy-filled. He uses our neediness to bring us to our knees so He can fill our hearts and our lives with His abundant lovingkindness. We can honestly rejoice in our trials and tribulations because they always end in the sweet atmosphere of prayer in His Throne Room.

CHAPTER 5

THE PRAYER OF FAITH

What is a prayer of faith and what role does my faith have on my prayer life? Let us return to James 5 and examine James' exhortation on prayer. Within the closing verses of his book, he gives examples of several types of prayer. In the middle of his admonition is this startling statement, "… and the prayer offered in faith will restore the one who is sick, and the Lord will raise him up, and if he has committed sins, they will be forgiven him" (James 5:15). There it is, "the prayer offered in faith."

My favorite definition of faith can be found in my faith card in the Prayer Card on page 132. Faith accepts, appropriates and applies the facts found in Scripture. But we have no right to be puffed up over our personal faith; it is a gift from God: "For by grace you have been saved through faith; and that not of yourselves, it is the gift of God" (Ephesians 2:8).

Over and over again, Our Savior clearly identifies the importance of personal faith in answered prayer. In the book of Mark, "… a woman who had had a hemorrhage for twelve years" (Mark 5:25) followed Jesus around. "For she thought, "If I just touch His garments, I shall get well" (Mark 5:28). When she received her healing, Jesus made this startling statement, "And He said to her, "Daughter, your faith has made you well; go in peace, and be healed of your affliction" (Mark 5:34). Did you catch that? Her faith made her well. Over and over again in Matthew 9:22, Luke 7:50 and Mark 11:23 He makes the same statement. Whether we seek healing, forgiveness, salvation, or a miracle, the requirement does not change. We need to exercise faith. God will answer in His wisdom and sovereignty.

Jesus makes an amazing promise. He says, "... Have faith in God. "Truly I say to you, whoever says to this mountain, 'Be taken up and cast into the sea,' and does not doubt in his heart, but believes that what he says is going to happen, it shall be granted him. "Therefore I say to you, all things for which you pray and ask, believe that you have received them, and they shall be granted you" (Mark 11:22-24). It is important to remember here, that God does not violate His own Scripture. We have already learned that prayer needs to be in accordance to His will, but here He is discussing an entirely different concept, our belief or personal faith.

Why is this personal faith so important? In the last chapter, Two-Way Communication, I pointed out that prayer changes us. Without faith in our omnipotent Father, our inclination is to think that our words or our walk entitle us to God's grace and blessings. Nothing could be further from the truth. In reality, we are weak and vacillating sinners, who do not even know how to pray. Therefore, even our faith is tarnished by our fallen character. When we acknowledge our inability to change our nature or our circumstances or our need for His guidance and provision, miraculous things occur!

In Mark 9, Jesus approaches a crowd gathered around His disciples. A father has brought his demon possessed son to be healed and the disciples could not heal him. Our compassionate Savior entered into this poor man's life as He so often does, to meet the physical need while at the same time edifying the spiritual realm: "And He asked his father, "How long has this been happening to him?" And he said, "From childhood. "And it has often thrown him both into the fire and into the water to destroy him. But if You can do anything, take pity on us and help us!" And Jesus said to him, "'If You can!' All things are possible to him who believes." Immediately the boy's father cried out and began saying, "I do believe; help my unbelief" (Mark 9:21-24).

Not exactly an impressive prayer is it? "I do believe; help my unbelief." But Jesus healed his son. Why? Because this father has, to the best of his ability, put his trust in Jesus' ability to heal. The father knew his faith was weak, and he had just seen Jesus' disciples fail in their attempt to heal through prayer. However, he also knew that there was no other power in heaven or on earth who could help his son so he timidly reached out for help.

Remember the definition of prayer from Chapter 4? Prayer is the meshing of human and divine will in accomplishing God's eternal purpose. Our Lord quickens our spirit, making us alive to His promises and His attributes, empowering us to ask for His intervention in our lives and in our world. His earnest desire is for us to know Him in all His majesty. He invites us to trust in His holiness, in His lovingkindness and in His sufficiency. It is not a matter of the size of our faith, but rather the size of our God that is important.

In a parallel passage to the healing of the demon-possessed son, Jesus' disciples asked Him, "... Why could we not cast it out?" And He said to them, "Because of the littleness of your faith; for truly I say to you, if you have faith as a mustard seed, you shall say to this mountain, 'Move from here to there,' and it shall move; and nothing shall be impossible to you" (Matthew 17:19-20). Lack of faith is the cause of unanswered prayer. A mustard seed is one of the smallest seeds God ever created, but one of the fastest growing plants. We need to keep the size of our God in our spiritual vision, not the size of our problem.

Returning once again to James 5, Jesus' half-brother gives us an illustration of just how powerful a prayer of faith can be. "Elijah was a man with a nature like ours, and he prayed earnestly that it might not rain; and it did not rain on the earth for three years and six months.

And he prayed again, and the sky poured rain, and the earth produced its fruit" (James 5:17-18). The complete story can be found in 1 Kings 17 and 18. The purpose of this extraordinary prayer was to prove to the evil King Ahab that Baal had no power over the rain; the maker of heaven and earth did!

George Muller[4] is one of my favorite examples of a man who had a firm grasp of the reality of the power of the prayer of faith. He was an English pastor who began a ministry to orphans in 1835. Mr. Muller was able to care for over 10,000 children in his lifetime raising approximately $7,200,000 through prayer alone. He never fundraised or asked for outside prayer support for his orphans. He prayed for their needs and taught the orphans to pray in faith. They were privileged to see their mighty God miraculously provide for them over and over again.

Listen to the heart of God. "If you then, being evil, know how to give good gifts to your children, how much more shall your Father who is in heaven give what is good to those who ask Him" (Matthew 7:11)! The prayer of faith is simply about asking our loving Father for what He already wants to provide.

CHAPTER 6

PRAYING IN THE SPIRIT

I would like to turn now to a topic that will be outside the comfort zone of many Christians. The Bible refers to something called, "praying in the Spirit." "With all prayer and petition pray at all times in the Spirit, and with this in view, be on the alert with all perseverance and petition for all the saints" (Ephesians 6:18).

But what exactly does it mean to pray in the Spirit? In essence it means that the Holy Spirit both guides and inspires our prayers and brings God's response to us. I like to use the archaic word, unction, to describe the process. Unction means to pour forth a divine or spiritual influence on a person. This is a powerful word picture! It is more than Christ or the Holy Spirit interceding for us, as powerful as that may be. It is the process the Holy Spirit works in us to enable us to possess a knowledge of the truth and to act upon it.

Here's how the apostle John describes it. "But ye have an unction from the Holy One, and ye know all things" (1 John 2:20 KJV). That is quite a statement. But he goes on to elaborate. "And as for you, the anointing which you received from Him abides in you, and you have no need for anyone to teach you; but as His anointing teaches you about all things, and is true and is not a lie, and just as it has taught you, you abide in Him" (1 John 2:27). This is not a license to ignore biblical doctrinal teaching, but it does mean that the Holy Spirit will help us discern truth from error and keep us from going astray. I have received this unction more times than I can count while hearing a sermon or reading a Christian book; when the Holy Spirit interrupts abruptly and says, "Don't receive that, it is error!" He always gives me a Bible verse or truth to edify me to prevent me from receiving and accepting false or unbalanced doctrine.

Paul has a wonderful and miraculous example of the unction of the Holy Spirit. In 2 Corinthians 12 he relates this experience: "I know a man in Christ who fourteen years ago-- whether in the body I do not know, or out of the body I do not know, God knows-- such a man was caught up to the third heaven... was caught up into Paradise, and heard inexpressible words, which a man is not permitted to speak" (2 Corinthians 12:2, 4). Whatever the Lord showed him, it was so compelling that he was given a "thorn in his flesh" to keep him from boasting about what he had received. God has a purpose for His every action. So, it is clear that Paul needed that knowledge to guide him or motivate him in his ministry. As a matter of fact, if you follow Paul's life subsequent to his miraculous conversion, he encountered many visions and trances throughout his life, visitations of the Lord to guide him.

Yet another such encounter is reported in Acts 10. Both Cornelius, a Roman centurion, and the apostle Peter were praying to the Lord and both received a vision regarding a holy appointment God was arranging between them. Both were given very clear directions as to where to go and whom to meet. The purpose was for Cornelius to receive crucial teaching about the Gospel and the result was miraculous. Peter shared the truth with Cornelius "Of Him (Jesus Christ) all the prophets bear witness that through His name everyone who believes in Him receives forgiveness of sins". While Peter was still speaking these words, the Holy Spirit fell upon all those who were listening to the message. And all the circumcised believers who had come with Peter were amazed, because the gift of the Holy Spirit had been poured out upon the Gentiles also" (Acts 10:43-45). The Gentiles were received into the Church!

God has provided the Holy Spirit to all believers to build up our faith and direct our prayers. "But you, beloved, building yourselves up on your most holy faith; praying in the Holy Spirit" (Jude 1:20). He even invites us to "Call to Me, and I will answer you, and I will tell you great and mighty things, which you do not know" (Jeremiah 33:3). As we learn to hear and instantly respond to His direction, He gives us more knowledge. It is the meshing of human and divine will in action.

I do have an illustration from my personal life that is indeed miraculous, but because of my spiritual history with Spirit-directed prayer and knowledge, I was not all that surprised by the Lord's intervention. I had seen it before. However there are several Emergency Medical Technicians in Catskill, New York that are still shaking their heads over it!

I was a member of an ambulance crew assigned to monitor two radio frequencies used by our teams in the field. The manager that day was out in the garage bay working on one of the vehicles. The radio crackled to life and I heard the driver of one of the rigs call in that he was experiencing mechanical trouble and to stand-by. The radio went dead. So I immediately attempted to radio him back, but could not successfully contact him. I informed the manager of the incident and we tried repeatedly to attempt to get him to repeat his transmission. Finally in frustration, we asked the driver in a one way S.O.S. to land-line the office immediately. This is an unusual request to make of a team on an active call. Shortly thereafter, a very shaken driver called in to report that when he received the urgent call, he was just approaching a toll booth phone at the side of the road on the New York State Thruway. When he went to slow down, he discovered that he had no brakes! Had he approached the actual toll booth farther down the road at full speed he would undoubtedly have crashed. Yet, he had never made the radio contact that I distinctly heard! When the crew returned to the office, the entire staff eyed me with awe and fear for the rest of the shift. There was no mistaking the fact that they had just witnessed a miracle and they knew it. If we are "prayed up" and have a submitted spirit, God can use us in amazing ways to achieve His will here on earth.

CHAPTER 7

GOD'S CREATIVITY

One of the reasons that this journey to know my Lord better has been so exciting is that He is infinitely creative. Now that may seem like a strange attribute to celebrate, but we mere mortals have a hard time relating to the spiritual realm and our attention naturally wanders from that which we cannot touch and see.

Think about how many different ways God interacted with man in Scripture. He spoke to Moses from a burning bush. He led Israel through the Sinai Peninsula from a pillar of cloud and fire. He spoke to many men through visions and He even spoke to a false prophet named Balaam through a donkey! My Father is a master at getting His children's attention.

I have prayed frequently over the years for the Lord to revive my prayer life. While it is true that we are admonished to "pray without ceasing," we must never forget that prayer is the principle means through which God communicates with us and we learn to depend on Him and participate in the eternal Church. Jesus taught us to pray, "Thy kingdom come. Thy will be done, on earth as it is in heaven" (Matthew 6:10).

The Lord's relationship with us is personal and full of lovingkindness. He desires our prayer life to be passionate and vital and wants us actively engaged in the process. He even warns against a stale, meaningless form of prayer. "And when you are praying, do not use meaningless repetition, as the Gentiles do, for they suppose that they will be heard for their many words" (Matthew 6:7). When I get into a spiritual rut, my prayers seem to bounce off the ceiling and my mind and heart are not actively engaged in the process. Can you identify? Yet, I know without a shadow of a doubt that my Lord and Savior is worth much more than a corner of my heart and mind!

What makes my relationship with Him so vital and exciting is the innumerable ways He has answered my pray to revive my prayer life. One of the first concepts that got my attention was to visualize being in His presence while I pray, which is in fact what is happening in the Spirit. Sometimes I picture myself kneeling before His heavenly throne and sometimes I picture Him walking into the room and sitting down beside me and conversing face-to-face. Sometimes I recall that famous picture of Jesus surrounded by children, loving on them. I have learned to trust the fact that if I have thought about an issue, He already knows it, so I may as well bring it up in prayer.

My heavenly Father and I have a long history together by now, and sometimes when I am feeling discouraged by my ministries or wondering why I feel distant and unloved, He holds me in His arms and reminds me of all the divine appointments we have had in the past, so miraculous that they are hard to fathom. I recall two occasions when, as part of a church visitation team, I had the opportunity to pray with two families who were in desperate need of prayer and fellowship. He gave me the privilege of being part of a holy prayer team. One family we visited had just learned that their father had just had a heart attack in Afghanistan and the mother was on the phone with the hospital trying to determine whether to leave him there or risk transporting him back to the United States for treatment. The two daughters answered the door when we knocked. One daughter was a senior in high school and the other was in kindergarten. The older daughter was clearly trying to hold herself together for her mother and younger sister's benefit. However, you could see the fear on her face. The little one was clinging desperately to her sister's leg overwhelmed with the news. We had a prayer meeting right there on their front stoop and though perfect strangers, (well maybe not perfect) received hugs and smiles through their tears when it was over.

The other divine appointment was a visit to a homeschooling family with numerous children. We were invited in and spent time getting to know them and speaking to them about our church. As we wound down our fellowship time with them, we asked as we always did, whether there were any prayer requests we could lift up before the throne together with them. The parents looked quietly at one another and I saw the father nod his head. The mother told us that they had just had a baby the previous Friday and they knew before the delivery that the baby was not going to survive. They planned for a birth and a funeral that Sunday at the same time! We were able to love on them, supply a gift basket to the family and met them at the door and escorted them into our church service the following Sunday. When we make ourselves available to serve, He puts us in the right place at the right time and there is nothing on earth so satisfying as to be used by God to further His kingdom here on earth.

The Lord has given me many creative ideas over the years to enhance both my prayer life and my personal worship. I have prayed through songs, worshipped my way through the psalms, laughed together over "spiritual coincidences," the list is endless. One time as I was struggling to confess "all my past sins," He sent me on a spiritual retreat to a hotel room where I spent 24 hours on my knees going over every event in my life, confessing sins all along the way. It turns out that the problem was not forgiveness, but rather not leaving the sins at the cross. They were covered by the blood of Christ. Satan was constantly bringing them back up again to sabotage my walk and incapacitate me. Now, if I am tempted to wallow in historical sins, God brings me right back to that hotel room in my spirit. Been there, done that. Buried! Corrie ten Boom, a Dutch believer who sheltered Jews in her home during World War II and served time in a concentration camp, later became a *Tramp for the Lord*,[5] visiting over sixty countries sharing about God's sufficiency even in a concentration camp and became a prolific Christian writer. One of my favorite quotes from her books is: "Maybe because the sea is never far from a Hollander's mind, I like to think that that's way into the deepest ocean, gone forever... Then God places a sign that says 'No Fishing Allowed!'" Apparently, this imaginative prayer idea has been around for a long time.[6]

God has infinite ways available to Him to teach us, encourage us and even admonish us. If we maintain a teachable spirit, He will show us many exciting sides to His holy character. Last night, as is my custom, I read a portion of Scripture just before lights out. I am currently reading through a list of *365 Key Bible Passages*.[7] I was excited to find that the passage for yesterday was my favorite Psalm, 139. As I read it, with new eyes, I realized that it would be relevant to this topic on creativity. But I've slept since then, so it immediately went wherever creative thoughts go when you don't write them down. As I pondered how to end this chapter, He brought that Psalm back up into my conscious mind. In verses 1 and 2 we read, "O Lord, Thou hast searched me and known me. Thou dost know when I sit down and when I rise up; Thou dost understand my thought from afar." My Father knows me thoroughly because He created me; "My frame was not hidden from Thee, when I was made in secret, and skillfully wrought in the depths of the earth" (Psalm 139:15). He is omniscient, (He knows all things). "How precious also are Thy thoughts to me, O God! How vast is the sum of them! If I should count them, they would outnumber the sand" (Psalm 139:17-18). He uses that intimate knowledge of my nature and His vast wisdom to direct every aspect of my spiritual life. "Search me, O God, and know my heart; try me and know my anxious thoughts; and see if there be any hurtful way in me, and lead me in the everlasting way" (Psalm 139:23-24). The Master of the Universe can keep our prayer life and our worship experience endlessly engaging and personal and tailor made to our own unique personality (which incidentally, He made as well).

CHAPTER 8

DAVID'S HEART

In Acts 13, we read an extraordinary statement about a man who was a murderer and an adulterer. Verse 22 says, "And after He had removed him (Saul), He raised up David to be their king, concerning whom He also testified and said, 'I have found David the son of Jesse, a man after my heart, who will do all My will'".

David started out on fire for the Lord as a teenager. He faced down a giant while the entire army of Israel hid in fear: "Then David said to the Philistine, "You come to me with a sword, a spear, and a javelin, but I come to you in the name of the Lord of hosts, the God of the armies of Israel, whom you have taunted. "This day the Lord will deliver you up into my hands, and I will strike you down and remove your head from you. And I will give the dead bodies of the army of the Philistines this day to the birds of the sky and the wild beasts of the earth, that all the earth may know that there is a God in Israel" (1 Samuel 17:45-46).

Later, after he had been king for a while, pride and independence from God led him to commit some unbelievable sins, but we have a record of his heart in the book of Psalms. "Be gracious to me, O God, according to Thy lovingkindness; according to the greatness of Thy compassion blot out my transgressions. Wash me thoroughly from my iniquity, and cleanse me from my sin. For I know my transgressions, and my sin is ever before me. Against Thee, Thee only, I have sinned, and done what is evil in Thy sight, so that Thou art justified when Thou dost speak, and blameless when Thou dost judge" (Psalm 51:1-4).

What are we to make of this dichotomy? Simply this, David was a sinner. We all have the capacity to commit all manner of sin. The question is, what do we do about it? Hide from it? Rationalize it away? Or own it, confess it, and throw ourselves on the mercy of our Lord and Savior who alone has the capacity to forgive? The book of Psalms is a beautiful account of a man who recognizes his condition and seeks hard after God. It has become my personal source of worship. Why? Because David was forgiven much; therefore, he loved much. Jesus speaks about this same issue when He points to an immoral woman who was bathing His feet with her tears saying, "For this reason I say to you, her sins, which are many, have been forgiven, for she loved much; but he who is forgiven little, loves little" (Luke 7:47).

In Chapter 2, God's Will, I mentioned that there needs to be a balance between praying Scripture back to the Lord and praying as David did. To put it more simply; "To every thing there is a season, and a time to every purpose under the heaven..." (Ecclesiastes 3:1 KJV). Sometimes we need to petition the Lord for needs to be met or guidance, and sometimes we need simply to seek the Lord. David learned this in the course of his lifetime. By spending time in His Throne room, he was able to worship with his whole heart:

"I will sing of the lovingkindness of the Lord forever; to all generations I will make known Thy faithfulness with my mouth" (Psalm 89:1). On another occasion, "David was dancing before the Lord with all his might" (2 Samuel 6:14).

There are times in my prayer life, when the Lord needs to remind me that Jesus withdrew to a quiet place to seek His Father's face. I presume that He did not lug a binder of prayer cards around with him. We are instructed, "... You shall love the Lord your God with all your heart, and with all your soul and with all your mind" (Matthew 22:37). The Lord has much to say about our heart attitude. He even warned the church in Laodicea, "I know your deeds, that you are neither cold nor hot; I would that you were cold or hot. 'So because you are lukewarm, and neither hot nor cold, I will spit you out of My mouth'" (Revelation 3:15-16). We need to seek the proper balance between praying without ceasing and rejoicing always. Both are necessary for our spiritual health. We need an attitude of gratitude every bit as much as we need to recognize our neediness.

I have found that the Prayer Cards give me a foundation to ground me in my spiritual walk and remind me of the many lessons the Lord has graciously taught me over several decades. I have even referred to them frequently as I prepared this Chapter. As He did for David, He has also given me a heart for worship. Remember what I said about God being endlessly creative? I have a huge notebook filled with materials which add immeasurably to my praise and worship time which include everything from attributes of God, names of Jesus Christ, reminders of who I am in Christ, gladness passages, aging promises, and a host of praise songs. There is no excuse in the Kingdom of God for apathy!

CHAPTER 9

PRAYING FOR MYSELF

Whoa, wait a minute. That does not sound right. Are we not supposed to pray for others first? I have written about the nature and purpose of prayer in general including how to maintain a balance between praying prayer needs and simply seeking the Lord. Now, it is time to turn to the subjects of our intercession. The ministry of intercession is the supreme privilege and duty of all believers to lift up others in prayer. But what does this ministry look like? What are the parameters?

When I look at the big picture, and read about great prayer warriors in Church History, one thing becomes clear. Prayer starts in the center and spreads to the far corners of the earth, kind of like the ripple effect of a drop of water in a bowl of water. The center of a prayer warrior's life is therefore, him or herself. If that sounds perhaps selfish, then let us take a look at the life of Jesus as a model. (That's always a good idea!)

Immediately after His baptism, "… Jesus was led up by the Spirit into the wilderness to be tempted by the devil. And after He had fasted forty days and forty nights, He then became hungry" (Matthew 4:1-2). We frequently miss two important facts which take place before Satan came onto the scene. First, Jesus was led by the Holy Spirit. This is the beginning point of all prayer. We are always, always to be guided by the Spirit. Resources and Scripture are all fine, but they are tools to be used under His divine direction.

Secondly, Jesus fasted for forty days and forty nights. What, you may ask was the purpose of that? Did you know that both Moses and Elijah also fasted forty days and forty nights? In all three cases, their lives were in transition and they were seeking the Lord's will. During this time of fasting, they were divinely sustained and were in direct communion with God. Immediately after this intense one-on-one time with their Heavenly Father, each began a new phase of their lives. Moses received the Ten Commandments which formed the foundation of the Word of God as we know it today. Elijah went from hiding in caves in fear of his life, to a bold prophet who anointed kings and proclaimed God's word to the nation of Israel. Jesus came out of the wilderness, having been tested and found worthy, to take up his earthly ministry which ultimately led to the Cross.

On another occasion, in the Garden of Gethsemane, Jesus prepared for His death. "... (He) fell on His face and prayed, saying, "My Father, if it is possible, let this cup pass from Me; yet not as I will, but as Thou wilt" (Matthew 26:39). Would you call that selfish prayer? When our souls are in turmoil or our bodies in danger, it makes perfect sense to reach out to the Lord in prayer. As He fulfilled all the necessary prophecies regarding the Messiah's early life, His Father sustained Him through the horrors of the next three days and nights. If Jesus felt it necessary to pray for Himself, it is safe to say that we would do well to do so regularly, in order to be ready to fulfill all the Lord has for us to accomplish.

There are very good reasons for beginning our prayer sessions with ourselves. First of all, we need to acknowledge that God the Father is in charge of our lives and not us. "Know that the Lord Himself is God; It is He who has made us, and not we ourselves; we are His people and the sheep of His pasture" (Psalm 100:3). This prepares us spiritually for all that is to follow. Confession is also crucial because unconfessed sin blocks our access to His presence. "If we confess our sins, He is faithful and righteous to forgive us our sins and to cleanse us from all unrighteousness" (1 John 1:9). Sin separates us from God. Drawing close to Him opens us up to His wisdom, His love and His guidance. When we are spiritually prepared to hear from Him as He edifies our lives, we are ready to intercede for the world around us.

There are two main ways the Lord taught me to be effective in praying for myself. The first is through Rhema. You may not be familiar with this term because it is not found in the Bible, but the concept is. Rhema is the specific Scripture the Holy Spirit brings to mind in order to direct and edify our lives. Another good definition of the term is an utterance of God occasioned by the Holy Spirit in the heart.[8] This is only possible if we have a good working knowledge of the Word to begin with. If memorizing Scripture is a challenge for you, here is a helpful hint that I tripped over by accident. With all my fancy Bible software, I discovered that the most efficient Bible Concordance is… Google! If you have a phrase running around your brain without a Scripture address, put what you remember into Google. I have a 90% success rate with this method. The good news is that Google doesn't care what version of the Bible you are familiar with. It seems to be able to find it regardless!

The second way the Lord has taught me to inform my prayer life is a stack of Bible verses that I have printed on 3 x 5 cards sorted by subject. There are, believe it or not, areas of my life that are still not sanctified; like my tongue, my thought life, my ability to forgive, my judgmental nature, the list goes on. But, He has given me about twenty verses to memorize, one per topic which I regularly review. God frequently brings one of these subjects up in my spirit as I wait for Him in the morning for my "marching orders." Usually one of two things happens as a result; either He gives me the opportunity to practice one of these themes, such as say patience, or He wants to expand my understanding of the truth in that area.

This brings me to the last thought I'd like to leave with you about my personal prayer time. Lately, I have been thinking frequently about the fact that Christianity is meant to be radical: it is meant to change the world in which we live. In order to do that, we need to allow the Lord to expand our horizons and explore the potential of carrying these Rhema verses out on a daily basis, without worrying about the world's response to it.

Are you getting excited yet?

CHAPTER 10

FAMILY MATTERS

Why is it so difficult to talk about the dynamics of the family when we attempt to be transparent about praying for them? Is it because of the emotional ties to various family members? Is it because we do not know where to begin or how to pray honestly without infusing our own desires in our prayers for our loved ones? Is it perhaps that we do not want to appear judgmental when we intercede on their behalf?

We are not alone. Jesus wrestled with the very same issues with His earthly family. He spoke about family dynamics when He shared this observation, "… a prophet is not without honor except in his home town and among his own relatives and in his own household" (Mark 6:4). As He hung on the cross, He arranged for His mother's care after His death. "When Jesus therefore saw His mother, and the disciple whom He loved standing nearby, He said to His mother, "Woman, behold, your son!" Then He said to the disciple, "Behold, your mother!" And from that hour the disciple took her into his own household" (John 19:26-27). Jesus chose John to care for His mother even though He had several brothers still living. He was very clear about the importance of the Christian bonds of love when He proclaimed, "… Who are My mother and My brothers?" And looking about on those who were sitting around Him, He said, "Behold, My mother and My brothers! For whoever does the will of God, he is My brother and sister and mother" (Mark 3:33-35).

However, God clearly designed His children to flourish in family units, which began with a husband and wife. "Then the Lord God said, "It is not good for the man to be alone; I will make him a helper suitable for him… For this cause a man shall leave his father and his mother, and shall cleave to his wife; and they shall become one flesh . . . And God saw all that He had made, and behold, it was very good…" (Genesis 2: 18, 24, 1:31). There is no doubt that He meant for us to be loved, raised and nurtured in family units. It is one of the Lord's many blessings to His children. He also expects us to carry out His purpose in our families. "Train up a child in the way he should go, even when he is old he will not depart from it" (Proverbs 22:6). Our Heavenly Father also addresses children's responsibility; "Honor your father and your mother, that your days may be prolonged in the land which the Lord your God gives you" (Exodus 20:12). His plan has not changed.

The problem, beginning with the first couple, Adam and Eve, is sin. Our families are ripe with tension because we are in rebellion against God. Peter even warns about this problem: "You husbands likewise, live with your wives in an understanding way, as with a weaker vessel, since she is a woman; and grant her honor as a fellow heir of the grace of life, so that your prayers may not be hindered. To sum up, let all be harmonious, sympathetic, brotherly, kindhearted, and humble in spirit; not returning evil for evil, or insult for insult, but giving a blessing instead; for you were called for the very purpose that you might inherit a blessing" (1 Peter 3: 7-9). Here is the issue. If we expect to receive grace from our Lord in the midst of our sin, we need to extend the same within our family units.

Divorce, being "unequally yoked", having a prodigal son or daughter, blended families, substance abuse, physical abuse, homosexuality, all make the very family that God meant for a safe-haven and a blessing, an adversarial camp instead. Does this change the fact that family is God's best plan for us? Absolutely not. However, it does present a challenge in being effective and hopeful in our intercession. There is one promise that we can hold onto. "… All things are possible to him who believes" (Mark 9:23).

Beginning with marriage, God desires that we demonstrate the love which He so freely gives to us and to one another. I Corinthians Chapter 13 speaks of the excellence of love. It is within the framework of a family that a believer learns to walk in that admonition. We are to treat one another with respect and unconditional love. We have the opportunity to role model what Christ taught us. For example, "In the same way, you wives, be submissive to your own husbands so that even if any of them are disobedient to the word, they may be won without a word by the behavior of their wives, as they observe your chaste and respectful behavior" (1 Peter 3:1-2). We have the privilege and the responsibility to seek the Lord's will in our prayers for our family members. Both Jesus Christ and the Holy Spirit act as our intercessors in this endeavor.

I had often wondered whether my prayers and my witness were having any effect in my family. But I recall two experiences that God gave me that encouraged me to keep on keeping on. As many daughters do, I worried about my father's health, since he had been a smoker since World War II. I prayed for years that he stop smoking and one day during a phone call he "casually" mentioned that he had stopped "just like that." For me, it was an opportunity to see God perform the seemingly impossible, in answer to persistent prayer. On another occasion, my mother unfortunately died unexpectedly in a hospital over the Christmas holidays, just before my father and I arrived for a visit. After the funeral, my older brother took me aside and said to me that he was glad that I was the one who was with my father when the incident occurred. When I tried to deflect the compliment by saying something like any of us would have done what was necessary under the circumstances, he stopped me. He repeated that there was a reason that I was the one who providentially was there to support my father. It may have been the first time that I recognized that my strength and calmness during family crises, which came directly from the Lord, was recognized by my own family.

I find that I need to pray about the needs I see in my family's lives and not project my solutions onto God. I need to make sure that I do not harbor bitterness or lack of grace which would inhibit my prayers. My Father wants the family unit to work even more than I do. Sometimes, I need to wait on His timing and give Him room to discipline one of His children in order to bring about transformation.

We all have the opportunity as spouses, parents, children and grandparents to pray with one another on a regular basis, demonstrating our dependence on our Lord to produce His fruit in our lives. Here's an amazing statistic for you. According to a study by the National Association of Marriage Enhancement,[9] couples who pray together daily have a divorce rate of 1 in 1156, or less than 1 hundredth of one percent. The divorce rate for the rest of the country is 50%.

How are we to pray? Whatever discernment God gives you regarding your loved ones should become the focus of your prayer. The list is endless; hope, confidence, freedom from fear, a teachable spirit, an obedient heart, freedom from anger or bitterness, the Lord's calling on their life, a suitable marriage partner, wisdom, or the ability to communicate. Most importantly, always partner that prayer with consistency in your walk, absence of judgment and unconditional love.

Finally, remember that there must be balance in your prayer ministry for your family. Your first commitment must be to the Lord. "And He said to him, "'You shall love the Lord your God with all your heart, and with all your soul, and with all your mind" (Matthew 22:37). Never let your concern for your family override your devotion to Him. Jesus warns us, "He who loves father or mother more than Me is not worthy of Me; and he who loves son or daughter more than Me is not worthy of Me" (Matthew 10:37).

CHAPTER 11

PRAYING FOR THE CHURCH

I consider praying for the church one of the highest privileges in a believer's life. I have read many biographies of missionaries and accounts of revivals within the Church and am convinced that prayer is the single most effective means by which the world is evangelized. Before I address this ministry however, I want to differentiate between the local church and what I call the Church with a capital "C."

Acts Chapter 2 contains my favorite passage describing the intimacy of the early church. "And all those who had believed were together, and had all things in common; and they began selling their property and possessions, and were sharing them with all, as anyone might have need. And day by day continuing with one mind in the temple, and breaking bread from house to house, they were taking their meals together with gladness and sincerity of heart, praising God, and having favor with all the people. And the Lord was adding to their number day by day those who were being saved" (verses 44-47). The local church is where we worship, fellowship, tithe, and hear the Word preached. It is also where we meet needs, encourage fellow believers, comfort the sick and hurting, counsel and most of all pray.

The Church with a capital "C" is the Bride of Christ worldwide. It is the entity created by the carrying out of the Great Commission. "Go therefore and make disciples of all the nations, baptizing them in the name of the Father and the Son and the Holy Spirit, teaching them to observe all that I commanded you... " (Matthew 28: 19-20). It is the Church with a capital "C" that is invited to the Marriage Feast. "Let us rejoice and be glad and give the glory to Him, for the marriage of the Lamb has come and His bride has made herself ready… And he said to me, "Write, 'Blessed are those who are invited to the marriage supper of the Lamb" (Revelation 19:7, 9). The Church triumphant is vast; is multi-national, multi-ethnic, multi-lingual, multi-generational and eternal!

How did the first church receive the power of the Holy Spirit at Pentecost? They gathered together with one spirit. "And they were continually devoting themselves to the apostles' teaching and to fellowship, to the breaking of bread and to prayer" (Acts 2:42). Did you catch that? They were devoted to one another in all things and they prayed. So, how do you pray for the church? One person at a time. I learned years ago that when someone asks you to pray for them, pray with them right then. Christian life is meant to be lived in the moment. Jesus frequently stopped on the way from point A to point B to minister to someone in tremendous need. And He usually got rebuked for it by His disciples who reminded Him of their schedule. We will miss many opportunities for prayer and service by waiting for Wednesday Prayer Meeting or Single Parent Car Clinic Night.

I had an interesting experience while on a mission trip to Mexico several years ago. Our group was staying at an old hotel in the town of Guzman. One of the teenagers was trying to unlock the door to her room and she couldn't get it open. My roommate and I went down the hall to see if we could help. She said that the key only worked if you placed it in the lock in a certain way and only one of her roommates (who was not present) knew how to do it. After my roommate and I tried without any success, I suggested we lay hands on the door and pray. This was business as usual for me, but my two fellow missionaries looked at me as if I had lost my senses. Well, you can probably guess the result. The Lord opened the door, quick as you please, and as I walked away, I praised the Lord. I thought no more about the incident until we returned to our church in Tennessee and shared our experiences in the mission field. When it was this teenager's turn to share, of all things, she said she learned about the power of prayer through the locked door incident! The Lord taught her that He is concerned about anything that concerns us, in any emergency, no matter how large or small. God used this object lesson to change her perspective on praying without ceasing.

Praying for church members, one-on-one, is very much like praying for family and friends. Listen to the prayer need, but also pray for discernment from the Lord, so you can be precise as to what the actual need is from His perspective. Remember, there is power in numbers. "Again I say to you, that if two of you agree on earth about anything that they may ask, it shall be done for them by My Father who is in heaven. "For where two or three have gathered together in My name, there I am in their midst" (Matthew 18:19-20). For myself, I try to make sure that whatever group I am leading; whether it be a Bible Study, Mentoring, Women's Fellowship or Visitation Team, we always begin in prayer. We pray both for the Lord's presence and blessing on our gathering and to pray for any urgent prayer needs among us. Our Bible Class which meets weekly on Sunday has a Prayer Chain for urgent prayer needs that can get a request out to the entire class in about 15 minutes. Not only has this brought the class close together in times of crisis, but we have all been privileged to see miraculous answers to our prayers over and over again. It is exciting to be part of that kind of fellowship!

It is also important to get to know those in your small group or ministry team well so that you can be effective in prayer. My husband and I have made it a practice to invite any new members to our Bible Study to our home for a "Newbie Dinner." Not only have we enjoyed rich fellowship over the years, but we have a much better sense of where our brothers and sisters are coming from which informs our prayer life. Take every opportunity to get to know your church staff, ministry partners, and small group members and their family to better enable you to intercede with knowledge.

One of the difficulties about praying for the local church is that we may have prayer lists for urgent needs and prayer requests from various ministries for success in upcoming scheduled events. However, praying in the Spirit for the eternal work of the Lord in our midst seems to get little priority. Notice what the Lord had to say to several of the local congregations about their church in Revelation. One had lost their first love, another did not eliminate idol worship in their midst, another tolerated false prophets in their midst, yet another was dead in good works, and yet another was lukewarm in their faith. Do you see any pattern here? These are flaws in the local body with eternal ramifications. Can you imagine the damage done in the hearts of new believers in such a church? We must pray for discernment and insight to know the heart of God for our church. We need to pray that our church has His vision for carrying out the Great Commission in our midst as well as making disciples for Christ.

A vibrant, active, powerful, evangelical church will have a powerful prayer ministry. Whether the corporate prayer is in a sanctuary, a prayer room, a virtual prayer room or at a retreat, regular unified prayer is necessary for a powerful witness. Pray for your pastors, worship leaders, elders, Bible teachers, anyone who has influence over the spiritual wellbeing of the members. Pray for wisdom, freedom from pride, freedom from the love of the world, freedom from spiritual warfare. Pray for strong families and godly fathers. Pray especially for the love of the Lord Jesus Christ to be evident in every aspect of church ministry. Pray for holiness and submission. In short, pray that we as a body become more and more transformed into the image of Jesus Christ. If that is not our goal in all our endeavors, then something is seriously wrong. These are eternal values and God's heart.

I was part of a prayer meeting in a church once where the entire sanctuary was turned into prayer stations. There were signs in big block letters representing all the different departments all over the room. We were encouraged to kneel before any sign that God had placed on our heart to pray for. After doing this for some time, I felt an overwhelming urge to go up to the baptistery and lay hands on it and pray for the baptismal candidates who would next "stir the waters" in baptism. Needless to say, there was no sign over the baptistery, and I certainly had no idea who would be baptized next. It was a huge church. I was a teacher in a large class of mentally challenged adults at the time. Talk about excited believers! They loved to worship! I was teaching on the subject of Jesus' baptism and the Roman Road. Would you believe the next two Sundays about ten of the students in the class were baptized! This had never occurred in that class ever before. The baptismal counselors came up to me and said it was a rare pleasure to see believers so excited about declaring their faith in public as these precious saints were doing! I have learned, incidentally, never ever to ignore the unction of the Holy Spirit when it comes to obedience. Unfortunately, it took a graphic illustration of how He works in a church setting to cure me of reluctance, which is simply a fancy word for disobedience. I was at a massive prayer meeting for the family members of the head of the board of elders in a large church who had died suddenly at an early age. We were arranged in large circles with a family member seated in each circle. Two of the many children of this family were in my Sunday School class at this time. As we prayed quietly over these precious family members, the Holy Spirit told me to start singing Amazing Grace quietly. I was startled and argued within my spirit that it would be inappropriate. We were praying. As soon as I had made that decision in my heart, what do I hear from the opposite corner of the room? Amazing Grace. What a beautiful witness it was as three hundred people started singing softly and reverently throughout the room. I felt outside of the moment and have vowed that I will never knowingly quench the Holy Spirit in that way again.

The Lord has expanded my prayer ministry over the decades to include a love for the Church worldwide. I am sad to observe that we do not do a good job, in general, in the American Church with recognizing our responsibility to pray for, support and offer comfort and fellowship to the Church around the world. There are many without a local church, many without a translation of the Bible in their own heart language, many in prison for preaching the Gospel, many persecuted and killed for their faith, and many serving in areas that have no access to communication with the outside world. Tithing money as a church to the mission field is a good beginning, but that is not nearly enough. We will spend eternity with the Bride of Christ and many in the Church are forgotten. If we do not invite missionaries into our churches to tell their story and be loved on and prayed over, how will our children and young people know there is a Church out there? Where will the next generation of missionaries and Bible translators come from? There is much we can do to become more personally involved.

I currently have the privilege to be part of a large church that tithes to the mission field, supports many additional worldwide outreaches, hosts an annual Missions Conference and has many short term mission opportunities throughout the year, all over the world. Our Bible Study class had the rare privilege of hosting a couple from Zambia who came to visit our church during the Missions Conference. My husband and I took them out for breakfast locally to get to know them and find out how to pray for them effectively. While I was in the shower, the Lord started preparing my heart for this encounter. (I have no idea why, but He frequently directs my thoughts for the day while I am soaking wet, without a pen or paper to record His directions!) Anyway, He told me to ask two questions. The first was, do you have an adequate reference library for your many responsibilities? We knew from their biographical sketch that they ran two Bible Schools for Pastors as well as preaching on a weekly basis. The second question was, what do you do for personal worship time? I don't think they would be the first things I would ask missionaries from the field, but there you have it. When I asked these questions during our wonderful fellowship breakfast, the wife teared-up immediately. In a quiet voice, she said, "It is very difficult." I had no idea that she had been a Reference Librarian in South Korea before she "married into the mission field." They also, as it turned out, had beautiful singing voices which we were to be treated to later in the week.

As a result of my obedience (this time) and our Bible Class's generosity, we met all of their needs on their wish list; sending them home with two very extensive Bible Software programs, two MP3's loaded with Christian music, which they now use in church services, two complete sets of Children's Bible Story booklets, and dozens of DVD movies depicting various Bible Stories. Every attempt to love on them seemed to be just right. During the special service we held to honor all the visiting missionaries, we were encouraged to make up posters with words of encouragement. I love a good crafts project, so I went on-line, found their website and enlarged pictures of them in Zambia teaching, preaching, worshipping and fellowshipping. As soon as the service was over, the husband came up to me asking for the posters. He had never had a visual presentation to share with the churches they visited to share their story. He immediately hung them over his table in our atrium! God is so good!

I believe in the truth, "… where your treasure is, there will your heart be also" (Matthew 6:21). I would encourage you to learn about the many worldwide ministries out there who are engaging in Church building, Bible Translation, Pastoral support, Medical Missionaries, and many other fine programs. I would also suggest that when you do find one (or two or three) which touch your heart, support them with your prayers, letters of encouragement, and finances. This is truly an eternal investment! Sometimes in my personal prayer time for the Church, I make use of the excellent material put out by the Voice of the Martyrs which has a map of the countries where the Church is persecuted as well as suggestions as to what to pray for specifically.

Prayer is the best gift we saints can offer to the Bride of Christ. Be consistent, be informed, and rejoice that there will be a great cloud of believers one day celebrating at the Marriage of the Lamb. I believe we will meet many whom we have personally prayed for someday and marvel over God's grace!

CHAPTER 12

PRAYING FOR YOUR COMMUNITY

When I think about the Great Commission, I tend to think in terms of the local church and the unsaved world, but I cannot say that I have spent much time considering my immediate neighborhood or my town. At least that used to be the case. Two things have changed in my life recently that caused me to reconsider my role as a Christian in my community; I am now retired, and I moved to a retirement community within the last year.

Jesus walked all over Israel teaching, preaching, praying, and meeting needs. He demonstrated what Christian compassion looked like. In the book of Luke, Jesus exorcized a demon from a man, healed many people He met, helped a fisherman, forgave sinners, calmed the sea, raised the dead, fed thousands, called disciples, and taught people how to pray. He carried out these ministries as He walked among the people to glorify God.

I do not believe it is possible to pray for others outside of our church, family and friends unless the Lord enlarges our compassion and our vision for those whom we do not know. One of the easiest ways to get to know the needs of your community is to investigate volunteer opportunities. There is no better way to pray for your neighbors than in the course of ministry. There are food pantries, schools which need tutors, kids who need coaching, mentoring and scouts needing leaders. The possibilities are endless. I have tutored orphans, transported people in ambulances (as an Emergency Medical Technician), responded to local disasters, ministered to widows and opened my home for Women's

Bible Devotion and Prayer Meetings in my new neighborhood. Take every opportunity to get to know where there are needs and roll up your sleeves and get to work. It may be something as simple as driving a senior citizen to physical therapy, visiting someone in the hospital and praying for them, or visiting a lonely widow. What it says is, "someone cares," and you have the privilege of being a blessing in the name of the Father. The Lord will fill your heart with love for others and enrich your prayer life as you intercede for your community.

As a side note, early on in my retirement, the Lord answered my prayer for guidance on how He wanted me to serve Him. He gave me this Rhema: "This is pure and undefiled religion in the sight of our God and Father, to visit orphans and widows in their distress, and to keep oneself unstained by the world" (James 1:27). This one verse has led me to serve first orphans and then widows for over 16 years. Serving the Lord according to His will and making use of your spiritual gifts brings about a deep satisfaction that has eternal blessings.

As the Lord has expanded my horizons, He has made it clear that knowledge is crucial in order to pray effectively. How do you get to know your community? Talk to people; get to know your neighbors, read the local newspaper, attend town meetings, attend school board meetings, library meetings, community events and anything that gives you insight into the inner workings of your town. Know your community leaders, read about their "platforms" and vote in local elections. As you gain an understanding of the issues, you will be both motivated and enlightened to becoming an effective prayer warrior. Do not stop at the local level. Become informed about your city and state issues as well. Many of the recent state laws enacted across the country are in direct violation to the Word of God. Become vocal in standing up for the Lord where school, health, finances, and civil laws violate our Christian heritage. A nation whose Christian citizens will not stand up for those who cannot stand up for themselves or will not protest the disintegration of the Judeo-Christian ethic upon which our nation was founded become part of the problem. Jesus became salt in His community. He was never afraid to take on the establishment wherever they interfered with His Father's business. My Prayer Card on salt (p. 244) defines salt figuratively, as making a difference in the world because of our sanctification. Christians are supposed to have a purifying influence on society. Be careful, however, to avoid promoting a political agenda within the context of sharing the Gospel. Ours is a Kingdom battle with eternal ramifications, but our influence in our community as well as our nation is to be salt in a fallen world. Let the Lord guide you in the details.

Prayer changes us. Corporate prayer changes our environment. God honors those who love their communities enough to pray for them and reach out to share the love of the Lord. Organize corporate prayer through your church for our schools with "Rally Round the Flagpole" on the first day of school. Take neighborhood prayer walks praying for the residents of the houses. Pray for the teachers, policemen, firefighters, government leaders and business owners that they may withstand Satan's lies and uphold truth and justice. Be a visible influence for Christ taking every opportunity to share the Gospel and pray for one another. Converse with those whom you see on a regular basis; your bank teller, your butcher, the store greeter, your landscaper, your doctor, your dentist and your waitress. Find out about their lives and pray for them. If you are willing, God will make use of your availability to teach you how to pray for each one of His precious children.

As Christians, we tend to dream of doing something great for the Lord. But if you take a look at the first church in Acts 2, our ministry and our prayers begin in our own backyard. This is where we all have a sphere of influence where we can make a real difference in the lives of those whom God has placed around us.

CHAPTER 13

PRAYING FOR OUR NATION

I just love it when my day begins with a God Wink. If you are not familiar with the term, I first ran across it in Squire Rushnell's book *When God Winks* (2002).[10] A God Wink is a message of assurance from the Lord, a gift from the Heavenly Father to His beloved children, reminding us of how much He loves us and wants to give us good gifts. From a human perspective, they may seem like coincidences, but from a spiritual perspective, they are God's love kisses. I am in the habit lately of waking up and spending the first moments of each day asking God for His marching orders. This morning, He reminded me that the next chapter in this book would be, "Praying for Our Nation," and by the way, Happy Memorial Day! Now this might seem like a planned event to the unsuspecting, but I have other ministry commitments which necessitate my putting my writing aside periodically to write a lesson plan, or spend a day with a sister in the Lord. God is the one who brings about these happy coincidences to remind me of His providence.

As I considered the question of praying for our nation, I wondered about how American's view their citizenship and what affect it has (if any) on our Christian walk. First of all, I firmly believe that most of our citizens, when asked, would readily enough agree that they would rather live here than in any other country. Secondly, there is enough patriotism, even today, to stir the hearts of this nation when we are under physical attack. Memorial Day and Veterans Day were designed to pay honor to those who served in the various branches of the military. We had a common sense of duty when we responded to the attack on Pearl Harbor in 1941 and the attack on New York City and the Pentagon in 2001. Being an American citizen is an important part of our personal identity.

As Christians we also have responsibilities. We are directed in Scripture to pray for our government leaders. "First of all, then, I urge that entreaties and prayers, petitions and thanksgivings, be made on behalf of all men, for kings and all who are in authority, in order that we may lead a tranquil and quiet life in all godliness and dignity. This is good and acceptable in the sight of God our Savior" (1 Timothy 2:1-3).

I don't think most Americans who call themselves Christians find this admonition a stretch. But how many of us regularly pray for our country and its leaders? I find it interesting that our nation's motto is, "In God We Trust" and our Pledge of Allegiance includes the words, "One Nation Under God." This would seem to indicate that we are deeply rooted in our Judeo-Christian origin. When our motto was changed to "In God We Trust" in 1956, there was significant vocal opposition. One writer commented "commanding people's children to trust in a god is not the job of the state… this (is) a misuse of government power".[11] "One Nation Under God" was added to the Pledge of Allegiance in 1954, and at the time, a writer for the New York Times ridiculed the addition by calling it, "a petty attempt to link patriotism with religious piety." He pointed out that the United States Court of Appeals for the Ninth District in California ruled that these words in the pledge violated the First Amendment.[12] In recent decades there is increasing agreement with these opinions. So where does God stand on the subject of nationality? As usual, I turn to Jesus as our model in all things Christian. When the Pharisees tried to trap him on the subject of submission to government authority, He answered them in this way:

"Shall we pay (a poll-tax to Caesar), or shall we not pay?" But He, knowing their hypocrisy, said to them, "Why are you testing Me? Bring Me a denarius to look at." And they brought one. And He said to them, "Whose likeness and inscription is this?" And they said to Him,

"Caesar's." And Jesus said to them, "Render to Caesar the things that are Caesar's, and to God the things that are God's" (Mark 12:15-17).

Jesus is clearly differentiating between our responsibilities to our nation and its leaders and our responsibility toward God. Does that mean that God does not approve of national identity in general? That's a difficult question to answer. In the days of Noah immediately after the flood we read, "These are the sons of Shem, according to their families, according to their languages, by their lands, according to their nations. These are the families of the sons of Noah, according to their genealogies, by their nations; and out of these the nations were separated on the earth after the flood" (Genesis 10:31-32). The flood, as well as the multitude of languages which we have to this day, are the direct result of disobedience to God and pride. The result is a division among those whom God created. Yet at the same time, we cannot say that this was not His will. "… He made from one, every nation of mankind to live on all the face of the earth, having determined their appointed times, and the boundaries of their habitation, that they should seek God, if perhaps they might grope for Him and find Him, though He is not far from each one of us" (Acts 17: 26-27).

But our Creator is still sovereign. "… O Lord, the God of our fathers, art Thou not God in the heavens? And art Thou not ruler over all the kingdoms of the nations? Power and might are in Thy hand so that no one can stand against Thee" (2 Chronicles 20:6). He determines who our rulers will be. "Let every person be in subjection to the governing authorities. For there is no authority except from God, and those which exist are established by God" (Romans 13:1). That is a hard truth to grasp as we look around the world. Does that mean that He approves of all the nations? No. "Why are the nations in an uproar, and the peoples devising a vain thing? The kings of the earth take their stand, and the rulers take counsel together against the Lord and against His Anointed" (Psalm 2:1-2). Because man is fallen, God ordained that there would be leaders over the multitudes. God will judge each nation according to how they live in relation to His law. "Thou hast rebuked the nations; Thou hast destroyed the wicked; Thou hast blotted out their name forever and ever" (Psalm 9:5).

Alex de Tocqueville, a 19th century French historian, offered this observation on America. "America is great because America is good. If America ceases to be good, America will cease to be great."[13] How prophetic is that? God will judge America, not according to our Constitution, but according to His Word. Incidentally, de Tocqueville also had this to offer, "The American Republic will endure until the day that Congress discovers that it can bribe the public with the public's money."[14] How's that for insight?

So what does this all have to do with praying for our nation? We need to have God's clear perspective on America. I have always appreciated Watchman Nee's writings on our spiritual life. He was a Chinese Christian Teacher who lived in the first half of the twentieth century. His book *Spiritual Man*[15] is very powerful. He is uncompromising with regard to our duty to obey God regardless of the cost and without compromising in order to be acceptable citizens in the country of our birth. He spent the last twenty years of his life in prison for his stand. Christian Americans should be the best patriots our country has to offer, but that is because we should have the character and mind of Christ. God is not partisan, except in standing for justice and truth. These are not concepts originally defined by our Declaration of Independence and codified in our Constitution and the Bill of Rights. They originated in the mind of God and have been communicated to us through His Word, the Bible.

In practical terms then, how do we pray effectively for America? We must recognize that part of America's heritage is a can-do attitude that sometimes borders on arrogance. Our patriotism too often informs our Church rather than the reverse. A good place to begin in prayer is this: "(If) My people who are called by My name humble themselves and pray, and seek My face and turn from their wicked ways, then I will hear from heaven, will forgive their sin, and will heal their land" (2 Chronicles 7:14).

Are there problems in America? You bet. Are we worse than any other nation? Probably not. But just as personal salvation is not weighed on a scale, neither is our judgment as a nation weighed by God in relation to others (with one exception). This verse above is proclaimed the first Thursday of every May at the National Day of Prayer celebrations and it should be. However, are we serious about the prerequisites for healing what is wrong with our land? Are we a praying nation, a humble nation and a repentant nation? Are we willing to change to conform to His revealed standards for our personal and national life? Personally, I don't see a concerted effort in this direction. However, revivals have changed the course of our nation at least for a period of time (generally referred to as the Great Awakenings). Our nation has had four well known, "Great Awakenings;" in the 1730's, the early 1800's, the mid and late 1800's and the late 1960's.[16] What do they all have in common? God's Church prayed purposefully, unitedly, and consistently. Is there any reason that we could not see a repeat of that phenomenon? Absolutely none, except perhaps our commitment to corporate prayer and repentance has waned. It requires faith in God that is larger than our problems as a nation. It requires commitment to seek His wisdom to see where we went off track and faithful obedience to change whatever He directs us to change.

As I have indicated in previous chapters, it is crucial to become informed about the subject you are praying for and it is equally true in praying for America. The problem however, is that we have become so partisan that obtaining godly information on the issues is more and more difficult. I would suggest finding out what your favorite Christian leaders, writers and Christian Organizations use as their source for news with a Christian Worldview. Have an attitude of prayer as you gather information. Let the Word of God inform you as to the righteous path in each situation.

What we pray is determined by the Holy Spirit as we come before Him in our quiet time. I would like to suggest another rich source of prayer needs as well as Scripture verses. I have placed in my Prayer Notebook a copy of the National Day of Prayer Brochure from 2008. I have added items so there are thirty-one needs and Scriptures to pray for, corresponding to the days in a month. Each year the National Day of Prayer.org offers a new version for your use. I would also suggest that you research the names of your U.S. Senators, U.S. Representatives, Supreme Court Judges, and add them to a list, including the President, Vice President, and Major Cabinet Secretaries. Pray for our leaders regularly that they may be guided by His Law either written on their hearts through God's Word or on their consciences, since we are all created in His image. "For when Gentiles who do not have the Law do instinctively the things of the Law, these, not having the Law, are a law to themselves, in that they show the work of the Law written in their hearts, their conscience bearing witness, and their thoughts alternately accusing or else defending them" (Romans 2:14-15).

I can think of no better benediction to this chapter than to quote from Irving Berlin's song "God Bless America".[17]

God bless America, land that I love.
Stand beside her and guide her,
Thru the night with a light from above.

CHAPTER 14

PRAYING FOR THE WORLD

The nations of our world are in chaos. I believe this to be literally true. Every nation on earth is in rebellion against our Creator, some more so than others. Yet, we have established that God is sovereign over the nations of the world in Chapter 13, Praying For Our Nation. I believe that in many if not most Christian populations around the world, the culture of the nation or tribe has so infiltrated the Church that its witness has been all but silenced. But if we look ahead at the description of the new earth, we read, "And the city (New Jerusalem) has no need of the sun or of the moon to shine upon it, for the glory of God has illumined it, and its lamp is the Lamb. And the nations shall walk by its light, and the kings of the earth shall bring their glory into it" (Revelation 21:23-24).

There is hope. God's plan will prevail. I believe that our solemn responsibility before God is to stand in the gap and pray for the nations to be open to God's wisdom before they are exposed to His wrath. "And I searched for a man among them who should build up the wall and stand in the gap before Me for the land, that I should not destroy it; but I found no one" (Ezekiel 22:30).

Regardless of what nation we reside in, we have an admonition from the Lord to pray for the peace of one specific nation. God has always had a special place in His heart for Israel. He refers to Israel as the "apple of His eye." "For thus says the Lord of hosts, "After glory He has sent me against the nations which plunder you, for he who touches you, touches the apple of His eye" (Zechariah 2:8). While Israel has had just

51

as much of a history of rebellion against God as many other nations, we are told to "Pray for the peace of Jerusalem: "May they prosper who love you" (Psalm 122:6). It would not be an overstatement to say that part of God's judgment of the nations will be determined by their treatment of Israel.

Israel will be at the center of the Battle of Armageddon on the Plain of Megiddo. This will literally be the final battle between the forces of good and evil; "for they are spirits of demons, performing signs, which go out to the kings of the whole world, to gather them together for the war of the great day of God, the Almighty" (Revelation 16:14). Jesus Himself will return to defend Israel: "Then the Lord will go forth and fight against those nations, as when He fights on a day of battle. And in that day His feet will stand on the Mount of Olives, which is in front of Jerusalem on the east... And the Lord will be king over all the earth; in that day the Lord will be the only one, and His name the only one" (Zechariah 14:3-4, 9). We do not yet know what will precipitate the Battle of Armageddon, but it will be no surprise, given the current climate in the Middle East, that Israel will have few defenders.

We cannot talk realistically about praying for the world without addressing the issue of hopelessness, even among Christians, regarding praying for significant change among the nations. If hope is the confidence of expectation in the Lord's intention of fulfilling all His promises, then hopelessness is a sense of futility, an abandonment to one's "fate." It suggests a lack of trust in God's power. I frequently hear the argument, but what about Hitler? Are we saying that tyrants are more powerful than God? What happened to Hitler? God will deal with every tyrant in His own time. As Christians, we can play a vital part in the outcome of such evil regimes. Can we honestly say that there was sustained and unified prayer during these horrific reigns of terror?

I absolutely believe without reservation that if the Church, worldwide, prays with unity of spirit for three principles to be incorporated in each nation's rules of government, we will see the power of God released in a miraculous way. These three principles are truth, justice, and freedom. Naive you say? What if I told you I could prove it through examples from Scripture and modern history? This is where the rubber meets the road. Either we have faith to move mountains in obedience to the Word or we do not.

We think of truth in the abstract, but God's Truth has been established before the creation of the world and encompasses all of reality. His Word establishes Truth's parameters. To distinguish Truth as God's non-negotiable worldview, I will capitalize it for the purpose of this discourse. Man's search for Truth leads him to his Creator. Throughout history, Satan's agents have tried to substitute lies for the Truth and national leaders have always been a chosen vehicle to carry out his agenda. Whenever citizens of any nation are persecuted, evicted or killed for pursuing Truth, the Church has a spiritual obligation to intercede and defend their afflicted brothers and sisters.

In the first three chapters of the book of Daniel, we read of the history of Nebuchadnezzar, King of Babylon. He besieged Jerusalem and took many captives, among whom were Daniel, Shadrach, Meshach, and Abed-nego. After three years of intense education, they entered the king's service as advisors to the king. Because of God's protection and blessing, these four young men became his wisest counselors. But Nebuchadnezzar was an idol worshipper and a violent, proud man. When he was bothered by repeated disturbing dreams, he called his seers to his palace to both recount and interpret his dream. Since this is an impossible task, apart from God's divine knowledge, he quickly ordered the slaying of all his wise men, including the Hebrew youth. Does this qualify as the act of a tyrant? What did Daniel do when he was informed of his fate? Did he pray that God would strike down the king? Did he take up arms and fight? No, he did not. "Then Daniel went to his house and informed his friends, Hananiah, Mishael and Azariah, about the matter, in order that they might request compassion from the God of heaven concerning this mystery, so that Daniel and his friends might not be destroyed with the rest of the wise men of Babylon" (Daniel 2:17-18). He was given the understanding necessary to fulfill King Nebuchadnezzar's demands and disaster was diverted.

Was the king's character changed? Not yet! In the very next chapter we read, "Nebuchadnezzar the king made an image of gold … To you the command is given, O peoples, nations and men of every language, that at the moment you hear the sound of the horn, flute, lyre, trigon, psaltery, bagpipe, and all kinds of music, you are to fall down and worship the golden image that Nebuchadnezzar the king has set up" (Daniel 3:1, 4-5). When Daniel's friends refused to worship the golden idol, they were thrown into a furnace and miraculously delivered by God. After this second confrontation, we see a distinct change in Nebuchadnezzar:

"Nebuchadnezzar responded and said, "Blessed be the God of Shadrach, Meshach and Abed-nego, who has sent His angel and delivered His servants who put their trust in Him, violating the king's command, and yielded up their bodies so as not to serve or worship any god except their own God. Therefore, I make a decree that any people, nation or tongue that speaks anything offensive against the God of Shadrach, Meshach and Abed-nego shall be torn limb from limb and their houses reduced to a rubbish heap, inasmuch as there is no other god who is able to deliver in this way. Then the king caused Shadrach, Meshach and Abed-nego to prosper in the province of Babylon" (Daniel 3:28-30). As a direct result of witnessing God intervening in His children's lives, the king changed his tyrannical ways and protected and prospered God's people.

The second principle that Christians can intervene for is justice. Justice is simply applying God's standards to our personal and national lives. From a civil standpoint, it is lawfulness, moral uprightness and being equitable in our actions. In the book of Esther, we read about King Ahasuerus (or King Xerxes) who ruled over Persia. He married Esther, a Jewess who was raised by her cousin Mordecai. Mordecai was a just man and a good citizen who overheard a plot to harm the king and through Queen Esther warned him in time to thwart the plan. King Ahasuerus promoted a man by the name of Haman to be prime minister. As a result of Haman's promotion, "… all the king's servants who were at the king's gate bowed down and paid homage to Haman; for so the king had commanded concerning him. But Mordecai neither bowed down nor paid homage" (Esther 3:2). Mordecai would not bow down to Haman, and honor him as a god, since his faith forbade it. Haman responded according to his nature.

"When Haman saw that Mordecai neither bowed down nor paid homage to him, Haman was filled with rage. But he disdained to lay hands on Mordecai alone, for they had told him who the people of Mordecai were; therefore Haman sought to destroy all the Jews, the people of Mordecai, who were throughout the whole kingdom of Ahasuerus" (Esther 3:5-6). King Ahasuerus gave him permission to send out a decree ordering the annihilation of all the Jews, not realizing that both Queen Esther and her faithful cousin Mordecai where among them. To add insult to injury, King Ahasuerus inadvertently poured oil on the flame of Haman's hatred by ordering him to honor Mordecai for his prior service to the king. So what did Mordecai and Esther do to intervene for their people? Did they plot against the king or pray for God to destroy the kingdom? No, once again they resorted to corporate prayer. "Then Esther told them to reply to Mordecai, "Go, assemble all the Jews who are found in Susa, and fast for me; do not eat or drink for three days, night or day. I and my maidens also will fast in the same way. And thus I will go in to the king, which is not according to the law; and if I perish, I perish" (Esther 4:15-16).

Now the king's decree could not be revoked, even after Haman's wicked jealousy was revealed (go figure). But God changed the king's heart! (Do you sense a pattern here?) King Ahasuerus recognized the injustice of Haman. Haman was hanged, and the king transferred all Haman's honor and power to Queen Esther and Mordecai saying, "Now you write to the Jews as you see fit, in the king's name, and seal it with the king's signet ring; for a decree which is written in the name of the king and sealed with the king's signet ring may not be revoked" (Esther 8:8). The Jewish population successfully defended themselves and a holocaust was averted.

This brings us to the third principle, freedom. Freedom is the liberation of someone from the domination of sin or the tyranny of another. Believers may seek freedom from sin or tyranny, but not independence from God. This concept was vividly illustrated in the book of Exodus. The Jews had been slaves in Egypt for four hundred years. They were forbidden to worship their God and their midwives were even told to murder their baby boys. "Then the king of Egypt spoke to the Hebrew midwives... and he said, "When you are helping the Hebrew women to give birth and see them upon the birthstool, if it is a son, then you shall put him to death; but if it is a daughter, then she shall live" (Exodus 1:15-16). What did the Hebrews do in their misery? You got it. Corporate Prayer.

"And the Lord said, "I have surely seen the affliction of My people who are in Egypt, and have given heed to their cry because of their taskmasters, for I am aware of their sufferings. So I have come down to deliver them from the power of the Egyptians, and to bring them up from that land to a good and spacious land, to a land flowing with milk and honey, to the place of the Canaanite and the Hittite and the Amorite and the Perizzite and the Hivite and the Jebusite" (Exodus 3:7-8). The Hebrews' cry may not have been an actual prayer. They may have conveyed their heartfelt yearning for divine deliverance as David did. "O Lord, Thou hast heard the desire of the humble; Thou wilt strengthen their heart, Thou wilt incline Thine ear" (Psalm 10:17). The Lord heard their cry and answered. He miraculously delivered them from the Pharaoh's hand and brought them into the Promised Land. We have every right to pray for freedom from tyranny wherever it is found and to inquire of the Lord what our role is in securing the freedom of God's children wherever they are being held against their will.

But that is Bible history, you may say. God does not respond to a nation's cry for help in the same way today. Really? Let me give you a little glimpse into my past, in regard to freedom from the fear of tyranny. As a junior in high school in the late 1960's, I remember being sure that the Cold War would result in someone pushing the "button" which would start a nuclear holocaust long before I had the chance to live my adult life. I was not a Christian then and could see no way around the overwhelming sense of hopelessness that seemed to surround the international community in overcoming the Communist Bloc's quest for world domination. Then in 1989, as a married believer, my husband and I were driving to a supermarket to do our weekly food shopping, and we heard the absolutely electric announcement that Poland had overthrown their communist government! I had tears in my eyes, and remember thinking that I never expected to hear that announcement in my lifetime. Then the communist governments fell one by one, every few months.

What does this have to do with prayer and faith in God's sovereign intervention in the affairs of nations? Have you ever heard of a woman by the name of Feliksa Kaminska Walesa? She was Lech Walesa's mother. Lech Walesa was a human rights activist and trade-union organizer who became the President of Poland. He co-founded an organization named Solidarity, which eventually brought about Poland's independence. He has some interesting things to say about his mother. He credits his mother with passing on her great faith which led to her strong sense of justice. "Mother was very religious. My faith can be said almost to have flowed into me with my mother's milk."[18] Lech Walesa learned to yearn for justice at his mother's knee. He looked back on Polish history and made this observation: "We could only survive as a nation thanks to our deep belief in God, because we lived through some absolutely hopeless situations in history, and on several occasions, we were erased as a country from the map of the world. But thanks to our religious beliefs we survived."[19]

Feliksa Walesa followed a simple precept in raising her children. "Train up a child in the way he should go, even when he is old he will not depart from it" (Proverbs 22:6). God used a mother's faith to raise a son whose faith was strong enough to endure prison, and communist repression, whose vision and determination would be instrumental in changing the map of the world! Walesa's tenacity in resisting tyranny in Poland had a domino effect, which led to the downfall of the Iron Curtain. We have been blessed throughout history with those men and women who dare to see what is possible when God works through them. When Ronald Reagan challenged Mikhail Gorbachev to "tear down this wall"[20] (referring to the Berlin Wall), how many shared his optimism? God still works among the nations and responds to the prayers and faith of His people.

So how are we to pray for the nations? I would suggest that the most obvious starting point would be to pray for unbelievers to be exposed to the Gospel message, whether through Christian witnessing, Bible distribution and tracts, or Christian Radio broadcasting. Pray against spiritual warfare which blinds the eyes and ears of government leaders so they receive Satan's lies and emboldens them to lash out at their own citizens. Pray for kings and leaders to have their hearts miraculously changed through God's divine intervention. Learn about tyranny's face around the world and speak out whenever you have the opportunity. Pray for the needs of oppressed people around the world in Jesus' name. Use materials such as those available through Voice of the Martyrs (www.persecution.com) to become informed about the conditions in repressed countries around the globe. Pray without ceasing! Prayer works because our God is an awesome and powerful King!

CHAPTER 15

SPIRITUAL WARFARE AND PRAYER

Here is where the rubber really meets the road. The Lord pointed out a spiritual truth to me this morning during my "Quiet Time" with Him. I have been reading the Life Application Bible Commentary, 1 and 2 Corinthians, and came across this statement: "As Christians, we are running toward our heavenly reward. The essential disciplines of prayer, Bible Study, and worship equip us to run with vigor and stamina."[21]

This is not something I did not know. I have made these disciplines the cornerstone of my Christian walk a long time ago. But then I read the following statement later in the same commentary: "Believers must not become lazy – for Satan seeks to cause them to stumble, sin continues to buffet, and sorrow and pain are a daily reality."[22]

I am faced with an uncomfortable reality. While it is true that prayer, Bible Study and worship are crucial to my Christian walk, it is also true that I have not exactly, "… Run in such a way that you (I) may win" (I Corinthians 9: 24, parenthesis added by me). Busyness, my physical state, my emotional state, my spiritual state (especially unforgiveness and unconfessed sin), or a crisis in my life can quickly undermine my spiritual discipline. Why am I sharing all this with you? Because every time we stumble and fail to return to God's throne for refreshment and encouragement, Satan wins!

The truth is that Satan battles against anyone who loves God. It is as simple as that. The good news is that God has already won the war. The bad news is that every day we must make the conscientious choice to put

59

on the "Full Armor of God" and walk in that victory. Satan trembles when Christians get on their knees, so he does everything he can to distract us or entice us away from our prayer closet.

Preparing the manuscript for this book is very time consuming, even though the Prayer Cards themselves have been in existence for decades. While I am working on editing this material, I am also preparing a Bible Study Lesson each Sunday, word processing my husband's Bible Study Lesson, (we co-teach a Bible Study Class), and remaining involved in multiple ministries as well. Maintaining the discipline of meeting all my obligations in each of these areas as well as housekeeping chores and being a Christian wife can be overwhelming at times. They should be. That is what keeps us dependent on the Lord. However, Satan can easily tempt us to cut ourselves some slack, give ourselves a well-deserved break. Next thing you know, as you review your busy day as you lay in bed waiting to fall asleep, you realize, once again, that the Lord got the short end of your attention today. Nothing makes me angrier than to realize that Satan won another round!

What do we do about this devious spiritual warfare? The very first step is to recognize it for what it is. "Be of sober spirit, be on the alert. Your adversary, the devil, prowls about like a roaring lion, seeking someone to devour" (1 Peter 5:8). If you belong to the Lord, then you are by definition Satan's adversary. If your life is running smoothly and you face no trials or obstacles, you are not a threat to Satan's kingdom, and that in itself is a problem!

If, on the other hand, you find yourself questioning your effectiveness as a Christian witness, struggling with praying and living according to God's will, and find yourself distracted by both events and your own thought life, congratulations, you are definitely human and have much in common with the apostle Paul. There is hope for you: "For I joyfully concur with the law of God in the inner man, but I see a different law in the members of my body, waging war against the law of my mind, and making me a prisoner of the law of sin which is in my members. Wretched man that I am! Who will set me free from the body of this death? Thanks be to God through Jesus Christ our Lord! So then, on the one hand I myself with my mind am serving the law of God, but on the other, with my flesh the law of sin" (Romans 7:22-25). God knows about our spiritual battles. He offers us His personal promise, "No temptation has overtaken you but such as is common to man; and God is faithful, who will not allow you to be tempted beyond what you are able, but with the temptation will provide the way of escape also, that you may be able to endure it" (1 Corinthians 10:13). God is faithful and will come through for us, but we have a part to play as well. What is the "way of escape?"

God has provided the "Armor of God" to equip us to defeat Satan's attempts to sabotage our walk:

"Put on the full armor of God, that you may be able to stand firm against the schemes of the devil. For our struggle is not against flesh and blood, but against the rulers, against the powers, against the world forces of this darkness, against the spiritual forces of wickedness in the heavenly places. Therefore, take up the full armor of God, that you may be able to resist in the evil day, and having done everything, to stand firm. Stand firm therefore, having girded your loins with truth, and having put on the breastplate of righteousness, and having shod your feet with the preparation of the gospel of peace; in addition to all, taking up the shield of faith with which you will be able to extinguish all the flaming missiles of the evil one. And take the helmet of salvation, and the sword of the Spirit, which is the word of God. With all prayer and petition pray at all times in the Spirit, and with this in view, be on the alert with all perseverance and petition for all the saints" (Ephesians 6:11-18).

It is not my intention to introduce an in-depth commentary on the Armor of God, there are plenty of them out there for you to consult. I do, however, wish to point out two facts. Firstly, God has provided the tools for every believer to withstand the assault of Satan, which include salvation, faith and the Word of God. (I would also add worship. Satan hates to hear the Church worshipping, too.) Secondly, notice how this passage of Scripture ends; praying in the Spirit for all the saints! Why is that so important? If Satan can disrupt prayer, Bible Study and worship among the believers, then he can undermine the spreading of the Gospel. With wisdom, we can direct our prayers against the strongholds Satan tries to trip us up with.

I discussed the meaning of praying in the Spirit in Chapter 6, but it is important to recognize that God has given us a plethora of information about, as well as promises regarding, how to combat Satan. We are living in the enemy's camp. "We know that we are of God, and the whole world lies in the power of the evil one" (1 John 5:19). Prayer is the action resulting from submitting to God, and that act is rewarded with a promise, "Submit therefore to God. Resist the devil and he will flee from you" (James 4:7).

While we are to be aware of spiritual warfare, we are not to be afraid of it, we are to overcome it with the power of the Holy Spirit living in us. As He reveals areas under satanic attack in our personal lives, our family, our church and our nation; we are to intercede for divine protection and guidance. Our Heavenly Father offers us great hope, "You are from God, little children, and have overcome them; because greater is He who is in you than he who is in the world" (1 John 4:4). The victory has already been assured. "And the God of peace will soon crush Satan under your feet... " (Romans 16:20).

CHAPTER 16

WHY DOES JESUS PRAY?

This is the chapter that almost did not get written. I was busy editing my Prayer Cards for the second time with my eyes on the finish line. I began the day with my usual Bible Reading and God drew my attention to a verse in Mark 1:

"And in the early morning, while it was still dark, He (Jesus) arose and went out and departed to a lonely place, and was praying there" (Mark 1:35).

Jesus had a full day performing miracles of healing and casting out demons. He clearly had the power of God upon Him to carry out all that His Father had for Him to do. Why did Jesus need to pray? After all, He is God! He was without sin even when He was incarnate (in human form), and He obeyed His Father in all things, so why did He need to pray? God asked me how I could possibly write a book about prayer without considering Christ's example of dependence on prayer. I know that when God issues a challenge, He always provides the resources to meet that challenge.

As I meditated on this question, it became obvious that there were two separate issues to consider. Jesus prayed regularly while He dwelt among us and Jesus still prays to the Father today. Now, if I ran the world (I know, scary thought), God would simply act, whether God the Father, Son or Holy Spirit. I would imagine the three persons being equal, would automatically know what the Others thought and would be in agreement. But God's ways are higher than my ways (Isaiah 55:9), and there is much more involved than I ever considered.

When Jesus took on a mortal body, He also took on physical frailty. I am not just talking about the hunger, and tiredness. Jesus, who is omniscient (all-knowing), had to learn, step-by-step, just like we did.

"And Jesus kept increasing in wisdom and stature, and in favor with God and men" (Luke 2:52). If Jesus had to increase in wisdom, then He had clearly humbled Himself in order to become the Son of Man. He also had an indwelling experience, just like every believer has when they are born again; an initial indwelling by the Holy Spirit. For Jesus, that indwelling occurred long before Pentecost, at His baptism: "Now it came about when all the people were baptized, that Jesus also was baptized, and while He was praying, heaven was opened, and the Holy Spirit descended upon Him in bodily form like a dove, and a voice came out of heaven, "Thou art My beloved Son, in Thee I am well-pleased" (Luke 3:21-22).

John the Baptist referred to this experience, "And John bore witness saying, "I have beheld the Spirit descending as a dove out of heaven, and He remained upon Him" (John 1:32). Clearly this verse indicates that Jesus did not come to earth with the Spirit dwelling in Him. He was anointed for His public ministry which began with his public baptism.

Jesus retreated from the busyness of the world frequently to spend time with His Father in a quiet, lonely place. He prayed for wisdom, strength and His Father's will throughout His ministry. Communication with Abba Father was essential for the success of His mission here on earth. "But He Himself would often slip away to the wilderness and pray (Luke 5:16).

In the next chapter of Luke, we have an example of Jesus praying for wisdom. "And it was at this time that He went off to the mountain to pray, and He spent the whole night in prayer to God. And when day came, He called His disciples to Him; and chose twelve of them, whom He also named as apostles" (Luke 6:12-13). Clearly, the calling and naming of the twelve apostles was the direct result of an all-night vigil with God the Father. Jesus sought His Father's wisdom for this historical selection.

On another occasion, Jesus drew strength, confirmed His calling, and demonstrated the importance of prayer when He raised His friend Lazarus from the dead. "And so they removed the stone. And Jesus raised His eyes, and said, "Father, I thank Thee that Thou heardest Me. "And I knew that Thou hearest Me always; but because of the people standing around I said it, that they may believe that Thou didst send Me." And when He had said these things, He cried out with a loud voice, "Lazarus, come forth" (John 11:41-43).

Jesus demonstrated both His emotional turmoil and His need to reconfirm His Father's will during the most critical event in His earthly life; His sacrifice on the cross. In the Garden of Gethsemane, immediately preceding His arrest, He asked His three closest disciples, Peter, James and John to watch and pray with Him:

"Then Jesus came with them to a place called Gethsemane, and said to His disciples, "Sit here while I go over there and pray." And He took with Him Peter and the two sons of Zebedee, and began to be grieved and distressed. Then He said to them, "My soul is deeply grieved, to the point of death; remain here and keep watch with Me. "And He went a little beyond them, and fell on His face and prayed, saying, "My Father, if it is possible, let this cup pass from Me; yet not as I will, but as Thou wilt" (Matthew 26:36-39).

Although the 'inner circle' fell asleep and did not support their Master in prayer, by the time Jesus had finished His prayer vigil, He was ready for His mission and well aware of His fate.

Jesus gives us ample reason to bathe our Christian walk in prayer. If He demonstrated the priority of communication with His Father in His sinless, obedient walk here on earth, then clearly we have a desperate need for God's wisdom, guidance, comfort, power, will and forgiveness in our own lives. Only deep regular times of coming before the Lord to hear from Him and receive His instructions will equip us to finish the course He has set before each one of us.

What about today? Jesus still prays, even though He no longer has to contend with weakness which is inherent in having a physical body i.e. susceptibility to physical and emotional frailty. Why? Romans 8:34 states that, "… Christ Jesus is He who died, yes, rather who was raised, who is at the right hand of God, who also intercedes for us" (Romans 8:34). Why must He spend time praying for us? Why does He not just exercise His majesty and cause all things to work according to His Father's will? The answer the Lord gave me is both simple and breathtakingly appropriate. The same Savior who became our Paschal Lamb (who took away the sins of the world) is also by Divine Decree, our High Priest:

"but He, on the other hand, because He abides forever, holds His priesthood permanently. Hence, also, He is able to save forever those who draw near to God through Him, since He always lives to make intercession for them. For it was fitting that we should have such a high priest, holy, innocent, undefiled, separated from sinners and exalted above the heavens; who does not need daily, like those high priests, to offer up sacrifices, first for His own sins, and then for the sins of the people, because this He did once for all when He offered up Himself" (Hebrews 7:24-27).

What a perfect plan! The Paschal Lamb, the perfect sacrifice for our sins has become the only High Priest who does not need to offer up a sacrifice before He goes into the presence of the Holy God of Israel to offer prayers for the people of God.

Stephen Cole, a Baptist pastor, has recently published a Bible study on the subject of Jesus as our High Priest, from Hebrews 5.[23] He states, "Jesus Christ perfectly fulfills the qualifications for the kind of high priest that we all need." He goes on to say that, "the qualifications for human high priests were to mediate between men and God and to sympathize with his fellow sinners, and to be called by God to the office."[24]

Jesus Christ is fulfilling one of His many roles today in heaven as our High Priest, "being designated by God as a high priest according to the order of Melchizedek" (Hebrews 5:10). He will also return to earth to fulfill another of His divine roles, as our King of Kings. It is clear that Jesus' days of praying are not over. He is praying before the throne of God continually in heaven.

What about us? Did you know that we too are priests? "... you also, as living stones, are being built up as a spiritual house for a holy priesthood, to offer up spiritual sacrifices acceptable to God through Jesus Christ... But you are a chosen race, a royal priesthood, a holy nation, a people for God's own possession, that you may proclaim the excellencies of Him who has called you out of darkness into His marvelous light" (1 Peter 2:5, 9).

What does it mean that we are part of a holy priesthood? We believers offer up spiritual sacrifices of worship, obedience and prayer because we have been cleansed by the indwelling Holy Spirit. Therefore, we may enter into the presence of the Lord at any time, unlike the Old Testament priests. Because of Christ's work on the cross, we have direct access to our High Priest without a mediator. "For we do not have a high priest who cannot sympathize with our weaknesses, but One who has been tempted in all things as we are, yet without sin. Let us therefore draw near with confidence to the throne of grace, that we may receive mercy and may find grace to help in times of need" (Hebrews 4:15-16). According to Revelation 1:6, "He has made us to be a kingdom, priest to His God and Father; to Him be the glory and the dominion forever and ever." As part of Christ's priesthood, it is our privilege to offer up prayers as God's earthly intercessors.

Jesus is our model in the art of prayer. We cannot understand the importance of the role of prayer in a believer's life without considering how Jesus fulfilled His responsibility as a Prayer Warrior here on earth. He went off to a quiet place to get alone with God, receive His marching orders, and be refreshed and strengthened throughout His ministry. Jesus is still petitioning the throne on our behalf from heaven. If Jesus demonstrated that every aspect of His life was bathed in prayer, can we treat the privilege of prayer with any less seriousness?

CHAPTER 17

WRITING PRAYER CARDS

I know what you're thinking. "Why would I want to write a Prayer Card? That is why I bought this book." Remember me telling you In Chapter 3, Effective Prayer, about creating a Prayer Card box full of index cards? The reason for that format was for the purpose of adding new cards as the Lord led me in prayer. As a matter of fact, once I word processed all the cards in that box, guess what happened? Immediately, as I went to the Lord in intercessory prayer, He gave me three new topics to pray about within the next ten days. I now had Prayer Card Addendums to two of my Prayer Card Letters. (Incidentally, you can pencil in the topic where it belongs alphabetically in the Prayer Card section, and add your own Prayer Cards at the end of book in an Addendum section).

I want to walk you through the process and the resources I use to create new Prayer Cards in case you want to actively pursue expanding your Prayer Card inventory as the Holy Spirit leads. Just be forewarned, if you become a committed Prayer Warrior, He will take you places you never imagined before, but I promise you it is an exciting journey you won't want to miss.

The first issue I need to address in establishing a reference library for this purpose is to suggest that you see what you already have available in your home. Whether you prefer (or own) physical books or own Bible software may determine which route you select, or as in my case, a combination of both. There are two parts to every Prayer Card; the definition and the actual Scriptures. In some cases, there are also antonyms (opposites) provided with Scripture as well, which are useful in bringing balance to prayer requests. I am reminded of a Scripture here; "Now when the unclean spirit goes out of a man, it passes through waterless places, seeking rest, and does not find it." Then it says, 'I will return to my house from which I came'; and when it comes, it finds it unoccupied, swept, and put in order." Then it goes, and takes along with it seven other spirits more wicked than itself, and they go in and live there; and the last state of that man becomes worse than the first… " (Matthew 12:43-45). We may not be praying against evil spirits, but the concept is the same; praying against a particular sin may be only half the job, praying for the "Christian Character Trait" to replace the sin may be equally important.

I will illustrate the process of writing a Prayer Card by walking you through one, step by step, but first I want to suggest that if you own a computer and prefer to research using twenty-first century technology, you are very fortunate, because there are many good choices out there.

The first resource you will need is a dictionary. The two simplest ones I know of are dictionary.com[25] and Google.[26] To use Google search, all you need to do is type the word you wish to define in the search bar with the word define after it, which will return a brief definition. The advantage of dictionary.com is that it also includes a thesaurus which can sometimes be very helpful. Most of the time, however, the term you are defining is a Bible or Christian theology term and for that you need a different source.

There are a few free Bible software programs available online which will provide the basics. E-Sword,[27] The Word,[28] and WordsearchBibleBasic,[29] are three of the most popular. I use Quicksearch 10,[30] because it is very user friendly and has an extensive free library you can download. It might be more cost effective in the long run to invest in a Bundle Package which includes a wide variety of Bible Study tools.

The first order of business is to define the term. Let us use the term wrath and generate a Prayer Card to demonstrate the steps involved. The first place I look for a definition is in the Bible dictionaries. My personal favorites would be Holman,[31] Unger's,[32] Easton's[33] and AMG Concise[34] Dictionaries. The reason I start with the Bible Dictionaries is that they come closer to the biblical meaning. By way of example, the Google definition of wrath simply says extreme anger; dictionary.com adds the dimensions of resentment, vengeance and punishment, which comes closer to the Bible definition but leaves out some valuable information. I love Holman's definition: "The emotional response to perceived wrong and injustice, often translated "anger," "indignation," "vexation," and "irritation."[35] Both humans and God express wrath." That is a good basic definition for the purposes of a Prayer Card. A second step you might want to pursue; would be to look up the opposite of wrath in dictionary.com. In this case the Thesaurus offers happiness as an antonym for wrath which does not quite match the biblical teaching on the subject of wrath, so it would not be a useful line of pursuit in this case. If finding a working definition of a term becomes allusive using the usual sources, I sometimes find myself going to my go-to reference, the Life Application Bible Notes[36] after I have located one solid Bible Verse on the topic which sometimes contains definitions within the commentary.*

Now that you have a working definition, the next step is to find Bible verses that edify the subject and also lend themselves to being used as a prayer back to God on the subject. I have a whole host of favorite resources to locate Bible verses, but I tripped over the easiest one quite by accident. Google has the uncanny ability to find almost any Bible verse the Lord puts in my head, regardless of the translation of the Bible I may be familiar with. I recall a verse that speaks of leaving room for the wrath of God. When I type that phrase into the Google search, up pops Romans 12:19! "Never take your own revenge, beloved, but leave room for the wrath of God, for it is written," Vengeance is Mine, I will repay," says the Lord."

At this point you can either look up the verse in your favorite version of the Bible or click on the verse in the Google result and the verse will pop up. I looked farther down the search results, and found a reference to Acts 17:11 which led me to a Bible Study on wrath[37] which included Nahum 1:2; "A jealous and avenging God is the Lord; the Lord is avenging and wrathful. The Lord takes vengeance on His adversaries, and He reserves wrath for His enemies." Incidentally, that same Bible study pointed out two aspects of wrath that are edifying; 1) The purpose of God's wrath is not discipline… but to destroy and eternally judge, and 2) Christians need not fear the wrath of God.[38] We have God's promise that we are His chosen.

Other sources for appropriate Scripture include Topical Indexes which list Bible verses according to the subject. My personal favorites are NASB Topical[39] and Nave's Topics.[40] When I looked up wrath in the New American Standard Bible,[41] for instance, I found John 3:36 which says, "He who believes in the Son has eternal life; but he who does not obey the Son shall not see life, but the wrath of God abides on him." This verse authenticates the second statement in the above Bible Study reference. Additional sources for locating Bible Verses include concordances, my favorites being Zondervan NASB Concordance[42] and Strong's Comprehensive Concordance.[43] Sometimes, when specific verses are hard to locate, I use Roget's Thesaurus of the Bible[44] which has the ability to suggest an alternate word to look up. For instance, wrath is not listed in Roget's Thesaurus, but the subject index[45] suggests looking up anger, and there the very first entry is, "for the Law brings about wrath… " (Romans 4:15).[46] As I read down the list of entries in Roget's Thesaurus, I notice that God admonishes man not to engage in wrathful behavior. "… But let everyone be quick to hear, slow to speak and slow to anger; for the anger of man does not achieve the righteousness of God" (James 1:19-20).[47]

So with the information I just looked up on the subject of wrath, the Prayer Card might look like this:

wrath: 1) the emotional response to perceived wrong and injustice, often translated anger, indignation, vexation, and irritation; 2) God's purpose for wrath is destruction, not discipline, but Christians need not fear God's wrath

"A jealous and avenging God is the Lord; the Lord is avenging and wrathful. The Lord takes vengeance on His adversaries, and He reserves wrath for His enemies" (Nahum 1:2).

"Never take your own revenge, beloved, but leave room for the wrath of God, for it is written, "Vengeance is Mine, I will repay," says the Lord" (Romans 12:19).

"Wherefore, my beloved brethren, let every man be swift to hear, slow to speak, slow to wrath: For the wrath of man worketh not the righteousness of God" (James 1:19-20 KJV).

Notice that the last verse is from the King James Version of the Bible. When the topic is not specifically indicated in the verse, I sometimes check other versions of the Bible. In this case, the King James used the exact term wrath, where my Bible version of choice, the New American Standard Version does not.

While researching a Prayer Card may seem labor intensive, I promise you this. Firstly, you will learn more and more about how God's kingdom works. Secondly, looking back you will be astounded by the knowledge you have accumulated. Thirdly, you will feel increasingly more confident that you are praying the Lord's will, and will be able to rejoice with Him in answered prayers. Remember, prayers never go unheard and they outlast our finite lifetime!

William Borden is an example of a man committed to following after God. He graduated from both Yale and Princeton Theological Seminary and had a heart for the Muslims of Northern China. His life ended at the age of twenty-five, while studying in Egypt in 1913 after contracting cerebral meningitis. A good biography of his short life is called *Borden of Yale.*[48] Were his prayers for those lost souls in Northern China unheard? Definitely not. Borden himself bequeathed one million dollars to the Chinese Missions. In 2004, a Church Planting Movement in a northern Chinese province has seen 20,000 new believers and 500 new churches planted in less than five years.[49] Borden's burden for those precious non-believers was heard!

God honors our prayers in His own time. Since our lives are eternal, whether they are answered this side of heaven or not does not diminish their effectiveness! So keep praying, fellow Prayer Warriors! It is our highest privilege to be part of God's eternal plans for His kingdom!

*Note:
For more information please refer to the Prayer Card Endnotes on page 313.

A PRAYER CARDS

__Abba:__ **1)** translated "Father", but the closeness of the relationship conveys the warm sense of intimacy; "Daddy"[50]

"For you have not received a spirit of slavery leading to fear again, but you have received a spirit of adoption as sons by which we cry out, "Abba! Father"! (Romans 8:15)

"And because you are sons, God has sent forth the Spirit of His Son into our hearts, crying, "Abba! Father!" Therefore you are no longer a slave, but a son; and if a son, then an heir through God." (Galatians 4:6-7)

__abide:__ 1) to stand fast or remain in; 2) making the conscious decision to follow Christ; 3) surrendering our independence to receive all from Him

"But now abide faith, hope, love, these three; but the greatest of these is love." (1 Corinthians 13:13)

"And the world is passing away, and also its lusts; but the one who does the will of God abides forever." (1 John 2:17)

"… If what you heard from the beginning abides in you, you also will abide in the Son and in the Father." (1 John 2:24)

"Abide in Me, and I in you. As the branch cannot bear fruit of itself, unless it abides in the vine, so neither can you, unless you abide in Me . . . "By this is My Father glorified, that you bear much fruit, and so prove to be My disciples." (John 15:4, 8)

abundant life: 1) bountiful blessings and joy in serving Christ now; 2) eternal life with Christ in the future

"The thief comes only to steal, and kill, and destroy; I came that they might have life, and might have it abundantly." (John 10:10)

"The Lord is my shepherd, I shall not want. He makes me lie down in green pastures; He leads me beside quiet waters. He restores my soul; He guides me in the paths of righteousness For His name's sake." (Psalm 23:1-3)

"but whoever drinks of the water that I shall give him shall never thirst; but the water that I shall give him shall become in him a well of water springing up to eternal life." (John 4:14)

"… we are children of God, and if children, heirs also, heirs of God and fellow heirs with Christ, if indeed we suffer with Him in order that we may also be glorified with Him." (Romans 8:16-17)

accountability: 1) to be answerable to another for our conduct; especially to God

"And I say to you, that every careless word that men shall speak, they shall render account for it in the day of judgment." (Matthew 12:36)

"Obey your leaders, and submit to them; for they keep watch over your souls, as those who will give an account... " (Hebrews 13:17)

"For the time already past is sufficient for you to have carried out the desire of the Gentiles, having pursued a course of sensuality, lusts, drunkenness, carousals, drinking parties and abominable idolatries… but they shall give account to Him who is ready to judge the living and the dead." (1 Peter 4:3, 5)

"But because of your stubbornness and unrepentant heart you are storing up wrath for yourself in the day of wrath and revelation of the righteous judgment of God, who will render to every man according to his deeds" (Romans 2:5-6)

adultery: 1) a sexual relationship between a man and a woman outside of marriage

"You have heard that it was said, 'you shall not commit adultery'; but I say to you, that everyone who looks on a woman to lust for her has committed adultery with her already in his heart." (Matthew 5:27-28)

advocate: 1) in legal terms, an attorney or defender; 2) Both Christ and the Holy Spirit defend us before the throne of God, ensuring us of God's acceptance.

"My little children, I am writing these things to you that you may not sin. And if anyone sins, we have an Advocate with the Father, Jesus Christ the righteous; and He Himself is the propitiation for our sins; and not for ours only, but also for those of the whole world." (1 John 2:1-2)

"And I will ask the Father, and He will give you another Helper, that He may be with you forever." (John 14:16)

agape: 1) deep, self-sacrificing love especially where it is not merited; 2) required by God of all believers

"A new commandment I give to you, that you love one another, even as I have loved you, that you also love one another. "By this all men will know that you are My disciples, if you have love for one another." (John 13:34-35)

"And if I give all my possessions to feed the poor, and if I deliver my body to be burned, but do not have love, it profits me nothing. Love is patient, love is kind, and is not jealous; love does not brag and is not arrogant, does not act unbecomingly; it does not seek its own, is not provoked, does not take into account a wrong suffered, does not rejoice in unrighteousness, but rejoices with the truth; bears all things, believes all things, hopes all things, endures all things." (1 Corinthians 13:3-7)

aging: 1) a human's lifespan, especially the latter part of life

"Bless the Lord, O my soul; and all that is within me, bless His holy name… Who pardons all your iniquities; who heals all your diseases… Who satisfies your years with good things, so that your youth is renewed like the eagle." (Psalm 103:1-5)

"The righteous man will flourish like the palm tree, He will grow like a cedar in Lebanon. Planted in the house of the Lord, they will flourish in the courts of our God. They will still yield fruit in old age; they shall be full of sap and very green." (Psalm 92:12-14)

"For I know the plans that I have for you,' declares the Lord, 'plans for welfare and not for calamity to give you a future and a hope." (Jeremiah 29:11)

alcoholism: 1) drinking too much liquor especially on a regular basis; overindulgence

"Wine is a mocker, strong drink a brawler, and whoever is intoxicated by it is not wise." (Proverbs 20:1)

"And do not get drunk with wine, for that is dissipation, but be filled with the Spirit" (Ephesians 5:18)

altar of incense: 1) gold covered piece of furniture in the Temple which became the symbol of all believers prayers in the New Testament

"We have an altar, from which those who serve the tabernacle have no right to eat… Through Him then, let us continually offer up a sacrifice of praise to God, that is, the fruit of lips that give thanks to His name." (Hebrews 13: 10, 15)

"And another angel came and stood at the altar, holding a golden censer; and much incense was given to him, that he might add it to the prayers of all the saints upon the golden altar which was before the throne. And the smoke of the incense, with the prayers of the saints, went up before God out of the angel's hand." (Revelation 8:3-4)

angelic protection: 1) angels are charged with watching over believers as guardians especially in times of danger and stress

"For He will give His angels charge concerning you, to guard you in all your ways. They will bear you up in their hands, lest you strike your foot against a stone." (Psalm 91:11-12)

"But an angel of the Lord during the night opened the gates of the prison, and taking them out he said, "Go your way, stand and speak to the people in the temple the whole message of this Life." (Acts 5:19-20)

"My God sent His angel and shut the lions' mouths, and they have not harmed me, inasmuch as I was found innocent before Him; and also toward you, O king, I have committed no crime." (Daniel 6:22)

"Now when they had departed, behold, an angel of the Lord appeared to Joseph in a dream, saying, "Arise and take the Child and His mother, and flee to Egypt, and remain there until I tell you; for Herod is going to search for the Child to destroy Him." (Matthew 2:13-14)

anger: 1) strong passion of displeasure sometimes excited by perceived injury or insult; 2) not sin in itself, but may result in evil actions if not controlled

"Wherefore, my beloved brethren, let every man be swift to hear, slow to speak, slow to wrath: For the wrath of man worketh not the righteousness of God." (James 1:19-20 KJV)

"Cease from anger, and forsake wrath; do not fret, it leads only to evildoing." (Psalm 37:8)

"be angry, and yet do not sin; do not let the sun go down on your anger" (Ephesians 4:26)

"Let all bitterness and wrath and anger and clamor and slander be put away from you, along with all malice." (Ephesians 4:31)

anointing: 1) pouring oil over someone for a specific occasion; 2) to consecrate as king, pray for healing, appoint to a duty, or to prepare for burial; 3) the Holy Spirit in each believer's life

"The Spirit of the Lord God is upon me, because the Lord has anointed me to bring good news to the afflicted; He has sent me to bind up the brokenhearted, to proclaim liberty to captives, and freedom to prisoners." (Isaiah 61:1)

"Now He who establishes us with you in Christ and anointed us is God, who also sealed us and gave us the Spirit in our hearts as a pledge." (2 Corinthians 1:21-22)

"And as for you, the anointing which you received from Him abides in you, and you have no need for anyone to teach you; but as His anointing teaches you about all things, and is true and is not a lie, and just as it has taught you, you abide in Him." (1 John 2:27)

anxiety: 1) restless agitation or uneasiness brought on by the storms of life; 2) fear without adequate cause, lack of trust in God's protection and provision

"Be anxious for nothing, but in everything by prayer and supplication with thanksgiving let your requests be made known to God. And the peace of God, which surpasses all comprehension, shall guard your hearts and your minds in Christ Jesus." (Philippians 4:6-7)

"Therefore do not be anxious for tomorrow; for tomorrow will care for itself. Each day has enough trouble of its own." (Matthew 6:34)

"Look at the birds of the air, that they do not sow, neither do they reap, nor gather into barns, and yet your heavenly Father feeds them. Are you not worth much more than they? "And which of you by being anxious can add a single cubit to his life's span?" (Matthew 6:26-27)

apathy: 1) being without spiritual zeal; 2) doubt or indifference to God's grace

"I know your deeds, that you are neither cold nor hot; I would that you were cold or hot. 'So because you are lukewarm, and neither hot nor cold, I will spit you out of My mouth... Those whom I love, I reprove and discipline; be zealous therefore, and repent." (Revelation 3:15-16, 19)

"And He saw that there was no man, and was astonished that there was no one to intercede; then His own arm brought salvation to Him; and His righteousness upheld Him." (Isaiah 59:16)

"And I searched for a man among them who should build up the wall and stand in the gap before Me for the land, that I should not destroy it; but I found no one." (Ezekiel 22:30)

"And because lawlessness is increased, most people's love will grow cold." (Matthew 24:12)

appearance of evil: 1) those activities which God considers an abomination; 2) those situations which might tempt a believer to disobey God and allow Satan to gain a foothold

"Prove all things; hold fast that which is good. Abstain from all appearance of evil." (1 Thessalonians 5:21-22 KJV)

"Let love be without hypocrisy. Abhor what is evil; cling to what is good." (Romans 12:9)

"Therefore let us not judge one another anymore, but rather determine this-- not to put an obstacle or a stumbling block in a brother's way." (Romans 14:13)

application: 1) learning the principles found in the Word and understanding its deep implications in order to take proper action

"All Scripture is inspired by God and profitable for teaching, for reproof, for correction, for training in righteousness; that the man of God may be adequate, equipped for every good work." (2 Timothy 3:16-17)

"But prove yourselves doers of the word, and not merely hearers who delude themselves." (James 1:22)

"For the word of God is living and active and sharper than any two-edged sword, and piercing as far as the division of soul and spirit, of both joints and marrow, and able to judge the thoughts and intentions of the heart." (Hebrews 4:12)

armor of God: 1) the supernatural power of God given to all believers through the Holy Spirit to defeat Satan and every form of evil

"Put on the full armor of God, that you may be able to stand firm against the schemes of the devil. For our struggle is not against flesh and blood, but against the rulers, against the powers, against the world forces of this darkness, against the spiritual forces of wickedness in the heavenly places." (Ephesians 6:11-12)

"Stand firm therefore, having girded your loins with truth, and having put on the breastplate of righteousness, and having shod your feet with the preparation of the Gospel of peace; in addition to all, taking up the shield of faith with which you will be able to extinguish all the flaming missiles of the evil one. And take the helmet of salvation, and the sword of the Spirit, which is the Word of God." (Ephesians 6:14-17)

arrogance: 1) making claims of superior intelligence or importance due to pride; independence from God

"Boast no more so very proudly, do not let arrogance come out of your mouth; for the Lord is a God of knowledge, and with Him actions are weighed." (1 Samuel 2:3)

"The fear of the Lord is to hate evil; pride and arrogance and the evil way, and the perverted mouth, I hate." (Proverbs 8:13)

"For the wrath of God is revealed from heaven against all ungodliness and unrighteousness of men, who suppress the truth in unrighteousness... haters of God, insolent, arrogant, boastful, inventors of evil, disobedient to parents, without understanding, untrustworthy, unloving, unmerciful." (Romans 1: 18, 30-31)

"For men will be lovers of self, lovers of money, boastful, arrogant, revilers, disobedient to parents, ungrateful, unholy... treacherous, reckless, conceited, lovers of pleasure rather than lovers of God" (2 Timothy 3:2, 4)

assurance: 1) a declaration designed to inspire confidence; 2) the Word gives believers confidence in their future with Christ

"And we desire that each one of you show the same diligence so as to realize the full assurance of hope until the end, that you may not be sluggish, but imitators of those who through faith and patience inherit the promises." (Hebrews 6:11-12)

"let us draw near with a sincere heart in full assurance of faith, having our hearts sprinkled clean from an evil conscience and our bodies washed with pure water. Let us hold fast the confession of our hope without wavering, for He who promised is faithful" (Hebrews 10:22-23)

"For I am confident of this very thing, that He who began a good work in you will perfect it until the day of Christ Jesus." (Philippians 1:6)

attitude: 1) the disposition or action of an individual which indicate his feelings or intentions; 2) Christ expects us to have an attitude of obedience and surrender to Him

"Behold, how good and how pleasant it is for brothers to dwell together in unity!" (Psalm 133:1)

"(Love) does not act unbecomingly; it does not seek its own, is not provoked, does not take into account a wrong suffered." (1 Corinthians 13:5)

"But no one can tame the tongue; it is a restless evil and full of deadly poison. With it we bless our Lord and Father; and with it we curse men, who have been made in the likeness of God; from the same mouth come both blessing and cursing. My brethren, these things ought not to be this way." (James 3:8-10)

authoritarian: 1) persons who exercise power over others in a stern, cruel or tyrannical manner; demanding unquestioning obedience

"And He answered and said to them, "And why do you yourselves transgress the commandment of God for the sake of your tradition? ... "You hypocrites, rightly did Isaiah prophesy of you, saying, 'This people honors Me with their lips, but their heart is far away from Me. 'But in vain do they worship Me, teaching as doctrines the precepts of men." (Matthew 15:3, 7-9)

"The scribes and the Pharisees... tie up heavy loads, and lay them on men's shoulders; but they themselves are unwilling to move them with so much as a finger. But they do all their deeds to be noticed by men; for they broaden their phylacteries, and lengthen the tassels of their garments." (Matthew 23:2, 4-5)

authority: 1) legal or rightful power of persons or bodies in government, judicial courts or church matters

"But Jesus called them to Himself, and said, "You know that the rulers of the Gentiles lord it over them, and their great men exercise authority over them. "It is not so among you, but whoever wishes to become great among you shall be your servant." (Matthew 20:25-26)

"But he who boasts, let him boast in the Lord. For not he who commends himself is approved, but whom the Lord commends." (2 Corinthians 10:17-18)

"And He gave some as apostles, and some as prophets, and some as evangelists, and some as pastors and teachers, for the equipping of the saints for the work of service, to the building up of the body of Christ." (Ephesians 4:11-12)

available: 1) usable; willingness to serve for a purpose; 2) sufficient to meet the objective

"I urge you therefore, brethren, by the mercies of God, to present your bodies a living and holy sacrifice, acceptable to God, which is your spiritual service of worship." (Romans 12:1)

"And since we have gifts that differ according to the grace given to us, let each exercise them accordingly." (Romans 12:6)

"… whoever serves, let him do so as by the strength which God supplies; so that in all things God may be glorified through Jesus Christ." (1 Peter 4:11)

"All Scripture is inspired by God and profitable for teaching, for reproof, for correction, for training in righteousness; that the man of God man be adequate, equipped for every good work." (2 Timothy 3:16-17)

awe: 1) amazement, fear of the Lord; 2) our response to the presence of God

"You shall not dread them, for the Lord your God is in your midst, a great and awesome God." (Deuteronomy 7:21)

"Princes persecute me without cause, but my heart stands in awe of Thy words." (Psalm 119:161)

"You who fear the Lord, praise Him; all you descendants of Jacob, glorify Him, and stand in awe of Him, all you descendants of Israel." (Psalm 22:23)

B PRAYER CARDS

backbiting: 1) slander, bearing false witness, saying spiteful things behind someone's back

"The north wind brings forth rain, and a backbiting tongue, an angry countenance." (Proverbs 25:23)

"For the wrath of God is revealed from heaven against all ungodliness and unrighteousness of men, who suppress the truth in unrighteousness... gossips, slanderers, haters of God, insolent, arrogant, boastful, inventors of evil, disobedient to parents." (Romans 1:18, 29-30)

"A gentle answer turns away wrath, but a harsh word stirs up anger. The tongue of the wise makes knowledge acceptable, but the mouth of fools spouts folly. The eyes of the Lord are in every place, watching the evil and the good." (Proverbs 15:1-3)

balance: 1) to compare in importance or value; 2) to settle or make appropriate adjustments

"There is an appointed time for everything. And there is a time for every event under heaven... A time to tear apart, and a time to sew together; a time to be silent, and a time to speak." (Ecclesiastes 3:1, 7)

"Rejoice always; pray without ceasing; in everything give thanks; for this is God's will for you in Christ Jesus. Do not quench the Spirit; do not despise prophetic utterances. But examine everything carefully;

hold fast to that which is good; abstain from every form of evil." (1 Thessalonians 5:16-22)

"… And I show you a still more excellent way… But now abide faith, hope, love, these three; but the greatest of these is love." (1 Corinthians 12:31, 13:13)

Berean: 1) to evaluate sermons, books, teachings, and practices according to God's Word

"Now these were more noble-minded than those in Thessalonica, for they received the word with great eagerness, examining the Scriptures daily, to see whether these things were so." (Acts 17:11)

"And she (Martha) had a sister called Mary, who moreover was listening to the Lord's word, seated at His feet . . . for Mary has chosen the good part, which shall not be taken away from her." (Luke 10:39, 42)

"Be diligent to present yourself approved to God as a workman who does not need to be ashamed, handling accurately the word of truth." (2 Timothy 2:15)

"do not despise prophetic utterances. But examine everything carefully; hold fast to that which is good; abstain from every form of evil." (1 Thessalonians 5:20-22)

best: 1) the highest quality, the most excellence

"But now abide faith, hope, love, these three; but the greatest of these is love." (1 Corinthians 13:13)

"seeing that His divine power has granted to us everything pertaining to life and godliness, through the true knowledge of Him who called us by His own glory and excellence." (2 Peter 1:3)

"But this I admit to you, that according to the Way which they call a sect I do serve the God of our fathers, believing everything that is in accordance with the Law, and that is written in the Prophets... "In view of this, I also do my best to maintain always a blameless conscience both before God and before men." (Acts 24:14, 16)

"... Mary has chosen the good part, which shall not be taken away from her." (Luke 10:42)

(neglect of) Bible study: 1) rejecting meditation in God's Word; wanting no part of God's demand for a regular disciplined life

"To whom shall I speak and give warning, that they may hear? Behold, their ears are closed, and they cannot listen. Behold, the word of the Lord has become a reproach to them; they have no delight in it." (Jeremiah 6:10)

"For the time will come when they will not endure sound doctrine; but wanting to have their ears tickled, they will accumulate for themselves teachers in accordance to their own desires; and will turn away their ears from the truth, and will turn aside to myths." (2 Timothy 4:3-4)

"But his delight is in the law of the Lord, and in His law he meditates day and night." (Psalm 1:2)

"You, however, continue in the things you have learned and become convinced of, knowing from whom you have learned them; and that from childhood you have known the sacred writings which are able to give you the wisdom that leads to salvation through faith which is in Christ Jesus. All Scripture is inspired by God and profitable for teaching, for reproof, for correction, for training in righteousness." (2 Timothy 3:14-16)

bitterness: 1) resentfulness, sarcasm, enmity especially toward God

"Let all bitterness and wrath and anger and clamor and slander be put away from you, along with all malice." (Ephesians 4:31)

"Pursue peace with all men, and the sanctification without which no one will see the Lord. See to it that no one comes short of the grace of God; that no root of bitterness springing up causes trouble, and by it many be defiled." (Hebrews 12:14-15)

blessing: 1) approved by God, divine favor especially in the future

"And I will make them and the places around My hill a blessing. And I will cause showers to come down in their season; they will be showers of blessing." (Ezekiel 34:26)

"Blessings are on the head of the righteous... " (Proverbs 10:6)

"May you be blessed of the Lord, maker of heaven and earth." (Psalm 115:15)

"The Lord bless you, and keep you; the Lord make His face shine on you, and be gracious to you; the Lord lift up His countenance on you, and give you peace." (Numbers 6:24-26)

boasting: 1) glorifying oneself rather than God, to brag

"For who regards you as superior? And what do you have that you did not receive? But if you did receive it, why do you boast as if you had not received it?" (1 Corinthians 4:7)

"Do nothing from selfishness or empty conceit, but with humility of mind let each of you regard one another as more important than himself" (Philippians 2:3)

body: 1) figuratively, the spiritual unity of all Christians into the Church universal

"There is one body and one Spirit, just as also you were called in one hope of your calling; one Lord, one faith, one baptism, one God and Father of all who is over all and through all and in all." (Ephesians 4:4-6)

"For even as the body is one and yet has many members, and all the members of the body, though they are many, are one body, so also is Christ. For by one Spirit we were all baptized into one body, whether Jews or Greeks, whether slaves or free, and we were all made to drink of one Spirit." (1 Corinthians 12:12-13)

"Holy Father, keep them in Thy name, the name which Thou hast given Me, that they may be one, even as We are... that they may all be one; even as Thou, Father, art in Me, and I in Thee, that they also may be in Us; that the world may believe that Thou didst send Me." (John 17:11, 21)

(harming the) body: 1) figuratively, destroying the Church through false teaching, creating dissension or slandering individual believers

"Do you not know that you are a temple of God, and that the Spirit of God dwells in you? If any man destroys the temple of God, God will destroy him, for the temple of God is holy, and that is what you are." (1 Corinthians 3:16-17)

boldness: 1) being forthright about the Truth of the Gospel without regard for personal consequences

"but sanctify Christ as Lord in your hearts, always being ready to make a defense to everyone who asks you to give an account for the hope that is in you, yet with gentleness and reverence." (1 Peter 3:15)

"For God has not given us a spirit of timidity, but of power and love and discipline." (2 Timothy 1:7)

"And when they had prayed, the place where they had gathered together was shaken, and they were all filled with the Holy Spirit, and began to speak the word of God with boldness. And the congregation of those who believed were of one heart and soul; and not one of them claimed that anything belonging to him was his own; but all things were common property to them." (Acts 4:31-32)

"Only be strong and very courageous; be careful to do according to all the law which Moses My servant commanded you; do not turn from it to the right or to the left, so that you may have success wherever you go. "This book of the law shall not depart from your mouth, but you shall meditate on it day and night, so that you may be careful to do according to all that is written in it; for then you will make your way prosperous, and then you will have success. Have I not commanded you? Be strong and courageous! Do not tremble or be dismayed, for the Lord your God is with you wherever you go." (Joshua 1:7-9)

bond: 1) that influence which binds us together in fellowship; either through personal attraction or covenant

"And beyond all these things put on love, which is the perfect bond of unity. And let the peace of Christ rule in your hearts, to which indeed you were called in one body; and be thankful." (Colossians 3:14-15)

"with all humility and gentleness, with patience, showing forbearance to one another in love, being diligent to preserve the unity of the Spirit in the bond of peace." (Ephesians 4:2-3)

bondservant: 1) a slave who has been set free, but gives up that freedom to become devoted to his master for his entire life

"And it shall come about if he says to you, 'I will not go out from you,' because he loves you and your household, since he fares well with you; then you shall take an awl and pierce it through his ear into the door, and he shall be your servant forever. And also you shall do likewise to your maidservant." (Deuteronomy 15:16-17)

"So you too, when you do all the things which are commanded you, say, 'We are unworthy slaves; we have done only that which we ought to have done." (Luke 17:10)

"Blessed are those slaves whom the master shall find on the alert when he comes; truly I say to you, that he will gird himself to serve, and have them recline at the table, and will come up and wait on them... "You too, be ready; for the Son of Man is coming at an hour that you do not expect." (Luke 12:37)

bread: 1) figuratively Jesus, the bread of life who meets our daily spiritual needs; 2) Old Testament equivalent- manna, God's supernatural provision for His people

"For the bread of God is that which comes down out of heaven, and gives life to the world."... Jesus said to them, "I am the bread of life; he who comes to Me shall not hunger, and he who believes in Me shall never thirst." (John 6:33, 35)

"He who has an ear, let him hear what the Spirit says to the churches. To him who overcomes, to him I will give some of the hidden manna" (Revelation 2:17)

"How sweet are Thy words to my taste! Yes, sweeter than honey to my mouth!" (Psalm 119:103)

bride (of Christ): 1) the Church, promised to the Bridegroom Christ, who will return for His bride

"Let us rejoice and be glad and give the glory to Him, for the marriage of the Lamb has come and His bride has made herself ready." And it was given to her to clothe herself in fine linen, bright and clean; for the fine linen is the righteous acts of the saints." (Revelation 19:7-8)

"For I am jealous for you with a godly jealousy; for I betrothed you to one husband, that to Christ I might present you as a pure virgin." (2 Corinthians 11:2)

"And one of the seven angels who had the seven bowls full of the seven last plagues, came and spoke with me, saying, "Come here, I shall show you the bride, the wife of the Lamb." And he carried me away in the Spirit to a great and high mountain, and showed me the holy city, Jerusalem, coming down out of heaven from God, having the glory of God. Her brilliance was like a very costly stone, as a stone of crystal-clear jasper." (Revelation 21:9-11)

brokenness: 1) God desires a broken and repentant heart; 2) humble dependence on God for forgiveness and eternal life

"Blessed are the poor in spirit, for theirs is the kingdom of heaven." (Matthew 5:3)

"For we who live are constantly being delivered over to death for Jesus' sake, that the life of Jesus also may be manifested in our mortal flesh." (2 Corinthians 4:11)

"For the word of God is living and active and sharper than any two-edged sword, and piercing as far as the division of soul and spirit, of both joints and marrow, and able to judge the thoughts and intentions of the heart." (Hebrews 4:12)

"The sacrifices of God are a broken spirit; a broken and a contrite heart, O God, Thou wilt not despise." (Psalm 51:17)

brokenhearted: 1) God is our source of help when we grieve, or are troubled, or have failed. He is our source of solace, wisdom and courage

"He heals the brokenhearted, and binds up their wounds." (Psalm 147:3)

"The Spirit of the Lord God is upon me, because the Lord has anointed me to bring good news to the afflicted; He has sent me to bind up the brokenhearted... " (Isaiah 61:1)

"The Lord is near to the brokenhearted, and saves those who are crushed in spirit." (Psalm 34:18)

"For thus says the high and exalted One Who lives forever, whose name is Holy, "I dwell on a high and holy place, And also with the contrite and lowly of spirit in order to revive the spirit of the lowly and to revive the heart of the contrite." (Isaiah 57:15)

busyness: 1) religious activity or keeping of rules which enslave us and rob us of freedom in Christ

"But Martha was distracted with all her preparations... " (Luke 10:40)

"Unless the Lord builds the house, they labor in vain who build it" (Psalm 127:1)

"But seek first His kingdom and His righteousness; and all these things shall be added to you." (Matthew 6:33)

"For all of us have become like one who is unclean, and all our righteous deeds are like a filthy garment; and all of us wither like a leaf, and our iniquities, like the wind, take us away." (Isaiah 64:6)

C PRAYER CARDS

<u>call:</u> 1) chosen by God and equipped by the Holy Spirit to perform a special work; 2) God's choosing all nations to become part of His family; 3) God's selecting of individuals to receive salvation and represent Christ to the world

"And while they were ministering to the Lord and fasting, the Holy Spirit said, "Set apart for Me Barnabas and Saul for the work to which I have called them." (Acts 13:2)

"And we know that God causes all things to work together for good to those who love God, to those who are called according to His purpose." (Romans 8:28)

"There is one body and one Spirit, just as also you were called in one hope of your calling; one Lord, one faith, one baptism, one God and Father of all who is over all and through all and in all. But to each one of us grace was given according to the measure of Christ's gift. Therefore it says, "When He ascended on high, He led captive a host of captives, and He gave gifts to men.".… And He gave some as apostles, and some as prophets, and some as evangelists, and some as pastors and teachers, for the equipping of the saints for the work of service, to the building up of the body of Christ." (Ephesians 4:4-8, 11-12)

"But we should always give thanks to God for you, brethren beloved by the Lord, because God has chosen you from the beginning for salvation through sanctification by the Spirit and faith in the truth. And it was for this He called you through our gospel, that you may gain the glory of our Lord Jesus Christ." (2 Thessalonians 2:13-14)

calm: 1) freedom from fear or agitation; 2) quiet, serene

"He makes me lie down in green pastures; He leads me beside quiet waters." (Psalm 23:2)

"The Lord is my strength and my shield; my heart trusts in Him, and I am helped; therefore my heart exults, and with my song I shall thank Him." (Psalm 28:7)

"and to make it your ambition to lead a quiet life and attend to your own business and work with your hands, just as we commanded you." (1 Thessalonians 4:11)

"And the work of righteousness will be peace, and the service of righteousness, quietness and confidence forever. Then my people will live in a peaceful habitation, and in secure dwellings and in undisturbed resting places" (Isaiah 32:17-18)

carnal: 1) fleshly, sinful; 2) spiritually immature, unable to receive deeper truths

"For that which I am doing, I do not understand; for I am not practicing what I would like to do, but I am doing the very thing I hate." (Romans 7:15)

"For the flesh sets its desire against the Spirit, and the Spirit against the flesh; for these are in opposition to one another, so that you may not do the things that you please." (Galatians 5:17)

"Now the deeds of the flesh are evident, which are: immorality, impurity, sensuality, idolatry, sorcery, enmities, strife, jealousy, outbursts of anger, disputes, dissensions, factions, envying, drunkenness, carousing, and things like these, of which I forewarn you just as I have forewarned you that those who practice such things shall not inherit the kingdom of God." (Galatians 5:19-21)

change our hearts: 1) the change in our nature made possible by Jesus' sacrifice, and accomplished by the indwelling Holy Spirit when we turn our lives over to Christ and become obedient

"Purify me with hyssop, and I shall be clean; wash me, and I shall be whiter than snow. Make me to hear joy and gladness, let the bones which Thou hast broken rejoice... Create in me a clean heart, O God, and renew a steadfast spirit within me." (Psalm 51: 7-8, 10)

"Moreover, I will give you a new heart and put a new spirit within you; and I will remove the heart of stone from your flesh and give you a heart of flesh. "And I will put My Spirit within you and cause you to walk in My statutes, and you will be careful to observe My ordinances." (Ezekiel 36:26-27)

cheating: 1) to deceive, commit fraud, be dishonest

"And Zaccheus stopped and said to the Lord, "Behold, Lord, half of my possessions I will give to the poor, and if I have defrauded anyone of anything, I will give back four times as much." And Jesus said to him, "Today salvation has come to this house, because he, too, is a son of Abraham." (Luke 19:8-9)

childlike: 1) having the simple, humble faith and trust necessary to enter God's kingdom

"And He called a child to Himself and set him before them, and said, "Truly I say to you, unless you are converted and become like children, you shall not enter the kingdom of heaven. "Whoever then humbles

himself as this child, he is the greatest in the kingdom of heaven."
(Matthew 18:2-4)

"Therefore, putting aside all malice and all guile and hypocrisy and envy
and all slander, like newborn babes, long for the pure milk of the word,
that by it you may grow in respect to salvation, if you have tasted the
kindness of the Lord." (1 Peter 2:1-3)

"But when the chief priests and the scribes saw the wonderful things
that He had done, and the children who were crying out in the temple
and saying, "Hosanna to the Son of David, "they became indignant,
and said to Him, "Do You hear what these are saying?" And Jesus
said to them, "Yes; have you never read, 'Out of the mouth of infants
and nursing babes Thou hast prepared praise for Thyself'?" (Matthew
21:15-16)

chosen: 1) those selected by God who respond to the invitation to
follow Christ; 2) the elect; those God foreknew, who will be justified
and glorified

"My sheep hear My voice, and I know them, and they follow Me; and
I give eternal life to them, and they shall never perish; and no one shall
snatch them out of My hand. "My Father, who has given them to Me,
is greater than all; and no one is able to snatch them out of the Father's
hand." (John 10:27-29)

"but God has chosen the foolish things of the world to shame the wise,
and God has chosen the weak things of the world to shame the things
which are strong, and the base things of the world and the despised,
God has chosen, the things that are not, that He might nullify the
things that are, that no man should boast before God." (1 Corinthians
1:27-29)

church attendance: 1) God did not design Christians to be independent of one another, but rather to encourage, pray for, and meet one another's needs.

"and let us consider how to stimulate one another to love and good deeds, not forsaking our own assembling together, as is the habit of some, but encouraging one another; and all the more, as you see the day drawing near." (Hebrews 10:24-25)

"And all those who had believed were together, and had all things in common; and they began selling their property and possessions, and were sharing them with all, as anyone might have need. And day by day continuing with one mind in the temple, and breaking bread from house to house, they were taking their meals together with gladness and sincerity of heart, praising God, and having favor with all the people. And the Lord was adding to their number day by day those who were being saved." (Acts 2:44-47)

circumcision of the heart: 1) performed by the Holy Spirit inwardly, bringing about a love for God and obedience to the Law

"for we are the true circumcision, who worship in the Spirit of God and glory in Christ Jesus and put no confidence in the flesh." (Philippian 3:3)

"For he is not a Jew who is one outwardly; neither is circumcision that which is outward in the flesh. But he is a Jew who is one inwardly; and circumcision is that which is of the heart, by the Spirit, not by the letter; and his praise is not from men, but from God." (Romans 2:28-29)

clarity: 1) mental sharpness, brilliant insight, making truth clear

"And when Philip had run up, he heard him (an Ethiopian eunuch) reading Isaiah the prophet, and said, "Do you understand what you are reading?" And he said, "Well, how could I, unless someone guides me?" And he invited Philip to come up and sit with him... And Philip opened his mouth, and beginning from this Scripture he preached Jesus to him... and he (the eunuch) answered and said, "I believe that Jesus Christ is the Son of God." (Acts 8:30-31, 35, 37)

"For it is evident that our Lord was descended from Judah, a tribe with reference to which Moses spoke nothing concerning priests. And this is clearer still, if another priest arises according to the likeness of Melchizedek, who has become such not on the basis of a law of physical requirement, but according to the power of an indestructible life." (Hebrews 7:14-16).

"The unfolding of Thy words gives light; it gives understanding to the simple." (Psalm 119:130)

comfort: 1) to strengthen, help, encourage, impart hope

"Blessed be the God and Father of our Lord Jesus Christ, the Father of mercies and God of all comfort; who comforts us in all our affliction so that we may be able to comfort those who are in any affliction with the comfort with which we ourselves are comforted by God." (2 Corinthians 1:3-4)

"God is our refuge and strength, a very present help in trouble. Therefore we will not fear, though the earth should change, and though the mountains slip into the heart of the sea." (Psalm 46:1-2)

"Now may our Lord Jesus Christ Himself and God our Father, who has loved us and given us eternal comfort and good hope by grace, comfort and strengthen your hearts in every good work and word." (2 Thessalonians 2:16)

commitment: 1) single-minded loyalty, trust, a pledge of fidelity toward another

"Commit your way to the Lord, trust also in Him, and He will do it." (Psalm 37:5)

"And Jesus, crying out with a loud voice, said, "Father, into Thy hand I commit My Spirit." And having said this, He breathed His last." (Luke 23:46)

"Now all these things are from God, who reconciled us to Himself through Christ, and gave us the ministry of reconciliation." (2 Corinthians 5:18)

"… let us also lay aside every encumbrance, and the sin which so easily entangles us, and let us run with endurance the race that is set before us" (Hebrews 12:1)

compassion: 1) pity, conscious of another's distress, sympathy, together with a desire to alleviate it

"And so, as those who have been chosen of God, holy and beloved, put on a heart of compassion, kindness, humility, gentleness and patience; bearing with one another, and forgiving each other, whoever has a complaint against anyone; just as the Lord forgave you, so also should you." (Colossians 3:12-13)

"But a certain Samaritan, who was on a journey, came upon him; and when he saw him, he felt compassion, and came to him, and bandaged up his wounds, pouring oil and wine on them; and he put him on his own beast, and brought him to an inn, and took care of him." (Luke 10:33-34)

complacency: 1) self-satisfied; 2) compromising with the world, neglect of the things of God

"For they all seek after their own interests, not those of Christ Jesus." (Philippians 2:21)

"Do nothing from selfishness or empty conceit, but with humility of mind let each of you regard one another as more important than himself; do not merely look out for your own personal interests, but also for the interests of others." (Philippians 2:3-4)

"But I have this against you, that you have left your first love. 'Remember therefore from where you have fallen, and repent and do the deeds you did at first; or else I am coming to you, and will remove your lampstand out of its place-- unless you repent." (Revelation 2:4-5)

"So I will stretch out My hand against... those who have turned back from following the Lord, and those who have not sought the Lord or inquired of Him... at that time I will search Jerusalem with lamps and punish those who are stagnant in spirit." (Zephaniah 1: 4, 6, 12)

"I know your deeds, that you are neither cold nor hot; I would that you were cold or hot. 'So because you are lukewarm, and neither hot nor cold, I will spit you out of My mouth." (Revelation 3: 15-16)

"For through the grace given to me I say to every man among you not to think more highly of himself than he ought to think; but to think so as to have sound judgment." (Romans 12:3)

complete: 1) perfect, accomplished, fulfilled, lacking nothing

"The Lord will accomplish what concerns me; Thy lovingkindness, O Lord, is everlasting." (Psalm 138:8)

"For I am confident of this very thing, that He who began a good work in you will perfect it until the day of Christ Jesus." (Philippians 1:6)

"Owe nothing to anyone except to love one another; for he who loves his neighbor has fulfilled the law." (Romans 13:8)

"Consider it all joy, my brethren, when you encounter various trials, knowing that the testing of your faith produces endurance. And let endurance have its perfect result, that you may be perfect and complete, lacking in nothing." (James 1:2-4)

compromise: 1) to agree, adjust, settle; 2) there is no compromise regarding the truth found in Scripture, but in civil or political matters, compromise avoids the image of stubbornness which provokes resistance

"For truly I say to you, until heaven and earth pass away, not the smallest letter or stroke shall pass away from the Law, until all is accomplished." (Matthew 5:18)

"For I, the Lord, do not change." (Malachi 3:6)

"Jesus Christ is the same yesterday and today, yes and forever." (Hebrews 13:8)

confession: 1) acknowledging our sin and agreeing with God's verdict on sin

"If we say that we have no sin, we are deceiving ourselves, and the truth is not in us. If we confess our sins, He is faithful and righteous to forgive us our sins and to cleanse us from all unrighteousness." (1 John 1:8-9)

"... And if anyone sins, we have an Advocate with the Father, Jesus Christ the righteous; and He Himself is the propitiation for our sins." (1 John 2:1-2)

"For I joyfully concur with the law of God in the inner man, but I see a different law in the members of my body, waging war against the law of my mind, and making me a prisoner of the law of sin which is in my members. Wretched man that I am! Who will set me free from the body of this death? Thanks be to God through Jesus Christ our Lord!... " (Romans 7:22-25)

confidence: 1) trust, faith, belief in God's integrity; 2) which leads to boldness in sharing the Gospel

"This was in accordance with the eternal purpose which He carried out in Christ Jesus our Lord, in whom we have boldness and confident access through faith in Him." (Ephesians 3:11-12)

"for we are the true circumcision, who worship in the Spirit of God and glory in Christ Jesus and put no confidence in the flesh." (Philippians 3:3)

"For I am confident of this very thing, that He who began a good work in you will perfect it until the day of Christ Jesus." (Philippians 1:6)

consecration: 1) all believers are chosen by God as a holy priesthood, set apart for His service

"and do not go on presenting the members of your body to sin as instruments of unrighteousness; but present yourselves to God as those alive from the dead, and your members as instruments of righteousness to God." (Romans 6:13)

"Now may the God of peace Himself sanctify you entirely; and may your spirit and soul and body be preserved complete, without blame at the coming of our Lord Jesus Christ." (1 Thessalonians 5:23)

"But Jesus said to him, "No one, after putting his hand to the plow and looking back, is fit for the kingdom of God." (Luke 9:62)

consistency: 1) living according to one's beliefs, without wavering

"So then, my beloved, just as you have always obeyed, not as in my presence only, but now much more in my absence, work out your salvation with fear and trembling." (Philippians 2:12)

"the one who says he abides in Him ought himself to walk in the same manner as He walked." (1 John 2:6)

"This I say therefore, and affirm together with the Lord, that you walk no longer just as the Gentiles also walk, in the futility of their mind... and that you be renewed in the spirit of your mind, and put on the new self, which in the likeness of God has been created in righteousness and holiness of the truth." (Ephesians 4:17, 23-24)

"Blessed are those slaves whom the master shall find on the alert when he comes... for the Son of Man is coming at an hour that you do not expect." (Luke 12:37, 40)

consolation: 1) comfort, solace, refreshing the spirit, relieving mental distress

"When my anxious thoughts multiply within me, Thy consolations delight my soul." (Psalm 94:19)

"And behold, there was a man in Jerusalem whose name was Simeon; and this man was righteous and devout, looking for the consolation of Israel; and the Holy Spirit was upon him." (Luke 2:25)

"If therefore there is any encouragement in Christ, if there is any consolation of love, if there is any fellowship of the Spirit, if any affection and compassion, make my joy complete by being of the same mind, maintaining the same love, united in spirit, intent on one purpose." (Philippians 2:1-2)

constancy: 1) reliability, with orderliness; 2) steadfast, stable

"And He shall be the stability of your times, a wealth of salvation, wisdom, and knowledge; the fear of the Lord is his treasure." (Isaiah 33:6)

"… I am with you in spirit, rejoicing to see your good discipline and the stability of your faith in Christ. As you therefore have received Christ Jesus the Lord, so walk in Him, having been firmly rooted and now being built up in Him and established in your faith, just as you were instructed, and overflowing with gratitude." (Colossians 2:5-7)

contempt: 1) scorn, lack of respect, deliberate disobedience to rules

"… And I will bless those who bless you, and the one who curses you I will curse… " (Genesis 12:3)

"But if you do not obey Me and do not carry out all these commandments, if instead, you reject My statutes, and if your soul abhors My ordinances so as not to carry out all My commandments, and so break My covenant… then I will punish you… " (Leviticus 26:14-15, 18)

"'Because he has despised the word of the Lord and has broken His commandment, that person shall be completely cut off; his guilt shall be on him.'" (Numbers 15:31)

"Now when they heard of the resurrection of the dead, some began to sneer, but others said, "We shall hear you again concerning this." (Acts 17:32)

contentment: 1) being at peace with what God has given you; 2) recognizing and being grateful for the Lord's blessings

"Let your character be free from the love of money, being content with what you have; for He Himself has said, " I will never desert you, nor will I ever forsake you" (Hebrews 13:5)

"… I have learned to be content in whatever circumstances I am." (Philippians 4:11)

"But godliness actually is a means of great gain, when accompanied by contentment. For we have brought nothing into the world, so we cannot take anything out of it either. And if we have food and covering, with these we shall be content." (1 Timothy 6:6-8)

"Therefore I am well content with weaknesses, with insults, with distresses, with persecutions, with difficulties, for Christ's sake; for when I am weak, then I am strong." (2 Corinthians 12:10)

contrite: 1) deep repentance for one's sins; 2) being penitent for one's disobedience to God

"The Lord is near to the brokenhearted, and saves those who are crushed in spirit." (Psalm 34:18)

"For thus says the high and exalted One Who lives forever, whose name is Holy, "I dwell on a high and holy place, and also with the contrite and lowly of spirit in order to revive the spirit of the lowly and to revive the heart of the contrite." (Isaiah 57:15)

"The sacrifices of God are a broken spirit; a broken and a contrite heart, O God, Thou wilt not despise." (Psalm 51:17)

"… But to this one I will look, to him who is humble and contrite of spirit, and who trembles at My word." (Isaiah 66:2)

conviction: 1) having our conscience burdened by personal sin, resulting in confession and repentance; 2) the work of the Holy Spirit in one's heart

"Wash me thoroughly from my iniquity, and cleanse me from my sin. For I know my transgressions, and my sin is ever before me." (Psalms 51:2-3)

"And He, when He comes, will convict the world concerning sin, and righteousness, and judgment." (John 16:8)

"For I am ready to fall, and my sorrow is continually before me. For I confess my iniquity; I am full of anxiety because of my sin... Do not forsake me, O Lord; O my God, do not be far from me!" (Psalm 38:17-18, 21)

"For when Gentiles who do not have the Law do instinctively the things of the Law, these, not having the Law, are a law to themselves, in that they show the work of the Law written in their hearts, their conscience bearing witness, and their thoughts alternately accusing or else defending them, on the day when, according to my gospel, God will judge the secrets of men through Christ Jesus." (Romans 2:14-16)

countenance: 1) our facial expression; 2) our face should reflect the joy and peace which come from knowing the Lord

"And while He was praying, the appearance of His face became different, and His clothing became white and gleaming." (Luke 9:29)

"Thou hast made known to me the ways of life; Thou wilt make me full of gladness with Thy presence." (Acts 2:28)

"And Jacob sent and called Rachel and Leah to the field unto his flock, and said unto them, I see your father's countenance, that it is not toward me as before; but the God of my father hath been with me." (Genesis 31:4-5 KJV)

"But the Lord said to Samuel, "Do not look at his appearance or at the height of his stature, because I have rejected him; for God sees not as man sees, for man looks at the outward appearance, but the Lord looks at the heart." (1 Samuel 16:7)

"A merry heart maketh a cheerful countenance: but by sorrow of the heart the spirit is broken." (Proverbs 15:13 KJV)

(finish the) course: 1) completing the path in order to reach the goal; 2) for a believer – faithfully accomplishing the task God has assigned to us with the reward of eternal life

"But I do not consider my life of any account as dear to myself, in order that I may finish my course, and the ministry which I received from the Lord Jesus, to testify solemnly of the gospel of the grace of God." (Acts 20:24)

covetousness: 1) greed, being preoccupied with accumulating more possessions, self-indulgence

"And He (Jesus) said to them, "Beware, and be on your guard against every form of greed; for not even when one has an abundance does his life consist of his possessions." (Luke 12:15)

"You shall not covet your neighbor's wife, and you shall not desire your neighbor's house, his field or his male servant or his female servant, his ox or his donkey or anything that belongs to your neighbor." (Deuteronomy 5:21)

critical spirit: 1) being judgmental without mercy, having a self-righteous demeanor

"All Scripture is inspired by God and profitable for teaching, for reproof, for correction, for training in righteousness; that the man of God may be adequate, equipped for every good work." (2 Timothy 3:16-17)

"But if you bite and devour one another, take care lest you be consumed by one another." (Galatians 5:15)

"Do not judge lest you be judged. "For in the way you judge, you will be judged; and by your standard of measure, it will be measured to you. "And why do you look at the speck that is in your brother's eye, but do not notice the log that is in your own eye?" (Matthew 7:1-3)

"Therefore you are without excuse, every man of you who passes judgment, for in that you judge another, you condemn yourself; for you who judge practice the same things." (Romans 2:1)

cynical: 1) mean-spirited; 2) purposely taking an opposing view, distrustful

"And He also told this parable to certain ones who trusted in themselves that they were righteous, and viewed others with contempt." (Luke 18:9)

"See to it that no one comes short of the grace of God; that no root of bitterness springing up causes trouble, and by it many be defiled" (Hebrews 12:15)

D PRAYER CARDS

debt: 1) obligation to pay money, goods, or services to another, that which is owed; 2) we are obligated to repay any debt we owe, whether taxes or personal, we are not to incur debt we cannot repay

"Do not be among those who give pledges, among those who become sureties for debts." (Proverbs 22:26)

"Render to all what is due them: tax to whom tax is due; custom to whom custom; fear to whom fear; honor to whom honor." (Romans 13:7)

deception: 1) misleading, fraud, counterfeit

"But the Spirit explicitly says that in later times some will fall away from the faith, paying attention to deceitful spirits and doctrines of demons, by means of the hypocrisy of liars seared in their own conscience as with a branding iron." (1 Timothy 4:1-2)

"The heart is more deceitful than all else and is desperately sick; who can understand it?" (Jeremiah 17:9)

"As you therefore have received Christ Jesus the Lord, so walk in Him... See to it that no one takes you captive through philosophy and empty deception, according to the tradition of men, according to the elementary principles of the world, rather than according to Christ." (Colossians 2:6, 8)

decision-making: 1) the act of settling a controversy or giving a judgment in a matter; 2) if you find yourself wavering in an your opinion, consult God's Word with an attitude of prayer; 3) vacillating between two choices suggests a worldly thought process

"Therefore, I was not vacillating when I intended to do this, was I? Or that which I purpose, do I purpose according to the flesh, that with me there should be yes, yes and no, no at the same time? But as God is faithful, our word to you is not yes and no." (2 Corinthians 1:17-18)

"Yet they seek Me day by day, and delight to know My ways, as a nation that has done righteousness, and has not forsaken the ordinance of their God. They ask Me for just decisions, they delight in the nearness of God." (Isaiah 58:2)

deep things of God: 1) knowledge which the human senses cannot comprehend, revealed through the Holy Spirit

"Things which eye has not seen and ear has not heard, and which have not entered the heart of man, all that God has prepared for those who love Him." For to us God revealed them through the Spirit; for the Spirit searches all things, even the depths of God. For who among men knows the thoughts of a man except the spirit of the man, which is in him? Even so the thoughts of God no one knows except the Spirit of God." (1 Corinthians 2:9-11)

"For I would have you know, brethren, that the gospel which was preached by me is not according to man. For I neither received it from man, nor was I taught it, but I received it through a revelation of Jesus Christ." (Galatians 1:11-12)

delight: 1) that which brings pleasure or satisfaction, gratification

"He also brought me forth into a broad place; He rescued me, because He delighted in me." (2 Samuel 22:20)

"As for the saints who are in the earth, they are the majestic ones in whom is all my delight." (Psalm 16:3)

"Behold, My Servant, whom I uphold; My chosen one in whom My soul delights… " (Isaiah 42:1)

"O Lord, I beseech Thee, may Thine ear be attentive to the prayer of Thy servant and the prayer of Thy servants who delight to revere Thy name, and make Thy servant successful today, and grant him compassion before this man… " (Nehemiah 1:11)

"But his delight is in the law of the Lord, and in His law he meditates day and night." (Psalm 1:2)

deliverance: 1) freedom from captivity, evil, sin

"And do not lead us into temptation, but deliver us from evil. [For Thine is the kingdom, and the power, and the glory, forever…"] (Matthew 6:13)

"Blessed be the Lord, who daily bears our burden, the God who is our salvation. God is to us a God of deliverances; and to God the Lord belong escapes from death." (Psalm 68:19-20)

"Since I am afflicted and needy, let the Lord be mindful of me; Thou art my help and my deliverer; do not delay, O my God." (Psalm 40:17)

delusion: 1) misleading, false belief; 2) continual blindness to the truth

"If we say that we have no sin, we are deceiving ourselves, and the truth is not in us." (1 John 1:8)

"The heart is more deceitful than all else and is desperately sick; who can understand it?" (Jeremiah 17:9)

denial: 1) to surrender personal gratification in favor of determining who you are in Christ and desiring God's will; 2) to contradict, to declare something to be not true

"Keep deception and lies far from me, give me neither poverty nor riches; feed me with the food that is my portion, lest I be full and deny Thee and say, "Who is the Lord?" (Proverbs 30:8-9)

"But whoever shall deny Me before men, I will also deny him before My Father who is in heaven." (Matthew 10:33)

"For men will be lovers of self, lovers of money, boastful, arrogant, revilers, disobedient to parents, ungrateful, unholy... holding to a form of godliness, although they have denied its power; and avoid such men as these." (2 Timothy 3:2, 5)

depend: 1) to rely on God for our physical and spiritual needs

"That they should put their confidence in God, and not forget the works of God, but keep His commandments." (Psalm 78:7)

"... your faith should not rest on the wisdom of men, but on the power of God." (1 Corinthians 2:5)

"When I am afraid, I will put my trust in Thee. In God, whose word I praise, in God I have put my trust; I shall not be afraid." (Psalm 56:3-4)

"Some boast in chariots, and some in horses; but we will boast in the name of the Lord, our God." (Psalm 20:7)

depression: 1) debilitating emotional lows when physical or spiritual hardships occur, gloom

"But he himself went a day's journey into the wilderness, and came and sat down under a juniper tree; and he requested for himself that he might die, and said, "It is enough; now, O Lord, take my life..." (1 Kings 19:4)

"Trust in the Lord with all your heart, and do not lean on your own understanding... It will be healing to your body, and refreshment to your bones." (Proverbs 3:5, 8)

"Cast your burden upon the Lord, and He will sustain you; He will never allow the righteous to be shaken." (Psalm 55:22)

"For even when we came into Macedonia our flesh had no rest, but we were afflicted on every side: conflicts without, fears within. But God, who comforts the depressed, comforted us by the coming of Titus." (2 Corinthians 7:5-6)

"As the deer pants for the water brooks, so my soul pants for Thee, O God. My soul thirsts for God, for the living God; when shall I come and appear before God? My tears have been my food day and night..." (Psalm 42:1-3)

dignity: 1) being worthy of respect or honor, excellence of character

"Strength and dignity are her (an excellent wife's) clothing, and she smiles at the future." (Proverbs 31:25)

"He (an overseer) must be one who manages his own household well, keeping his children under control with all dignity" (1 Timothy 3:4)

"First of all, then, I urge that entreaties and prayers, petitions and thanksgivings, be made on behalf of all men, for kings and all who are in authority, in order that we may lead a tranquil and quiet life in all godliness and dignity." (1 Timothy 2:1-2)

"Deacons likewise must be men of dignity, not double-tongued, or addicted to much wine or fond of sordid gain, but holding to the mystery of the faith with a clear conscience." (1 Timothy 3:8-9)

diligence: 1) being careful, attending to the details, persevering

"The hand of the diligent will rule, but the slack hand will be put to forced labor." (Proverbs 12:24)

"He who spares his rod hates his son, but he who loves him disciplines him diligently." (Proverbs 13:24)

"At night my soul longs for Thee, indeed, my spirit within me seeks Thee diligently; for when the earth experiences Thy judgments the inhabitants of the world learn righteousness... " (Isaiah 26:9)

"Be devoted to one another in brotherly love; give preference to one another in honor; not lagging behind in diligence, fervent in spirit, serving the Lord; rejoicing in hope, persevering in tribulation, devoted to prayer." (Romans 12:10-12)

"Be diligent to present yourself approved to God as a workman who does not need to be ashamed, handling accurately the word of truth." (2 Timothy 2:15)

direct: 1) straightforward, true; 2) pointing toward a goal

"And may the Lord direct your hearts into the love of God and into the steadfastness of Christ." (2 Thessalonians 3:5)

"Lead me in Thy truth and teach me, for Thou art the God of my salvation; for Thee I wait all the day." (Psalm 25:5)

"Thus says the Lord, your Redeemer, the Holy One of Israel; "I am the Lord your God, who teaches you to profit, Who leads you in the way you should go." (Isaiah 48:17)

"For all who are being led by the Spirit of God, these are sons of God." (Romans 8:14)

"Thy word is a lamp to my feet, and a light to my path." (Psalm 119:105)

discernment: 1) making God-guided decisions based on the Word of God; reading the Bible for understanding and increasing our faith

"And this I pray, that your love may abound still more and more in real knowledge and all discernment, so that you may approve the things that are excellent, in order to be sincere and blameless until the day of Christ." (Philippians 1:9-10)

"Teach me good discernment and knowledge, for I believe in Thy commandments." (Psalm 119:66)

"… For if you cry for discernment, lift your voice for understanding; if you seek her as silver, and search for her as for hidden treasures; then you will discern the fear of the Lord, and discover the knowledge of God. For the Lord gives wisdom; from His mouth come knowledge and understanding." (Proverbs 2:3-6)

discipline: 1) submission to the Word of God on a regular basis in order to act according to God's will

"Whoever loves discipline loves knowledge, but he who hates reproof is stupid." (Proverbs 12:1)

"Do not hold back discipline from the child, although you beat him with the rod, he will not die. You shall beat him with the rod, and deliver his soul from Sheol." (Proverbs 23:13-14)

"Blessed is the man whom Thou dost chasten, O Lord, and dost teach out of Thy law; That Thou mayest grant him relief from the days of adversity, until a pit is dug for the wicked." (Psalm 94: 12-13)

"Those whom I love, I reprove and discipline; be zealous therefore, and repent." (Revelation 3:19)

discontent: 1) ungratefulness, being dissatisfied with God's provision

"Let your character be free from the love of money, being content with what you have; for He Himself has said, "I will never desert you, nor will I ever forsake you." (Hebrews 13:5)

discouragement: 1) having unrealistic expectations of the Christian walk; 2) failure to depend on prayer, studying the Word and relying on God's promises when times are hard

"Why are you in despair, O my soul? And why have you become disturbed within me? Hope in God, for I shall again praise Him for the help of His presence." (Psalm 42:5)

"Be anxious for nothing, but in everything by prayer and supplication with thanksgiving let your requests be made known to God. and the peace of God, which surpasses all comprehension, shall guard your hearts and your minds in Christ Jesus." (Philippians 4:6-7)

"I can do all things through Him who strengthens me." (Philippians 4:13)

discretion: 1) appropriate words and behavior; 2) having a lifestyle witness that avoids causing unnecessary offense or ridicule; 3) using God's wisdom to determine our path

"A man's discretion makes him slow to anger, and it is his glory to overlook a transgression." (Proverbs 19:11)

"For wisdom will enter your heart, and knowledge will be pleasant to your soul; discretion will guard you, understanding will watch over you, to deliver you from the way of evil, from the man who speaks perverse things." (Proverbs 2:10-12)

disobedience: 1) failure to obey God's laws; 2) complacency, stubbornness, hardness of heart

"And if you will not listen to the voice of the lord, but rebel against the command of the Lord, then the hand of the Lord will be against you, as it was against your fathers." (1 Samuel 12:15)

"He who believes in the Son has eternal life; but he who does not obey the Son shall not see life, but the wrath of God abides on him." (John 3:36)

disrespect for authority: 1) discourtesy, being uncivil toward those whom God has placed over us

"And Paul said, "I was not aware, brethren, that he was high priest; for it is written, 'you shall not speak evil of a ruler of your people.'" (Acts 23:5)

"Obey your leaders, and submit to them; for they keep watch over your souls, as those who will give an account. Let them do this with joy and not with grief, for this would be unprofitable for you." (Hebrews 13:17)

distracted: 1) failure to remain spiritually or morally alert to the task before you; 2) to be drawn away in different directions

"Give ear to my prayer, O God; and do not hide Thyself from my supplication. Give heed to me, and answer me; I am restless in my complaint and am surely distracted, because of the voice of the enemy because of the pressure of the wicked… " (Psalm 55:1-3)

"And she (Martha) had a sister called Mary, who moreover was listening to the Lord's word, seated at His feet. But Martha was distracted with all her preparations; and she came up to Him, and said, "Lord, do You not care that my sister has left me to do all the serving alone? Then tell her to help me." But the Lord answered and said to her, "Martha, Martha, you are worried and bothered about so many things; but only a few things are necessary, really only one, for Mary has chosen the good part, which shall not be taken away from her." (Luke 10: 39-42)

double-minded: 1) wavering between belief and unbelief; 2) inability to make a sound decision

"Draw near to God and He will draw near to you. Cleanse your hands, you sinners; and purify your hearts, you double-minded." (James 4:8)

"But if any of you lacks wisdom, let him ask of God who gives to all men generously and without reproach, and it will be given to him. But let him ask in faith without any doubting, for the one who doubts is like the surf of the sea driven and tossed by the wind. For let not that man expect that he will receive anything from the Lord, being a double-minded man, unstable in all his ways." (James 1:5-8)

doubt: 1) to be uncertain about what you believe; to question your faith in the truth

"And while they were telling these things, He Himself stood in their midst. But they were startled and frightened and thought that they were seeing a spirit. And He said to them, "Why are you troubled, and why do doubts arise in your hearts? "See My hands and My feet, that it is I Myself; touch Me and see, for a spirit does not have flesh and bones as you see that I have." (Luke 24:36-39)

And He said, "Come!" And Peter got out of the boat, and walked on the water and came toward Jesus. But seeing the wind, he became afraid, and beginning to sink, he cried out, saying, "Lord, save me!" And immediately Jesus stretched out His hand and took hold of him, and said to him, "O you of little faith, why did you doubt?" (Matthew 14:29-31)

"For I am confident of this very thing, that He who began a good work in you will perfect it until the day of Christ Jesus." (Philippians 1:6)

draw: 1) to influence, attract or call toward someone

"No one can come to Me, unless the Father who sent Me draws him; and I will raise him up on the last day." (John 6:44)

"Guard your steps as you go to the house of God, and draw near to listen rather than to offer the sacrifice of fools; for they do not know they are doing evil." (Ecclesiastes 5:1)

"Let us therefore draw near with confidence to the throne of grace, that we may receive mercy and may find grace to help in time of need." (Hebrews 4:16)

dross: 1) refuse, waste matter; 2) God promises to refine believers by removing our impurities so that we will reflect Him

"Like an earthen vessel overlaid with silver dross are burning lips and a wicked heart." (Proverbs 26:23)

"I will also turn My hand against you, and will smelt away your dross as with lye, and will remove all your alloy." (Isaiah 1:25)

"Thou hast removed all the wicked of the earth like dross; therefore I love Thy testimonies." (Psalm 119:119)

"And I will bring the third part through the fire, refine them as silver is refined, and test them as gold is tested. They will call on My name, and I will answer them; I will say, 'They are My people,' and they will say, 'The Lord is my God.'" (Zechariah 13:9)

dwell: 1) to reside in; 2) to take up permanent residence, linger

"Let me dwell in Thy tent forever; let me take refuge in the shelter of Thy wings." (Psalm 61:4)

"Surely the righteous will give thanks to Thy name; the upright will dwell in Thy presence." (Psalm 140:13)

"He who dwells in the shelter of the Most High will abide in the shadow of the Almighty. I will say to the Lord, "My refuge and my fortress, My God, in whom I trust!" (Psalms 91:1-2)

"And many nations will join themselves to the Lord in that day and will become My people. Then I will dwell in your midst, and you will know that the Lord of hosts has sent Me to you." (Zechariah 2:11)

E PRAYER CARDS

easily irritated: 1) looking for perfection in a fallen world; 2) becoming angry or provoked easily

"(Love)… does not act unbecomingly; it does not seek its own, is not provoked, does not take into account a wrong suffered." (1 Corinthians 13:5)

"A man's discretion makes him slow to anger, and it is his glory to overlook a transgression." (Proverbs 19:11)

edify: 1) to build others up spiritually, to encourage in the Lord

"A gentle answer turns away wrath, but a harsh word stirs up anger. The tongue of the wise makes knowledge acceptable, but the mouth of fools spouts folly . . . A fool rejects his father's discipline, but he who regards reproof is prudent." (Proverbs 15: 1-2, 5)

"The mouth of the righteous is a fountain of life… " (Proverbs 10:11)

"Let no unwholesome word proceed from your mouth, but only such a word as is good for edification according to the need of the moment, that it may give grace to those who hear." (Ephesians 4:29)

emotion: 1) feelings originating in the soul; 2) a spirit-filled life does not act on negative emotions

"Let all bitterness and wrath and anger and clamor and slander be put away from you, along with all malice. And be kind to one another, tender-hearted, forgiving each other, just as God in Christ also has forgiven you." (Ephesians 4:31-32)

"The heart is deceitful above all things, and desperately wicked: who can know it? (Jeremiah 17:9 KJV)

"(Love) . . . does not act unbecomingly; it does not seek its own, is not provoked, does not take into account a wrong suffered" (1 Corinthians 13:5)

empathy: 1) ability to sympathize with those who are suffering, especially as a result of enduring similar trials

"Jesus wept." (John 11:35)

"But go and learn what this means, 'I desire compassion, and not sacrifice,' for I did not come to call the righteous, but sinners." (Matthew 9:13)

"Rejoice with those who rejoice, and weep with those who weep. Be of the same mind toward one another; do not be haughty in mind, but associate with the lowly." (Romans 12:15-16)

"Blessed be the God and Father of our Lord Jesus Christ, the Father of mercies and God of all comfort; who comforts us in all our affliction so that we may be able to comfort those who are in any affliction with the comfort with which we ourselves are comforted by God." (2 Corinthians 1:3-4)

empty: 1) free, unburdened, poured out; 2) devote one's entire life toward serving others

"Have this attitude in yourselves which was also in Christ Jesus, who, although He existed in the form of God, did not regard equality with God a thing to be grasped, but emptied Himself, taking the form of a bond-servant, and being made in the likeness of men. And being found in appearance as a man, He humbled Himself by becoming obedient to the point of death, even death on a cross." (Philippians 2:5-8)

encouragement: 1) unconditional love, offer of help, words of hope, to console

"Now may the God who gives perseverance and encouragement grant you to be of the same mind with one another according to Christ Jesus." (Romans 15:5)

"Therefore encourage one another, and build up one another, just as you also are doing." (1 Thessalonians 5:11)

"But encourage one another day after day, as long as it is still called "Today," lest any one of you be hardened by the deceitfulness of sin." (Hebrews 3:13)

"So then let us pursue the things which make for peace and the building up of one another." (Romans 14:19)

endurance: 1) overcoming suffering, hardships, and afflictions with patience, gentleness and love

"For you have need of endurance, so that when you have done the will of God, you may receive what was promised." (Hebrews 10:36)

"If we endure, we shall also reign with Him… " (2 Timothy 2:12)

"Consider it all joy, my brethren, when you encounter various trials, knowing that the testing of your faith produces endurance. And let endurance have its perfect result, that you may be perfect and complete, lacking in nothing." (James 1:2-4)

enter in: 1) free access to into the presence of God through the blood of Jesus Christ; 2) being received into the kingdom of heaven

"For Christ did not enter a holy place made with hands, a mere copy of the true one, but into heaven itself, now to appear in the presence of God for us." (Hebrews 9:24)

"Blessed are those who wash their robes, that they may have the right to the tree of life, and may enter by the gates into the city." (Revelation 22:14)

"Since therefore, brethren, we have confidence to enter the holy place by the blood of Jesus, by a new and living way which He inaugurated for us through the veil, that is, His flesh, and since we have a great priest over the house of God, let us draw near with a sincere heart in full assurance of faith, having our hearts sprinkled clean from an evil conscience and our bodies washed with pure water." (Hebrews 10:19-22)

equip: 1) to outfit for service; 2) using the Word, sermons and spiritual gifts to prepare each of us to meet the needs of the Church

"All Scripture is inspired by God and profitable for teaching, for reproof, for correction, for training in righteousness; that the man of God may be adequate, equipped for every good work." (2 Timothy 3:16-17)

"Therefore, gird your minds for action, keep sober in spirit, fix your hope completely on the grace to be brought to you at the revelation of Jesus Christ." (1 Peter 1:13)

"And He gave some as apostles, and some as prophets, and some as evangelists, and some as pastors and teachers, for the equipping of the saints for the work of service, to the building up of the body of Christ; until we all attain to the unity of the faith, and of the knowledge of the Son of God, to a mature man, to the measure of the stature which belongs to the fulness of Christ." (Ephesians 4:11-13)

error: 1) falsehood, error, anything that does not line up with God's truth

"My brethren, if any among you strays from the truth, and one turns him back, let him know that he who turns a sinner from the error of his way will save his soul from death, and will cover a multitude of sins." (James 5:19-20)

"And Jesus answered and said to them, "See to it that no one misleads you." (Matthew 24:4)

"But Jesus answered and said to them, "You are mistaken, not understanding the Scriptures, or the power of God." (Matthew 22:29)

"Now these (Bereans) were more noble-minded than those in Thessalonica, for they received the word with great eagerness, examining the Scriptures daily, to see whether these things were so." (Acts 17:11)

eternity: 1) without beginning or end; 2) God exists outside of time. 3) We will all spend eternity somewhere, either in the presence of God or forever outside His kingdom.

"He has made everything appropriate in its time. He has also set eternity in their heart, yet so that man will not find out the work which God has done from the beginning even to the end." (Ecclesiastes 3:11)

"… we look not at the things which are seen, but at the things which are not seen; for the things which are seen are temporal; but the things which are not seen are eternal." (2 Corinthian 4:18)

"For this perishable must put on the imperishable, and this mortal must put on immortality." (1 Corinthians 15:53)

"And everyone who competes in the games exercises self-control in all things. They then do it to receive a perishable wreath, but we an imperishable." (1 Corinthians 9:25)

evil: 1) the opposite of moral goodness; 2) Satan is the author of evil; 3) that which God hates

"There are six things which the Lord hates, yes, seven which are an abomination to Him: haughty eyes, a lying tongue, and hands that shed innocent blood, a heart that devises wicked plans, feet that run rapidly to evil, a false witness who utters lies, and one who spreads strife among brothers." (Proverbs 6:16-19)

"Depart from evil, and do good; seek peace, and pursue it." (Psalms 34:14)

evil speaking: 1) using one's tongue to slander, judge, lie, or spread strife

"Do not speak against one another, brethren. He who speaks against a brother, or judges his brother, speaks against the law, and judges the law; but if you judge the law, you are not a doer of the law, but a judge of it." (James 4:11)

evil thoughts: 1) sinful intentions which come from the heart, which can lead to sinful acts

"For out of the heart come evil thoughts, murders, adulteries, fornications, thefts, false witness, slanders." These are the things which defile the man; but to eat with unwashed hands does not defile the man." (Matthew 15:19-20)

"Finally, brethren, whatever is true, whatever is honorable, whatever is right, whatever is pure, whatever is lovely, whatever is of good repute, if there is any excellence and if anything worthy of praise, let your mind dwell on these things." (Philippians 4:8)

examine: 1) to test, to inspect carefully, to discern, to prove

"Therefore whoever eats the bread or drinks the cup of the Lord in an unworthy manner shall be guilty of sinning against the body and blood of the Lord. But let a man examine himself, and so let him eat of the bread and drinks of the cup." (1 Corinthians 11:27-28)

"Test yourselves to see if you are in the faith; examine yourselves!" (2 Corinthians 13:5)

"Search me, O God, and know my heart; try me and know my anxious thoughts; and see if there be any hurtful way in me, and lead me in the everlasting way." (Psalms 139:23-24)

"But examine everything carefully; hold fast to that which is good; abstain from every form of evil." (1 Thessalonians 5:21)

excellence: 1) worthiness, merit, moral goodness

"An excellent wife is the crown of her husband, but she who shames him is as rottenness in his bones." (Proverbs 12:4)

"Whether, then, you eat or drink or whatever you do, do all to the glory of God." (1 Corinthians 10:31)

"And this I pray, that your love may abound still more and more in real knowledge and all discernment, so that you may approve the things that are excellent, in order to be sincere and blameless until the day of Christ." (Philippians 1:9-10)

"And whatever you do in word or deed, do all in the name of the Lord Jesus, giving thanks through Him to God the Father." (Colossians 3:17)

expectation: 1) what we look forward to, what we think the future may hold

"Rest in the Lord and wait patiently for Him... the Lord sustains the righteous. The Lord knows the days of the blameless; and their inheritance will be forever. They will not be ashamed in the time of evil; and in the days of famine they will have abundance." (Psalm 37: 7, 17-19)

"Yet those who wait for the Lord will gain new strength; they will mount up with wings like eagles, they will run and not get tired, they will walk and not become weary." (Isaiah 40:31)

"For our citizenship is in heaven, from which also we eagerly wait for a Savior, the Lord Jesus Christ; who will transform the body of our humble state into conformity with the body of His glory, by the exertion of the power that He has even to subject all things to Himself." (Philippians 3:20-21)

F PRAYER CARDS

<u>faith:</u> 1) belief, trust; 2) accepting Christ as God's Son and our Savior; 3) accepts, appropriates and applies the facts found in Scripture

"So faith comes from hearing, and hearing by the word of Christ." (Romans 10:17)

"in addition to all, taking up the shield of faith with which you will be able to extinguish all the flaming missiles of the evil one." (Ephesians 6:16)

"For this reason, I bow my knees before the Father, from whom every family in heaven and on earth derives its name, that He would grant you, according to the riches of His glory, to be strengthened with power through His Spirit in the inner man; so that Christ may dwell in your hearts through faith…" (Ephesians 3:14-17)

"But if God so arrays the grass in the field, which is alive today and tomorrow is thrown into the furnace, how much more will He clothe you, O men of little faith! "And do not seek what you shall eat, and what you shall drink, and do not keep worrying… "But seek for His kingdom, and these things shall be added to you." (Luke 12:28-29, 31)

"And without faith it is impossible to please Him, for he who comes to God must believe that He is, and that He is a rewarder of those who seek Him." (Hebrews 11:6)

"For through the grace given to me I say to every man among you not to think more highly of himself than he ought to think; but to think so as to have sound judgment, as God has allotted to each a measure of faith." (Romans 12:3)

faithful: 1) steadfast in adhering to the commands of God; 2) relying on His promises

"I thank Christ Jesus our Lord, who has strengthened me, because He considered me faithful, putting me into service." (1 Timothy 1:12)

"My eyes shall be upon the faithful of the land, that they may dwell with me; He who walks in a blameless way is the one who will minister to me." (Psalm 101:6)

"He who is faithful in a very little thing is faithful also in much... " (Luke 16:10)

faithfulness: 1) surrendering to God's will out of love; 2) being diligent in service according to the opportunities He presents to us

"... Be faithful until death, and I will give you the crown of life." (Revelation 2:10)

"He who is faithful in a very little thing is faithful also in much... " (Luke 16:10)

"But the fruit of the Spirit is . . . faithfulness." (Galatians 5:22)

"My eyes shall be upon the faithful of the land, that they may dwell with me; he who walks in a blameless way is the one who will minister to me." (Psalm 101:6)

faithlessness: 1) not following our expressed belief with action; being impulsive or doubting God's promises

"Then the disciples came to Jesus privately and said, "Why could we not cast it out?" And He said to them, "Because of the littleness of your faith; for truly I say to you, if you have faith as a mustard seed, you shall say to this mountain, 'Move from here to there,' and it shall move; and nothing shall be impossible to you." (Matthew 17:19-20)

"And they took offense at Him. But Jesus said to them, "A prophet is not without honor except in his home town, and in his own household." And He did not do many miracles there because of their unbelief." (Matthew 13:57-58)

"For the love of money is a root of all sorts of evil, and some by longing for it have wandered away from the faith, and pierced themselves with many a pang." (1 Timothy 6:10)

family: 1) a husband, wife and dependent children, a household; 2) spiritual family - the community of believers who follow and obey Jesus Christ

"But if anyone does not provide for his own, and especially for those of his household, he has denied the faith, and is worse than an unbeliever." (1 Timothy 5:8)

"And, fathers, do not provoke your children to anger; but bring them up in the discipline and instruction of the Lord." (Ephesians 6:4)

"Children, obey your parents in the Lord, for this is right." (Ephesians 6:1)

"Husbands, love your wives, just as Christ also loved the church and gave Himself up for her." (Ephesians 5:25)

"Wives, be subject to your own husbands, as to the Lord." (Ephesians 5:22)

"In the same way, you wives, be submissive to your own husbands so that even if any of them are disobedient to the word, they may be won without a word by the behavior of their wives." (1 Peter 3:1)

family of God: 1) all true believers, the Church worldwide

"So then, while we have opportunity, let us do good to all men, especially to those who are of the household of the faith." (Galatians 6:10)

"For you are all sons of God through faith in Christ Jesus… And if you belong to Christ, then you are Abraham's offspring, heirs according to promise." (Galatians 3:26, 29)

"And because you are sons, God has sent forth the Spirit of His Son into our hearts, crying, "Abba! Father!" Therefore you are no longer a slave, but a son; and if a son, then an heir through God." (Galatians 4:6-7)

"And answering them, He said, "Who are My mother and My brothers?" And looking about on those who were sitting around Him, He said, "Behold, My mother and My brothers! "For whoever does the will of God, he is My brother and sister and mother." (Mark 3:33-35)

"So then you are no longer strangers and aliens, but you are fellow citizens with the saints, and are of God's household" (Ephesians 2:19)

favor: 1) kind regard, support; 2) God's blessing or reward

"I entreated Thy favor with all my heart; be gracious to me according to Thy word." (Psalm 119:58)

"I kept looking, and that horn was waging war with the saints and overpowering them until the Ancient of Days came, and judgment was passed in favor of the saints of the Highest One, and the time arrived when the saints took possession of the kingdom." (Daniel 7:21-22)

fear: 1) the emotion accompanying the expectation of evil or imminent danger, dread

"I sought the Lord, and He answered me, and delivered me from all my fears." (Psalm 34:4)

"The fear of man brings a snare, but he who trusts in the Lord will be exalted." (Proverbs 29:25)

"I am the God of your father Abraham; do not fear, for I am with you..." (Genesis 26:24)

fear of the Lord: 1) awe, amazement, in the presence of such authority, together with a dread of displeasing God

"Surely His salvation is near to those who fear Him, that glory may dwell in our land." (Psalm 85:9)

"He will bless those who fear the Lord, the small together with the great." (Psalm 115:13)

"The fear of the Lord is the beginning of knowledge; fools despise wisdom and instruction." (Proverbs 1:7)

"For if you cry for discernment, lift your voice for understanding... then you will discern the fear of the Lord, and discover the knowledge of God." (Proverbs 2:3, 5)

fellowship: 1) to have a relationship with another based on common faith; 2) challenging, loving, helping, praying for and encouraging other believers

"And they were continually devoting themselves to the apostles' teaching and to fellowship, to the breaking of bread and to prayer." (Acts 2:42)

"So then you are no longer strangers and aliens, but you are fellow citizens with the saints, and are of God's household" (Ephesians 2:19)

"and recognizing the grace that had been given to me, James and Cephas and John, who were reputed to be pillars, gave to me and Barnabas the right hand of fellowship... " (Galatians 2:9)

"... if we walk in the light as He Himself is in the light, we have fellowship with one another... " (1 John 1:7)

fellowship with believers: 1) close association with other believers, involving sharing meals, praying together, helping one another, and worshipping; 2) mutual dependence

"and the life was manifested, and we have seen and bear witness and proclaim to you the eternal life, which was with the Father and was manifested to us-- what we have seen and heard we proclaim to you also, that you also may have fellowship with us; and indeed our fellowship is with the Father, and with His Son Jesus Christ." (1 John 1:2-3)

"be filled with the Spirit, speaking to one another in Psalms and hymns and spiritual songs, singing and making melody with your heart to the Lord." (Ephesians 5:18-19)

"And all those who had believed were together, and had all things in common; and they began selling their property and possessions, and were sharing them with all, as anyone might have need. And day by day continuing with one mind in the temple, and breaking bread from house to house, they were taking their meals together with gladness and sincerity of heart." (Acts 2:44-46)

fellowship with God: 1) an intimate, personal relationship with God the Father and Jesus Christ, a spiritual relationship renewed daily by the Holy Spirit, based on the Word of God

"God is faithful, through whom you were called into fellowship with His Son, Jesus Christ our Lord." (1 Corinthians 1:9)

"… indeed our fellowship is with the Father, and with His Son Jesus Christ." (1 John 1:3)

"The grace of the Lord Jesus Christ, and the love of God, and the fellowship of the Holy Spirit, be with you all." (2 Corinthians 13:14)

"And he said to me, "Write, 'Blessed are those who are invited to the marriage supper of the Lamb… " (Revelation 19:9)

"And I heard a loud voice from the throne, saying, "Behold, the tabernacle of God is among men, and He shall dwell among them, and they shall be His people, and God Himself shall be among them." (Revelation 21:3)

fellowship with unbelievers: 1) We must not form binding relationships with unbelievers, including legal and marriage relationships, because this might weaken our Christian commitment, integrity or moral standards.

"Do not be bound together with unbelievers; for what partnership have righteousness and lawlessness, or what fellowship has light with darkness? (2 Corinthians 6:14)

"Let no one deceive you with empty words, for because of these things the wrath of God comes upon the sons of disobedience. Therefore do not be partakers with them; for you were formerly darkness, but now you are light in the Lord; walk as children of light (for the fruit of the light consists in all goodness and righteousness and truth), trying to learn what is pleasing to the Lord." (Ephesians 5:6-10)

finances: 1) Our possessions or treasures all come from God, and we must hold them loosely as good stewards, learning to tithe and give generously as the Lord prompts us.

"Bring the whole tithe into the storehouse, so that there may be food in My house, and test Me now in this," says the Lord of hosts, "if I will not open for you the windows of heaven, and pour out for you a blessing until it overflows." (Malachi 3:10)

"Now this I say, he who sows sparingly shall also reap sparingly; and he who sows bountifully shall also reap bountifully." (2 Corinthians 9:6)

"For where your treasure is, there will your heart be also." (Luke 12:34)

"But if anyone does not provide for his own, and especially for those of his household, he has denied the faith, and is worse than an unbeliever." (1 Timothy 5:8)

"This book of the law shall not depart from your mouth, but you shall meditate on it day and night, so that you may be careful to do according to all that is written in it; for then you will make your way prosperous, and then you will have success." (Joshua 1:8)

"And if we have food and covering, with these we shall be content." (1 Timothy 6:8)

first love: 1) the great commandment to love the Lord and love your neighbor; 2) authentic proof of the Gospel; zeal for the Lord

"But I have this against you, that you have left your first love. Remember therefore from where you have fallen, and repent and do the deeds you did at first" (Revelation 2:4-5)

"You shall love the Lord your God with all your heart, and with all your soul, and with all your mind… you shall love your neighbor as yourself." (Matthew 22:37, 39)

(left) first love: 1) becoming halfhearted in our commitment to follow Jesus, looking back to the world, serving with reluctance

"But I have this against you, that you have left your first love." (Revelation 2:4)

"But Jesus said to him, "No one, after putting his hand to the plow and looking back, is fit for the kingdom of God." (Luke 9:62)

fleshly: 1) operating according to the human spirit, rather than by the power and wisdom of the indwelling Holy Spirit

"And He came to the disciples and found them sleeping, and said to Peter, "So, you men could not keep watch with Me for one hour? "Keep watching and praying, that you may not enter into temptation; the spirit is willing, but the flesh is weak." (Matthew 26:40-41)

"For the flesh sets its desire against the Spirit, and the Spirit against the flesh; for these are in opposition to one another, so that you may not do the things that you please." (Galatians 5:17)

"Set your mind on the things above, not on the things that are on earth. For you have died and your life is hidden with Christ in God." (Colossians 3:2-3)

flirtation: 1) casual relationships without commitment

"With her many persuasions she entices him; with her flattering lips she seduces him." (Proverbs 7:21)

"And let not your adornment be merely external-braiding the hair, and wearing gold jewelry, or putting on dresses; but let it be the hidden person of the heart, with the imperishable quality of a gentle and quiet spirit, which is precious in the sight of God." (1 Peter 3:3-4)

focus: 1) the center point; 2) to examine one's values and priorities in light of the Word

"In all your ways acknowledge Him, and He will make your paths straight." (Proverbs 3:6)

"You shall love the Lord your God with all your heart, and with all your soul, and with all your mind." (Matthew 22:37)

"If you were of the world, the world would love its own; but because you are not of the world, but I chose you out of the world, therefore the world hates you." (John 15:19)

following the crowd: 1) being enticed into sin for pleasure or prosperity to make us feel "one of the crowd"

"My son, if sinners entice you, do not consent." (Proverbs 1:10)

"And do not participate in the unfruitful deeds of darkness, but instead even expose them." (Ephesians 5:11)

foolishness: 1) unwise, silly, without understanding; 2) the truth of God's word is foolishness to those who do not have the Holy Spirit's discernment

"But if you... are confident that you yourself are a guide to the blind, a light to those who are in darkness, a corrector of the foolish, a teacher of the immature, having in the Law the embodiment of knowledge and of the truth, you, therefore, who teach another, do you not teach yourself?... " (Romans 2:17, 19-21)

"Wise men store up knowledge, but with the mouth of the foolish, ruin is at hand." (Proverbs 10:14)

forgetting: 1) to cease thinking about or doing something; 2) not completing a task or fulfilling a promise, especially in our commitment to follow after God

"While I was fainting away, I remembered the Lord; and my prayer came to Thee... But I will sacrifice to Thee with the voice of thanksgiving. That which I have vowed I will pay. Salvation is from the Lord." (Jonah 2:7, 9)

"Therefore now, O Lord, please take my life from me, for death is better to me than life. And the Lord said, "Do you have good reason to be angry?" (Jonah 4: 3-4)

"For if anyone is a hearer of the word and not a doer, he is like a man who looks at his natural face in a mirror; for once he has looked at himself and gone away, he has immediately forgotten what kind of person he was." (James 1:23-24)

forgiveness: 1) to give up resentment toward one who has wronged us; 2) Jesus pardons our sin when we confess and repent

"But I say to you who hear, love your enemies, do good to those who hate you, bless those who curse you, pray for those who mistreat you." (Luke 6:27-28)

"For if you forgive men for their transgressions, your heavenly Father will also forgive you. "But if you do not forgive men, then your Father will not forgive your transgressions." (Matthew 6: 14-15)

"Seek the Lord while He may be found; call upon Him while He is near. Let the wicked forsake his way, and the unrighteous man his thoughts; and let him return to the Lord, and He will have compassion on him; and to our God, for He will abundantly pardon." (Isaiah 55:6-7)

fountain: 1) figuratively a gift from God, Jesus Christ is the source of living water which is eternal life

"They drink their fill of the abundance of Thy house; and Thou dost give them to drink of the river of Thy delights. For with Thee is the fountain of life; in Thy light we see light." (Psalms 36:8-9)

"And I will pour out on the house of David and on the inhabitants of Jerusalem, the Spirit of grace and of supplication, so that they will look on Me whom they have pierced; and they will mourn for Him... In that day a fountain will be opened for the house of David and for the inhabitants of Jerusalem, for sin and for impurity." (Zechariah 12:10, 13:1)

freedom: 1) release from sin, sickness, and oppression through the intervention of Jesus Christ in this fallen world

"... If you abide in My word, then you are truly disciples of Mine; and you shall know the truth, and the truth shall make you free... If therefore the Son shall make you free, you shall be free indeed." (John 8:31-32, 36)

"For the law of the Spirit of life in Christ Jesus has set you free from the law of sin and of death... in hope that the creation itself also will be set free from its slavery to corruption into the freedom of the glory of the children of God." (Romans 8:2, 20-1)

(wrong) friends: 1) associates who draw us away from God, who mock God and have a sinful influence

"How blessed is the man who does not walk in the counsel of the wicked, nor stand in the path of sinners... " (Psalm 1:1)

"Do not enter the path of the wicked, and do not proceed in the way of evil men." (Proverbs 4:14)

friendship: 1) intimate relationships with others; sharing hearts, minds and opinions

"A man of many friends comes to ruin, but there is a friend who sticks closer than a brother." (Proverbs 18:24)

"A friend loves at all times... " (Proverbs 17:17)

"He who loves purity of heart and whose speech is gracious, the king is his friend." (Proverbs 22:11)

fruit of the Spirit: 1) the by-product of the Holy Spirit living inside a believer, producing Christlikeness

"But the fruit of the Spirit is love, joy, peace, patience, kindness, goodness, faithfulness, gentleness, self-control; against such things there is no law." (Galatians 5:22-23)

fruitfulness: 1) the proof of the power of the Holy Spirit working in you; 2) developing Christ-like characteristics in your daily walk

"Every branch in Me that does not bear fruit, He takes away; and every branch that bears fruit, He prunes it, that it may bear more fruit." (John 15:2)

"I am the vine, you are the branches; he who abides in Me, and I in him, he bears much fruit; for apart from Me you can do nothing." (John 15:5)

"By this is My Father glorified, that you bear much fruit, and so prove to be My disciples." (John 15:8)

"But the fruit of the Spirit is love, joy, peace, patience, kindness, goodness, faithfulness, gentleness, self-control; against such things there is no law." (Galatians 5:22-23)

fruitlessness: 1) religion without substance, having no evidence of a changed life

"For just as the body without the spirit is dead, so also faith without works is dead." (James 2:26)

fullness of God: 1) lacking nothing in your relationship with God; 2) living in His presence, experiencing His power and grace through faith and prayer

"so that Christ may dwell in your hearts through faith; and that you, being rooted and grounded in love... know the love of Christ which surpasses knowledge, that you may be filled up to all the fulness of God." (Ephesians 3:17, 19)

"For in Him all the fulness of Deity dwells in bodily form, and in Him you have been made complete, and He is the head over all rule and authority." (Colossians 2:9-10)

future: 1) the time to come; 2) for those who follow Christ, there is an eternity filled with hope and blessing

"For I know the plans that I have for you,' declares the Lord, 'plans for welfare and not for calamity to give you a future and a hope." (Jeremiah 29:11)

"Do not let your heart envy sinners, but live in the fear of the Lord always. Surely there is a future, and your hope will not be cut off." (Proverbs 23:17-18)

"Do not boast about tomorrow, for you do not know what a day may bring forth." (Proverbs 27:1)

"Therefore do not be anxious for tomorrow; for tomorrow will care for itself. Each day has enough trouble of its own." (Matthew 6:34)

G PRAYER CARDS

gambling: 1) to risk money on the chance outcome of a game or financial hunch rather than placing our trust in Jesus

"A faithful man will abound with blessings, but he who makes haste to be rich will not go unpunished." (Proverbs 28:20)

"A man with an evil eye hastens after wealth, and does not know that want will come upon him." (Proverbs 28:22)

gentleness: 1) a fruit of the Spirit; 2) humbleness, submission to God, being considerate of others even when they are unrighteous

"Remind them to be subject to rulers, to authorities, to be obedient, to be ready for every good deed, to malign no one, to be uncontentious, gentle, showing every consideration for all men." (Titus 3:1-2)

"but let it be (your adornment) be the hidden person of the heart, with the imperishable quality of a gentle and quiet spirit, which is precious in the sight of God." (1 Peter 3:4)

"And so, as those who have been chosen of God, holy and beloved, put on a heart of compassion, kindness, humility, gentleness and patience; bearing with one another, and forgiving each other, whoever has a complaint against anyone; just as the Lord forgave you, so also should you." (Colossians 3:12-13)

gladness: 1) that which produces joy; sinner's repentance, eternal life, God's promises, freedom from sin and worry

"Purify me with hyssop, and I shall be clean; wash me, and I shall be whiter than snow. Make me to hear joy and gladness, let the bones which Thou hast broken rejoice... Restore to me the joy of Thy salvation, and sustain me with a willing spirit." (Psalm 51: 7-8, 12)

glorify (God): 1) to bring honor to God by good deeds; 2) worship, praise and love for God's blessings

"Whoever speaks, let him speak, as it were, the utterances of God; whoever serves, let him do so as by the strength which God supplies; so that in all things God may be glorified through Jesus Christ, to whom belongs the glory and dominion forever and ever. Amen." (1 Peter 4:11)

"Now may the God who gives perseverance and encouragement grant you to be of the same mind with one another according to Christ Jesus; that with one accord you may with one voice glorify the God and Father of our Lord Jesus Christ. Wherefore, accept one another, just as Christ also accepted us to the glory of God." (Romans 15:5-7)

glorify (believers): 1) using one's Spiritual gifts to edify the Church and bring honor to Christ; 2) our new life in Christ as we are being sanctified through the Holy Spirit

"Whether, then, you eat or drink or whatever you do, do all to the glory of God." (1 Corinthians 10:31)

"For you have been bought with a price: therefore glorify God in your body." (1 Corinthians 6:20)

"Be diligent to present yourself approved to God as a workman who does not need to be ashamed, handling accurately the word of truth." (2 Timothy 2:15)

glory of the Lord: 1) God's holy attributes; 2) the majesty of His divine presence

"And to the eyes of the sons of Israel the appearance of the glory of the Lord was like a consuming fire on the mountain top." (Exodus 24:17)

"O God, Thou art my God; I shall seek Thee earnestly; My soul thirsts for Thee, my flesh yearns for Thee . . . Thus I have beheld Thee in the sanctuary, to see Thy power and Thy glory." (Psalm 63:1-2)

"And an angel of the Lord suddenly stood before them, and the glory of the Lord shone around them; and they were terribly frightened." (Luke 2:9)

"Then the glory of the Lord will be revealed, and all flesh will see it together; for the mouth of the Lord has spoken." (Isaiah 40:5)

glutton: 1) one who eats to excess with no restraint, greedy

"He who keeps the law is a discerning son, but he who is a companion of gluttons humiliates his father." (Proverbs 28:7)

"Do not be with heavy drinkers of wine, or with gluttonous eaters of meat; for the heavy drinker and the glutton will come to poverty... " (Proverbs 23:20-21)

goal: 1) purpose or aim to reach for; 2) a believer's goal should be to become more like Jesus and to glorify the Father

"And He said to him, "You shall love the Lord your God with all your heart, and with all your soul, and with all your mind . . . you shall love your neighbor as yourself." (Matthew: 22:37, 39)

"I urge you therefore, brethren, by the mercies of God, to present your bodies a living and holy sacrifice, acceptable to God, which is your spiritual service of worship." (Romans 12:1)

"Blessed be the God... who... caused us to be born again to a living hope... to obtain an inheritance which is imperishable . . . reserved in heaven for you... even though now for a little while, if necessary, you have been distressed by various trials that the proof of your faith being more precious than gold... tested by fire... found to result in praise and glory and honor at the revelation of Jesus Christ." (1 Peter 1:3-7)

goodness: 1) a fruit of the Spirit; 2) the Golden Rule in action; 3) our obedience reflects God's will

"Beloved, do not imitate what is evil, but what is good... " (3 John 1:11)

"... love your enemies, do good to those who hate you" (Luke 6:27)

"... every good tree bears good fruit... " (Matthew 7:17)

"With good will render service, as to the Lord, and not to men, knowing that whatever good thing each one does, this he will receive back from the Lord, whether slave or free." (Ephesians 6: 7-8)

Gospel: 1) the Good News of God's Messiah; Jesus came to give us eternal life when we acknowledge His claim over our destiny

"The time is fulfilled, and the kingdom of God is at hand; repent and believe in the gospel." (Mark 1:15)

"For God, who said, "Light shall shine out of darkness," is the One who has shone in our hearts to give the light of the knowledge of the glory of God in the face of Christ." (2 Corinthians 4:6)

"Grace to you and peace from God our Father, and the Lord Jesus Christ, who gave Himself for our sins, that He might deliver us out of this present evil age, according to the will of our God and Father..." (Galatians 1:3-4)

The Gospel: John 3:16, Romans 3:23, 6:23, 5:8, 10: 9-11

gossip: 1) verbal cruelty, spreading rumors, tattling

"And at the same time they also learn to be idle, as they go around from house to house; and not merely idle, but also gossips and busybodies, talking about things not proper to mention." (1 Timothy 5:13)

"Let no unwholesome word proceed from your mouth, but only such a word as is good for edification according to the need of the moment, that it may give grace to those who hear." (Ephesians 4:29)

grace: 1) God's spiritual enlightenment to understand and accept the Gospel of Jesus Christ; 2) salvation from the penalty of sin in spite of our sinful nature; 3) a gift from God, not due to our own merit

"And He has said to me, "My grace is sufficient for you, for power is perfected in weakness." (2 Corinthians 12:9)

"Therefore do not be ashamed of the testimony of our Lord, or of me His prisoner; but join with me in suffering for the gospel according to the power of God, who has saved us, and called us with a holy calling, not according to our works, but according to His own purpose and grace which was granted us in Christ Jesus from all eternity" (2 Timothy 1:8-9)

gratefulness: 1) having a thankful heart for all of God's blessings

"Oh give thanks to the Lord, call upon His name; make known His deeds among the peoples." (Psalm 105:1)

"Therefore, since we receive a kingdom which cannot be shaken, let us show gratitude, by which we may offer to God an acceptable service with reverence and awe." (Hebrews 12:28)

"in everything give thanks; for this is God's will for you in Christ Jesus." (1 Thessalonians 5:18)

"As you therefore have received Christ Jesus the Lord, so walk in Him, having been firmly rooted and now being built up in Him and established in your faith, just as you were instructed, and overflowing with gratitude." (Colossians 2:6-7)

guard our tongues: 1) speaking with humility and patience; 2) allowing the Holy Spirit to put a mental stopwatch on our mouth; 3) considering the impact of our words

"And the tongue is a fire, the very world of iniquity; the tongue is set among our members as that which defiles the entire body, and sets on fire the course of our life, and is set on fire by hell." (James 3:6)

"For, let him who means to love life and see good days refrain his tongue from evil and his lips from speaking guile." (1 Peter 3:10)

"Set a guard, O Lord, over my mouth; keep watch over the door of my lips." (Psalm 141:3)

"Let no unwholesome word proceed from your mouth, but only such a word as is good for edification according to the need of the moment, that it may give grace to those who hear." (Ephesians 4:29)

"The good man out of the good treasure of his heart brings forth what is good; and the evil man out of the evil treasure brings forth what is evil; for his mouth speaks from that which fills his heart." (Luke 6:45)

"If anyone thinks himself to be religious, and yet does not bridle his tongue but deceives his own heart, this man's religion is worthless." (James 1:26)

guide: 1) to lead or direct in the correct path; 2) God's Word and following Jesus' example will keep us in the center of His will

"Teach me to do Thy will, for Thou art my God; let Thy good Spirit lead me on level ground." (Psalm 143:10)

"With Thy counsel Thou wilt guide me, and afterward receive me to glory." (Psalm 73:24)

"For all who are being led by the Spirit of God, these are sons of God." (Romans 8:14)

"But when He, the Spirit of truth, comes, He will guide you into all the truth; for He will not speak on His own initiative, but whatever He hears, He will speak; and He will disclose to you what is to come." (John 16:13)

guile: 1) deceit, cunning, crafty, misleading to further one's own end

"Jesus saw Nathanael coming to Him, and said of him, "Behold, an Israelite indeed, in whom is no guile!" (John 1:47)

"For you have been called for this purpose, since Christ also suffered for you, leaving you an example for you to follow in His steps, who committed no sin, nor was any deceit found in his mouth." (1 Peter 2:21-22)

"Blessed is the man unto whom the Lord imputeth not iniquity, and in whose spirit there is no guile." (Psalm 32:2 KJV)

"And I looked, and behold, the Lamb was standing on Mount Zion, and with Him one hundred and forty- four thousand... These are the ones who follow the Lamb wherever He goes... And no lie was found in their mouth; they are blameless." (Revelation 14:1, 4-5)

H PRAYER CARDS

hardened heart: 1) an attitude of satisfaction with this life, feeling no guilt for sin and having no desire for forgiveness; 2) either takes God's blessings for granted or rebels against His dominion

"You men who are stiff-necked and uncircumcised in heart and ears are always resisting the Holy Spirit; you are doing just as your fathers did." (Acts 7:51)

"… Today if you hear His voice, do not harden your hearts, as when they (Israel) provoked Me." (Hebrews 3:15)

"And afterward He appeared to the eleven themselves as they were reclining at the table; and He reproached them for their unbelief and hardness of heart, because they had not believed those who had seen Him after He had risen." (Mark 16:14)

harmony: 1) being in agreement with the will of God; 2) of one mind or opinion, peace

"To sum up, let all be harmonious, sympathetic, brotherly, kindhearted, and humble in spirit." (1 Peter 3:8)

"And I looked, and I heard the voice of many angels around the throne and the living creatures and the elders; and the number of them was myriads of myriads, and thousands of thousands, saying with a loud voice, "Worthy is the Lamb that was slain to receive power and riches and wisdom and might and honor and glory and blessing." (Revelation 5:11-12)

harvest: 1) figuratively, the judgment of God at the end of time; 2) a spiritual harvest is an individual or group receptive to the Gospel message and open to the promises of eternal life

"And seeing the multitudes, He felt compassion for them, because they were distressed and downcast like sheep without a shepherd. Then He said to His disciples, "The harvest is plentiful, but the workers are few. "Therefore beseech the Lord of the harvest to send out workers into His harvest." (Matthew 9:36-38)

"So then, while we have opportunity, let us do good to all men, and especially to those who are of the household of the faith." (Galatians 6:10)

"All discipline for the moment seems not to be joyful, but sorrowful; yet to those who have been trained by it, afterwards it yields the peaceful fruit of righteousness." (Hebrews 12:11)

hatred: 1) enmity, strong dislike, regarding something (or someone) as evil

"Everyone who hates his brother is a murderer; and you know that no murderer has eternal life abiding in him." (1 John 3:15)

"Hatred stirs up strife, but love covers all transgressions." (Proverbs 10:12)

haughty: 1) high-minded, arrogant, proud, overbearing

"There are six things which the Lord hates... Haughty eyes... " (Proverbs 6:16-17)

"For though the Lord is exalted, yet He regards the lowly; but the haughty He knows from afar." (Psalms 138:6)

head: 1) authority, highest position, most important member; Jesus has authority over the Church; 2) the head of woman is man, the head of man is Christ, the head of Christ is God

"And He put all things in subjection under His feet, and gave Him as head over all things to the church." (Ephesians 1:22)

"But I want you to understand that Christ is the head of every man, and the man is the head of a woman, and God is the head of Christ." (1 Corinthians 11:3)

"For the husband is the head of the wife, as Christ also is the head of the church, He Himself being the Savior of the body. But as the church is subject to Christ, so also the wives ought to be to their husbands in everything. Husbands, love your wives, just as Christ also loved the church and gave Himself up for her." (Ephesians 5:23-25)

healing: 1) Jesus and the Holy Spirit have the power to perform the miracle of curing various diseases, birth defects, and demonic possession

"O Lord my God, I cried to Thee for help, and Thou didst heal me." (Psalm 30:2)

"For I will restore you to health and I will heal you of your wounds,' declares the Lord" (Jeremiah 30:17)

"He sent His word and healed them, and delivered them from their destructions." (Psalm 107:20)

"And Jesus was going about in all Galilee, teaching in their synagogues, and proclaiming the gospel of the kingdom, and healing every kind of disease and every kind of sickness among the people." (Matthew 4:23)

"Heal me, O Lord, and I will be healed; save me and I will be saved, for Thou art my praise." (Jeremiah 17:14)

health: 1) spiritual and physical wholeness, freedom from illness

"My son, give attention to my words; Incline your ear to my sayings... For they are life to those who find them, and health to all their whole body." (Proverbs 4:20, 22)

"Beloved, I pray that in all respects you may prosper and be in good health, just as your soul prospers." (3 John 1:2)

hear God: 1) to listen carefully to the Lord; which leads to spiritual understand and obedience

"While he was still speaking, behold, a bright cloud overshadowed them; and behold, a voice out of the cloud, saying, "This is My beloved Son, with whom I am well-pleased; listen to Him!" (Matthew 17:5)

"He who has an ear, let him hear what the Spirit says to the churches. To him who overcomes, to him I will give some of the hidden manna, and I will give him a white stone, and a new name written on the stone which no one knows but he who receives it." (Revelation 2:17)

heart: 1) the seat of affection, understanding and will; 2) those without faith have a heart of stone, those filled with the Holy Spirit receive a new heart, pliable in the hands of a loving Lord

"The heart is more deceitful than all else and is desperately sick; who can understand it?" (Jeremiah 17:9)

"Search me, O God, and know my heart; try me and know my anxious thoughts; and see if there be any hurtful way in me, And lead me in the everlasting way." (Psalms 139:23-24)

"And He said to him, "You shall love the Lord your God with all your heart, and with all your soul, and with all your mind." (Matthew 22:37)

heart after David: 1) having a heart for worship and obedience out of a love for the Lord

"And after He had removed him, He raised up David to be their king, concerning whom He also testified and said, ' I have found David the son of Jesse, a man after My heart, who will do all My will." (Acts 13:22)

"And David was dancing before the Lord with all his might..." (2 Samuel 6:14)

"I will sing of the lovingkindness of the Lord forever; to all generations I will make known Thy faithfulness with my mouth." (Psalm 89:1)

"And He said to him, "You shall love the Lord your God with all your heart, and with all your soul, and with all your mind." (Matthew 22:37)

heart after God: 1) a believer who is totally immersed in loving God, holding nothing back because God held nothing back

"And He said to him, "You shall love the Lord your God with all your heart, and with all your soul, and with all your mind.' "This is the great and foremost commandment." (Matthew 22:37-38)

"Let the words of my mouth and the meditation of my heart be acceptable in Thy sight, O Lord, my rock and my Redeemer." (Psalm 19:14)

"My soul, wait in silence for God only, for my hope is from Him... Trust in Him at all times, O people; pour out your heart before Him; God is a refuge for us." (Psalm 62:5, 8)

"O God, Thou art my God; I shall seek Thee earnestly; my soul thirsts for Thee, my flesh yearns for Thee... " (Psalm 63:1)

heart for worship: 1) the evidence of a deep spiritual relationship with God; inspired by the Holy Spirit

"for we are the true circumcision, who worship in the Spirit of God and glory in Christ Jesus and put no confidence in the flesh." (Philippians 3:3)

"And the twenty-four elders, who sit on their thrones before God, fell on their faces and worshiped God." (Revelation 11:16)

"After these things I looked, and behold, a great multitude, which no one could count, from every nation and all tribes and peoples and tongues, standing before the throne and before the Lamb, clothed in white robes, and palm branches were in their hands; and they cry out with a loud voice, saying, "Salvation to our God who sits on the throne, and to the Lamb." (Revelation 7:9-10)

"And I fell at his feet to worship him... " (Revelation 19:10)

hedge of protection: 1) God's protection of His children day and night, pictured in Exodus as the pillars of fire and cloud

"Hast Thou not made a hedge about him and his house and all that he has, on every side?... " (Job 1:10)

"The Lord will protect you from all evil; He will keep your soul. The Lord will guard your going out and your coming in from this time forth and forever." (Psalm 121:7-8)

Helper: 1) one who aids or relieves; 2) God the Father, Son and Holy Spirit are all referred to as Helpers in Scripture, who hold us up, comforts and guides us during times of confusion and trial

"And I will ask the Father, and He will give you another Helper, that He may be with you forever." (John 14:16)

"When the Helper comes, whom I will send to you from the Father, that is the Spirit of truth, who proceeds from the Father, He will bear witness of Me." (John 15:26)

"And He, when He comes, will convict the world concerning sin, and righteousness, and judgment; concerning sin, because they do not believe in Me; and concerning righteousness, because I go to the Father, and you no longer behold Me; and concerning judgment, because the ruler of this world has been judged." (John 16:8-11)

helpmeet: 1) King James term for a wife; 2) equal in honor, a companion perfectly suited to assist man

"Then the Lord God said, "It is not good for the man to be alone; I will make him a helper suitable for him." (Genesis 2:18)

"Wives, be subject to your own husbands, as to the Lord." (Ephesians 5:22)

"For this cause a man shall leave his father and mother, and shall cleave to his wife; and the two shall become one flesh... Nevertheless let each individual among you also love his own wife even as himself; and let the wife see to it that she respect her husband." (Ephesians 5:31, 33)

"An excellent wife, who can find? For her worth is far above jewels. The heart of her husband trusts in her, and he will have no lack of gain. She does him good and not evil all the days of her life." (Proverbs 31:10-12) (note: see Abigail in 1 Sam. 25:2-39)

heresy: 1) an opinion held which is in opposition to accepted doctrine of the Church; 2) mature believers must be able to determine false teachings which oppose the Word of God

"But in vain do they worship Me, teaching as doctrines the precepts of men." (Matthew 15:9)

"As a result, we are no longer to be children, tossed here and there by waves, and carried about by every wind of doctrine, by the trickery of men, by craftiness in deceitful scheming." (Ephesians 4:14)

"If anyone advocates a different doctrine, and does not agree with sound words, those of our Lord Jesus Christ, and with the doctrine conforming to godliness, he is conceited and understands nothing... " (1 Timothy 6: 3-4)

"Anyone who goes too far and does not abide in the teaching of Christ, does not have God; the one who abides in the teaching, he has both the Father and the Son." (2 John 1:9)

"Now I urge you, brethren, keep your eye on those who cause dissensions and hindrances contrary to the teaching which you learned, and turn away from them." (Romans 16:17)

hidden manna: 1) the secret wisdom of God, hidden from man in former times, revealed by the Holy Spirit

"To him who overcomes, to him I will give some of the hidden manna..." (Revelation 2:17)

"Yet we do speak wisdom among those who are mature; a wisdom, however, not of this age, nor of the rulers of this age, who are passing away; but we speak God's wisdom in a mystery, the hidden wisdom, which God predestined before the ages to our glory . . . but just as it is written, Things which eye has not seen and ear has not heard, and which have not entered the heart of man, all that God has prepared for those who love Him. "For to us God revealed them through the Spirit; for the Spirit searches all things, even the depths of God." (1 Corinthians 2:6-7, 9-10)

hiding place: 1) God is our shelter and protector who preserves us in times of danger and sin

"Keep me as the apple of the eye; hide me in the shadow of Thy wings." (Psalm 17:8)

"Thou art my hiding place; Thou dost preserve me from trouble; Thou dost surround me with songs of deliverance." (Psalm 32:7)

"Thou art my hiding place and my shield; I wait for Thy word." (Psalm 119:114)

holy: 1) without sin, spiritually whole, set apart or dedicated to God; 2) God is completely separated from sin and evil

". . . He chose us in Him before the foundation of the world, that we should be holy and blameless before Him." (Ephesians 1:4)

". . . the temple of God is holy, and that is what you are." (1 Corinthians 3:17)

"To grant us that we, being delivered from the hand of our enemies, might serve Him without fear, in holiness and righteousness before Him all our days." (Luke 1:74-75)

"be holy yourselves also in all your behavior; because it is written, "You shall be holy, for I am holy." (1 Peter 1:15-16)

Holy Spirit intercession: 1) The Holy Spirit knows how to approach the throne of God when we do not have the words to pray or know the will of God

"And in the same way the Spirit also helps our weakness; for we do not know how to pray as we should, but the Spirit Himself intercedes for us with groanings too deep for words; and He who searches the hearts knows what the mind of the Spirit is, because He intercedes for the saints according to the will of God." (Romans 8:26-27)

home: 1) both home base and our final goal; 2) our dwelling place and a place of refuge

"In My Father's house are many dwelling places; if it were not so, I would have told you; for I go to prepare a place for you." (John 14:2)

"Jesus answered and said to him, "If anyone loves Me, he will keep My word; and My Father will love him, and We will come to him, and make Our abode with him." (John 14:23)

"The eternal God is a dwelling place, and underneath are the everlasting arms... " (Deuteronomy 33:27)

"So then you are no longer strangers and aliens, but you are fellow citizens with the saints, and are of God's household, having been built upon the foundation of the apostles and prophets, Christ Jesus Himself being the corner stone, in whom you also are being built together into a dwelling of God in the Spirit." (Ephesians 2:19-22)

homosexuality: 1) to exchange or abandon natural sexual relations for that which God considers deviant

"For this reason God gave them over to degrading passions; for their women exchanged the natural function for that which is unnatural, and in the same way also the men abandoned the natural function of the woman and burned in their desire toward one another, men with men committing indecent acts and receiving in their own persons the due penalty of their error." (Romans 1: 26-27)

"You shall not lie with a male as one lies with a female; it is an abomination." (Leviticus 18:22)

honesty: 1) truthfulness, integrity, straightforward, candor, without guile

"And the seed in the good soil, these are the ones who have heard the word in an honest and good heart, and hold it fast, and bear fruit with perseverance." (Luke 8:15)

"Keep your behavior excellent among the Gentiles, so that in the thing in which they slander you as evildoers, they may on account of your good deeds, as they observe them, glorify God in the day of visitation." (1 Peter 2:12)

"Who may ascend into the hill of the Lord? And who may stand in His holy place? He who has clean hands and a pure heart, who has not lifted up his soul to falsehood, and has not sworn deceitfully. He shall receive a blessing from the Lord and righteousness from the God of his salvation." (Psalm 24:3-5)

honor: 1) respect, consideration, esteem, dignity, value highly; 2) We were created in God's image and reflect His glory, therefore we are to respect and treat one another with dignity.

"Then Moses said to Aaron, "It is what the Lord spoke, saying, 'By those who come near Me I will be treated as holy, and before all the people I will be honored... " (Leviticus 10:3)

"For Moses said, 'Honor your father and your mother'; and, 'He who speaks evil of father or mother, let him be put to death'. (Mark 7:10)

"Be devoted to one another in brotherly love; give preference to one another in honor." (Romans 12:10)

hope: 1) the promise of delivery from sin; 2) the expectation of good, the joyful anticipation of eternal salvation

"... hope does not disappoint, because the love of God has been poured out within our hearts through the Holy Spirit who was given to us." (Romans 5:5)

"Now may the God of hope fill you with all joy and peace in believing, that you may abound in hope by the power of the Holy Spirit." (Romans 15:13)

"... through Him are believers in God, who raised Him from the dead and gave Him glory, so that your faith and hope are in God." (1 Peter 1:21)

"For I am confident of this very thing, that He who began a good work in you will perfect it until the day of Christ Jesus." (Philippians 1:6)

hospitality: 1) welcoming a believer on God's mission; 2) feeding, clothing or sheltering someone in the name of Jesus; the duty of all disciples of Christ

"Be hospitable to one another without complaint." (1 Peter 4:9)

"Do not neglect to show hospitality to strangers, for by this some have entertained angels without knowing it." (Hebrews 13:2)

"Be devoted to one another in brotherly love; give preference to one another in honor... contributing to the needs of the saints, practicing hospitality." (Romans 12:10, 13)

humble: 1) unassuming, modest, meek, submissive; 2) being a servant, putting other people's needs first

"all of you, clothe yourselves with humility toward one another, for God is opposed to the proud, but gives grace to the humble." (1 Peter 5:5)

"Take My yoke upon you, and learn from Me, for I am gentle and humble in heart; and you shall find rest for your souls." (Matthew 11:29)

"... walk in a manner worthy of the calling with which you have been called, with all humility and gentleness, with patience, showing forbearance to one another in love." (Ephesians 4:1-2)

"And so, as those who have been chosen of God, holy and beloved, put on a heart of compassion, kindness, humility, gentleness and patience; bearing with one another, and forgiving each other, whoever has a complaint against anyone; just as the Lord forgave you, so also should you." (Colossians 3:12-13)

humility: 1) meekness, trusting in God rather than the flesh, not thinking too highly of oneself, waiting on the Lord with an attitude of submission

"... But to this one I will look, to him who is humble and contrite of spirit, and who trembles at My word." (Isaiah 66:2)

"… what does the Lord require of you but to do justice, to love kindness, and to walk humbly with your God?" (Micah 6:8)

"Do nothing from selfishness or empty conceit, but with humility of mind let each of you regard one another as more important than himself." (Philippians 2:3)

hurt feelings: 1) bearing the pain of unjust suffering with patience rather than exhibiting the fruit of the flesh, knowing our worth in the eyes of the Lord

"He came to His own, and those who were His own did not receive Him. But as many as received Him, to them He gave the right to become children of God, even to those who believe in His name." (John 1:11-12)

"Let all bitterness and wrath and anger and clamor and slander be put away from you, along with all malice. And be kind to one another, tender-hearted, forgiving each other, just as God in Christ also has forgiven you." (Ephesians 4:31-32)

"For what credit is there if, when you sin and are harshly treated, you endure it with patience? But if when you do what is right and suffer for it you patiently endure it, this finds favor with God. For you have been called for this purpose, since Christ also suffered for you, leaving you an example for you to follow in His steps, Who committed no sin, nor was any deceit found in His mouth; and while being reviled, He did not revile in return; while suffering, He uttered no threats, but kept entrusting Himself to Him who judges righteously." (1 Peter 2:20-23)

hypocrisy: 1) false piety, a religious phony whose heart is far from God but labors to appear holy

"Even so you too outwardly appear righteous to men, but inwardly you are full of hypocrisy and lawlessness." (Matthew 23:28)

"Let love be without hypocrisy. Abhor what is evil; cling to what is good." (Romans 12:9)

"But the wisdom from above is first pure, then peaceable, gentle, reasonable, full of mercy and good fruits, unwavering, without hypocrisy." (James 3:17)

I PRAYER CARDS

I AM: 1) a name of God; who has eternal power and an unchangeable character; 2) also used to identify Jesus, who is the same yesterday, today and tomorrow

"Then Moses said to God… "Now they (Israel) may say to me, 'What is His name?' What shall I say to them?" And God said to Moses, "I AM who I AM." (Exodus 3:13-14)

"Jesus said to them, "Truly, truly, I say to you, before Abraham was born, I am." (John 8:58)

"For since the creation of the world His invisible attributes, His eternal power and divine nature, have been clearly seen, being understood through what has been made, so that they are without excuse." (Romans 1:20)

"And God created man in His own image, in the image of God He created him; male and female He created them." (Genesis 1:27)

idolatry: 1) worshipping anything other than God; 2) rejection of God in favor of created things

"Beware, lest your hearts be deceived and you turn away and serve other gods and worship them." (Deuteronomy 11:16)

"The graven images of their gods you are to burn with fire; you shall not covet the silver or the gold that is on them, nor take it for yourselves,

lest you be snared by it, for it is an abomination to the Lord your God."
(Deuteronomy 7:25)

immaturity: 1) lack of understanding of Biblical truths, lack of self-discipline, reliance on the Law for salvation, never getting past spiritual "baby food" to the deeper things of God

"An overseer, then, must be above reproach... and not a new convert, lest he become conceited and fall into the condemnation incurred by the devil." (1 Timothy 3:2, 6)

"And I, brethren, could not speak to you as to spiritual men, but as to men of flesh, as to babes in Christ. I gave you milk to drink, not solid food; for you were not yet able to receive it. Indeed, even now you are not yet able, for you are still fleshly. For since there is jealousy and strife among you, are you not fleshly, and are you not walking like mere men? (1 Corinthians 3:1-3)

"For though by this time you ought to be teachers, you have need again for someone to teach you the elementary principles of the oracles of God, and you have come to need milk and not solid food ... But solid food is for the mature, who because of practice have their senses trained to discern good and evil." (Hebrews 5:12, 14)

immodest dress: 1) physical attractiveness without discretion; 2) indecent, obscene, without restraint in attire

"And you, O desolate one, what will you do? Although you dress in scarlet, although you decorate yourself with ornaments of gold, although you enlarge your eyes with paint, in vain you make yourself beautiful; Your lovers despise you; they seek your life." (Jeremiah 4:30)

"As a ring of gold in a swine's snout, so is a beautiful woman who lacks discretion." (Proverbs 11:22)

"And let not your adornment be merely external-- braiding the hair, and wearing gold jewelry, or putting on dresses; but let it be the hidden person of the heart, with the imperishable quality of a gentle and quiet spirit, which is precious in the sight of God." (1 Peter 3:3-4)

immortality: 1) lasting forever, unending existence; 2) the resurrection of the body and the soul for all eternity

"in a moment, in the twinkling of an eye, at the last trumpet; for the trumpet will sound, and the dead will be raised imperishable, and we shall be changed. For this perishable must put on the imperishable, and this mortal must put on immortality." (1 Corinthians 15:52-53)

"And many of those who sleep in the dust of the ground will awake, these to everlasting life, but the others to disgrace and everlasting contempt." (Daniel 12:2)

"... the Lord Jesus shall be revealed from heaven... dealing out retribution to those who do not know God and to those who do not obey the gospel of our Lord Jesus. And these will pay the penalty of eternal destruction, away from the presence of the Lord and from the glory of His power." (2 Thessalonians 1:7-9)

"and He has made us to be a kingdom, priests to His God and Father; to Him be the glory and the dominion forever and ever. Amen. Behold, He is coming with the clouds, and every eye will see Him, even those who pierced Him; and all the tribes of the earth will mourn over Him. Even so. Amen." (Revelation 1:6-7)

impatience: 1) restlessness, inability to tolerate delay, eagerness for change; 2) patience is foreign to our culture, we desire instant gratification and results, rather than mirror God's boundless grace and compassion

"Then they set out from Mount Hor by the way of the Red Sea, to go around the land of Edom; and the people became impatient because of the journey. And the people spoke against God and Moses... And the Lord sent fiery serpents among the people and they bit the people, so that many people of Israel died." (Numbers 21:4-6)

incest: 1) a sexual relationship between two individuals who are prohibited by law to marry

"None of you shall approach any blood relative of his to uncover nakedness; I am the Lord." (Leviticus 18:6)

"The nakedness of your sister, either your father's daughter or your mother's daughter, whether born at home or born outside, their nakedness you shall not uncover. The nakedness of your son's daughter or your daughter's daughter, their nakedness you shall not uncover; for their nakedness is yours... You shall not uncover the nakedness of your daughter-in-law; she is your son's wife, you shall not uncover her nakedness." (Leviticus 18:9-10, 15)

independence: 1) the world's rebellion against God, rather than deriving spiritual power from total dependence on God; 2) the Church is a model of mutual interdependence

"Jesus therefore said, "When you lift up the Son of Man, then you will know that I am He, and I do nothing on My own initiative, but I speak these things as the Father taught Me." (John 8:28)

"For I did not speak on My own initiative, but the Father Himself who sent Me has given Me commandment, what to say, and what to speak." (John 12:49)

"However, in the Lord, neither is woman independent of man, nor is man independent of woman. For as the woman originates from the man, so also the man has his birth through the woman; and all things originate from God." (1 Corinthians 11:11-12)

"And all those who had believed were together, and had all things in common... praising God, and having favor with all the people. And the Lord was adding to their number day by day those who were being saved." (Acts 2:44, 47)

inferiority: 1) having a sense of less importance or merit; 2) We were created in God's image and are all of equal value in our Father's eyes

"You did not choose Me, but I chose you, and appointed you, that you should go and bear fruit, and that your fruit should remain, that whatever you ask of the Father in My name, He may give to you." (John 15:16)

"For we are His workmanship, created in Christ Jesus for good works, which God prepared beforehand, that we should walk in them." (Ephesians 2:10)

"For I am confident of this very thing, that He who began a good work in you will perfect it until the day of Christ Jesus." (Philippians 1:6)

"I can do all things through Him who strengthens me." (Philippians 4:13)

inheritance: 1) every believer will receive salvation, eternal life and the kingdom of heaven freely given through the blood of Jesus Christ

"The Spirit Himself bears witness with our spirit that we are children of God, and if children, heirs also, heirs of God and fellow heirs with Christ, if indeed we suffer with Him in order that we may also be glorified with Him." (Romans 8:16-17)

"He saved us… according to His mercy by the washing of regeneration and renewing by the Holy Spirit… that being justified by His grace we might be made heirs according to the hope of eternal life." (Titus 3:5-7)

"And if you belong to Christ, then you are Abraham's offspring, heirs according to promise." (Galatians 3:29)

iniquity: 1) an unforgiving or spiteful attitude of the heart which disconnects us from the presence of God; 2) habitual actions which are displeasing to God; sin

"Establish my footsteps in Thy word, and do not let any iniquity have dominion over me." (Psalm 119:133)

"For Thy name's sake, O Lord, pardon my iniquity, for it is great." (Psalm 25:11)

"Hide Thy face from my sins, and blot out all my iniquities. Create in me a clean heart, O God, and renew a steadfast spirit within me." (Psalm 51:9-10)

"But He was pierced through for our transgressions, He was crushed for our iniquities; the chastening for our well-being fell upon Him, and by His scourging we are healed." (Isaiah 53:5)

innocence: 1) morally free from guilt, without sin; 2) purity of heart, blameless, especially in one's thought life

"Behold, I send you out as sheep in the midst of wolves; therefore be shrewd as serpents, and innocent as doves." (Matthew 10:16)

"I want you to be wise in what is good, and innocent in what is evil." (Romans 16:19)

"Jesus saw Nathanael coming to Him, and said of him, "Behold, an Israelite indeed, in whom is no guile!" (John 1:47)

integrity: 1) complete, morally sound, upright in character; 2) communicating our relationship with God through our daily walk

"O Lord, who may abide in Thy tent? Who may dwell on Thy holy hill? He who walks with integrity, and works righteousness, and speaks truth in his heart." (Psalm 15:1-2)

"Let integrity and uprightness preserve me, for I wait for Thee." (Psalm 25:21)

"Many a man proclaims his own loyalty, but who can find a trustworthy man? A righteous man who walks in his integrity-- How blessed are his sons after him." (Proverbs 20:6-7)

intercession: 1) prayer, petition, or seeking God's favor for another; 2) Jesus, the Holy Spirit and every believer have the privilege and duty to intercede for others before the Father

"With all prayer and petition pray at all times in the Spirit, and with this in view, be on the alert with all perseverance and petition for all the saints." (Ephesians 6:18)

"Therefore, confess your sins to one another, and pray for one another, so that you may be healed. The effective prayer of a righteous man can accomplish much." (James 5:16)

"... the Spirit also helps our weakness; for we do not know how to pray as we should, but the Spirit Himself intercedes for us with groanings too deep for words." (Romans 8:26)

"... Christ Jesus is He who died, yes, rather who was raised, who is at the right hand of God, who also intercedes for us." (Romans 8:34)

Intercessor: 1) both Jesus and the Holy Spirit search our hearts and make our deepest inarticulate needs known to God the Father

"Hence, also, He is able to save forever those who draw near to God through Him, since He always lives to make intercession for them." (Hebrews 7:25)

"... Christ Jesus is He who died, yes, rather who was raised, who is at the right hand of God, who also intercedes for us." (Romans 8:34)

irresponsibility: 1) refusal to be held accountable for our actions, attempting to cover up our indiscretions

"And if you have not been faithful in the use of that which is another's, who will give you that which is your own?" (Luke 16:12)

"So then each one of us shall give account of himself to God." (Romans 14:12)

"Therefore, to one who knows the right thing to do, and does not do it, to him it is sin." (James 4:17)

irreverence in the Church: 1) not acting with proper decorum and respect in church, out of order; 2) not coming to the house of the Lord with an open attitude to hear from Him, but rather to go through meaningless religious rites or to dictate what we expect from Him

"Guard your steps as you go to the house of God, and draw near to listen rather than to offer the sacrifice of fools; for they do not know they are doing evil. Do not be hasty in word or impulsive in thought to bring up a matter in the presence of God. For God is in heaven and you are on the earth; therefore let your words be few." (Ecclesiastes 5:1-2)

"Therefore, my brethren, desire earnestly to prophesy, and do not forbid to speak in tongues. But let all things be done properly and in an orderly manner." (1 Corinthians 14:39-40)

"But as for me, by Thine abundant lovingkindness I will enter Thy house, At Thy holy temple I will bow in reverence for Thee." (Psalm 5:7)

J PRAYER CARDS

jealousy: 1) rivalry, painful suspicion of another's faithfulness; 2) envious of affirmation received by others

"for you are still fleshly. For since there is jealousy and strife among you, are you not fleshly, and are you not walking like mere men?" (1 Corinthians 3:3)

"But if you have bitter jealousy and selfish ambition in your heart, do not be arrogant and so lie against the truth." (James 3:14)

Jesus our Intercessor: 1) As our eternal High Priest, Jesus acts as our advocate and mediator before God the Father, presenting our requests before Him.

"… He is able to save forever those who draw near to God through Him, since He always lives to make intercession for them." (Hebrews 7:25)

"… Christ Jesus is He who died, yes, rather who was raised, who is at the right hand of God, who also intercedes for us." (Romans 8:34)

joy: 1) cheerful, enthusiastic worship; 2) having your deepest needs met, facing the future with hope, a deep assurance of God's love; 3) a fruit of the Spirit

"Restore to me the joy of Thy salvation, and sustain me with a willing spirit." (Psalm 51:12)

"Rejoice always." (1 Thessalonians 5:16)

"If you keep My commandments, you will abide in My love; just as I have kept My Father's commandments, and abide in His love. These things I have spoken to you, that My joy may be in you, and that your joy may be made full." (John 15:10-11)

"Thou wilt make known to me the path of life; in Thy presence is fulness of joy; in Thy right hand there are pleasures forever." (Psalm 16:11)

judging others: 1) private willful attitudes toward others which build up self-esteem at the expense of tearing down others; 2) a critical spirit

"But you, why do you judge your brother? Or you again, why do you regard your brother with contempt? For we shall all stand before the judgment seat of God... So then each one of us shall give account of himself to God." (Romans 14:10,12)

"Do not judge lest you be judged. "For in the way you judge, you will be judged; and by your standard of measure, it will be measured to you. "And why do you look at the speck that is in your brother's eye, but do not notice the log that is in your own eye?... "You hypocrite, first take the log out of your own eye, and then you will see clearly to take the speck out of your brother's eye." (Matthew 7:1-3, 5)

judgment: 1) it is the responsibility of believers to deal with unrepentant sinners in their midst, confronting them with discipline and love as directed by the Holy Spirit

"But he who is spiritual appraises all things, yet he himself is appraised by no man. For who has known the mind of the Lord, that he should instruct Him? But we have the mind of Christ." (1 Corinthians 2:15-16)

"For what have I to do with judging outsiders? Do you not judge those who are within the church? But those who are outside, God judges. Remove the wicked man from among yourselves." (Corinthians 5:12-13)

"All Scripture is inspired by God and profitable for teaching, for reproof, for correction, for training in righteousness." (2 Timothy 3:16)

just: 1) fair, impartial, upright, honest, according to God's standards

"for not the hearers of the Law are just before God, but the doers of the Law will be justified." (Romans 2:13)

"But Peter and John answered and said to them, "Whether it is right in the sight of God to give heed to you rather than to God, you be the judge." (Acts 4:19)

"Finally, brethren, whatever is true, whatever is honorable, whatever is right, whatever is pure, whatever is lovely, whatever is of good repute, if there is any excellence and if anything worthy of praise, let your mind dwell on these things." (Philippians 4:8)

K PRAYER CARDS

kindness: 1) acts of good will, compassion, favor; 2) a fruit of the Spirit, responding to other's needs

"… in your faith supply… godliness; and in your godliness, brotherly kindness, and in your brotherly kindness, love." (2 Peter 1:5-7)

And so, as those who have been chosen of God, holy and beloved, put on a heart of compassion, kindness, humility, gentleness and patience; bearing with one another, and forgiving each other, whoever has a complaint against anyone; just as the Lord forgave you, so also should you." (Colossians 3:12-13)

kingdom of heaven: 1) the present experience of all believers who follow Jesus; 2) the rule and reign of God in a person's heart; 3) the future reward for believers at Christ's return

"Blessed are the poor in spirit, for theirs is the kingdom of heaven." (Matthew 5:3)

"But seek first His kingdom and His righteousness; and all these things shall be added to you." (Matthew 6:33)

"Whoever then humbles himself as this child, he is the greatest in the kingdom of heaven." (Matthew 18:4)

"so that you may walk in a manner worthy of the God who calls you into His own kingdom and glory." (1 Thessalonians 2:12)

knowledge: 1) believer's understanding of God's character, clear perception of Scripture

"we have not ceased to pray for you and to ask that you may be filled with the knowledge of His will in all spiritual wisdom and understanding, so that you may walk in a manner worthy of the Lord, to please Him in all respects, bearing fruit in every good work and increasing in the knowledge of God" (Colossians 1:9-10)

"… we know that we all have knowledge. Knowledge makes arrogant, but love edifies. If anyone supposes that he knows anything, he has not yet known as he ought to know; but if anyone loves God, he is known by Him." (1 Corinthians 8:1-3)

L PRAYER CARDS

laziness: 1) inactivity, disinclined to labor; 2) we are all to earn the bread we eat, (even Jesus had a job)

"The sluggard does not plow after the autumn, so he begs during the harvest and has nothing." (Proverbs 20:4)

"Laziness casts into a deep sleep, and an idle man will suffer hunger." (Proverbs 19:15)

"We must work the works of Him who sent Me, as long as it is day; night is coming, when no man can work." (John 9:4)

leaders: 1) spiritual overseers who teach the Word, and deal with discipline and false teachers within the church

"An overseer, then, must be above reproach, the husband of one wife, temperate, prudent, respectable, hospitable, able to teach, not addicted to wine or pugnacious, but gentle, uncontentious, free from the love of money. He must be one who manages his own household well, keeping his children under control with all dignity." (1 Timothy 3: 2-4)

"Deacons likewise must be men of dignity, not double-tongued… holding to the mystery of the faith with a clear conscience… beyond reproach." (1 Timothy 3:8-10)

"Therefore, I exhort the elders among you… shepherd the flock of God among you, exercising oversight not under compulsion, but voluntarily, according to the will of God; and not for sordid gain, but with eagerness; nor yet as lording it over those allotted to your charge, but proving to be examples to the flock." (1 Peter 5:1-3)

life: 1) the union of soul and body, animation; i.e. natural life; 2) spiritual life, in glorified bodies, transformed to suit our eternal existence

"Then the Lord God formed man of dust from the ground, and breathed into his nostrils the breath of life; and man became a living being." (Genesis 2:7)

"Therefore we have been buried with Him through baptism into death, in order that as Christ was raised from the dead through the glory of the Father, so we too might walk in newness of life." (Romans 6:4)

"He who believes in the Son has eternal life… " (John 3:36)

"For with Thee is the fountain of life; in Thy light we see light." (Psalm 36:9)

"In Him was life, and the life was the light of men." (John 1:4)

"Jesus said to them, "I am the bread of life; he who comes to Me shall not hunger, and he who believes in Me shall never thirst." (John 6:35)

"The thief comes only to steal, and kill, and destroy; I came that they might have life, and might have it abundantly." (John 10:10)

light: 1) figuratively, spiritual illumination; 2) enlightenment which the Holy Spirit provides to believers regarding the Gospel truth which we are to share with a darkened world

"For God, who said, "Light shall shine out of darkness," is the One who has shone in our hearts to give the light of the knowledge of the glory of God in the face of Christ." (2 Corinthians 4:6)

"You are the light of the world. A city set on a hill cannot be hidden. Nor do men light a lamp, and put it under the peck-measure, but on the lampstand; and it gives light to all who are in the house. "Let your light shine before men in such a way that they may see your good works, and glorify your Father who is in heaven." (Matthew 5:14-16)

"now you are light in the Lord; walk as children of light (for the fruit of the light consists in all goodness and righteousness and truth), trying to learn what is pleasing to the Lord." (Ephesians 5: 8-10)

listen: 1) to give close attention to, to heed; 2) we are to wait upon the Lord in prayer with a quiet spirit to hear from Him and obey

"Behold, I stand at the door and knock; if anyone hears My voice and opens the door, I will come in to him, and will dine with him, and he with Me." (Revelation 3:20)

"He who is of God hears the words of God… " (John 8:47)

"Then the Lord came and stood and called as at other times, "Samuel! Samuel!" And Samuel said, "Speak, for Thy servant is listening." (1 Samuel 3:10)

"He awakens Me morning by morning, He awakens My ear to listen as a disciple. The Lord God has opened My ear; and I was not disobedient, nor did I turn back." (Isaiah 50:4-5)

little children: 1) those who have a teachable spirit and humbly receive God's Truth; 2) those who recognize their complete dependence on God "like newborn babes, long for the pure milk of the word, that by it you may grow in respect to salvation." (1 Peter 2:2)

"Truly I say to you, unless you are converted and become like children, you shall not enter the kingdom of heaven. "Whoever then humbles himself as this child, he is the greatest in the kingdom of heaven." (Matthew 18:3-4)

lonely: 1) without companionship, having no intimate relationships

"And I will ask the Father, and He will give you another Helper, that He may be with you forever." (John 14:16)

"… and lo, I (Jesus) am with you always, even to the end of the age." (Matthew 28:20)

"for through Him we both have our access in one Spirit to the Father. So then you are no longer strangers and aliens, but you are fellow citizens with the saints, and are of God's household." (Ephesians 2:18-19)

long life: 1) according to Scripture, seventy to eighty years

"As for the days of our life, they contain seventy years, or if due to strength, eighty years… " (Psalm 90:10)

"Honor your father and your mother, that your days may be prolonged in the land which the Lord your God gives you." (Exodus 20:12)

"My son, do not forget my teaching, but let your heart keep my commandments; for length of days and years of life, and peace they will add to you." (Proverbs 3:1-2)

(no burden for the) lost: 1) the duty of every believer is to share the Gospel, teach new followers, and engage in compassionate service to the lost

"You are the light of the world. A city set on a hill cannot be hidden. "Nor do men light a lamp, and put it under the peck-measure, but on the lampstand; and it gives light to all who are in the house. "Let your light shine before men in such a way that they may see your good works, and glorify your Father who is in heaven." (Matthew 5:14-16)

"Go therefore and make disciples of all the nations, baptizing them in the name of the Father and the Son and the Holy Spirit, teaching them to observe all that I commanded you." (Matthew 28:19-20)

love: 1) strong attachment and devotion; 2) gratitude and reverence toward God; 3) both a fruit of the Spirit and every believer's privilege

"A new commandment I give to you, that you love one another, even as I have loved you, that you also love one another. By this all men will know that you are My disciples, if you have love for one another." (John 13:34-35)

"Beloved, if God so loved us, we also ought to love one another." (1 John 4:11)

"Love is patient, love is kind, and is not jealous; love does not brag and is not arrogant, does not act unbecomingly; it does not seek its own, is not provoked, does not take into account a wrong suffered, does not rejoice in unrighteousness, but rejoices with the truth; bears all things, believes all things, hopes all things, endures all things. Love never fails" (1 Corinthians 13:4-8)

"And so, as those who have been chosen of God, holy and beloved, put on a heart of compassion, kindness, humility, gentleness and patience;

bearing with one another, and forgiving each other, whoever has a complaint against anyone; just as the Lord forgave you, so also should you. And beyond all these things put on love, which is the perfect bond of unity." (Colossians 3:12-14)

"Hatred stirs up strife, but love covers all transgressions." (Proverbs 10:12)

lack of love: 1) clear evidence that the love of God is not evident in a person's heart

"Beloved, let us love one another, for love is from God; and everyone who loves is born of God and knows God. The one who does not love does not know God, for God is love... If someone says, "I love God," and hates his brother, he is a liar; for the one who does not love his brother whom he has seen, cannot love God whom he has not seen." (1 John 4:7-8, 20)

love of God: 1) God graciously demonstrated His love by stepping into this world in the form of a man to draw us to Himself and through His Son pay the penalty of our sin

"For God so loved the world, that He gave His only begotten Son, that whoever believes in Him should not perish, but have eternal life." (John 3:16)

"See how great a love the Father has bestowed upon us, that we should be called children of God; and such we are." (1 John 3:1)

"But God demonstrates His own love toward us, in that while we were yet sinners, Christ died for us." (Romans 5:8)

loveless: 1) without tenderness or kindness, no benevolent concern for others

"But I say to you, love your enemies, and pray for those who persecute you in order that you may be sons of your Father who is in heaven... " (Matthew 5:44-45)

"Beloved, let us love one another, for love is from God; and everyone who loves is born of God and knows God. The one who does not love does not know God, for God is love." (1 John 4:7-8)

"By this all men will know that you are My disciples, if you have love for one another." (John 13:35)

lovingkindness: 1) kindness, mercy, grace, God's love demonstrated toward His children; 2) believers should extend that same lovingkindness they receive from God toward others

"And be kind to one another, tender-hearted, forgiving each other, just as God in Christ also has forgiven you." (Ephesians 4:32)

"But as for me, I shall sing of Thy strength; yes, I shall joyfully sing of Thy lovingkindness in the morning, for Thou hast been my stronghold, and a refuge in the day of my distress. O my strength, I will sing praises to Thee; for God is my stronghold, the God who shows me lovingkindness." (Psalm 59:16-17)

"How precious is Thy lovingkindness, O God! And the children of men take refuge in the shadow of Thy wings." (Psalm 36:7)

lukewarm: 1) "Christians" without faith, without spiritual growth, apathetic, self-satisfied, neglecting the work of the church

"I know your deeds, that you are neither cold nor hot; I would that you were cold or hot. 'So because you are lukewarm, and neither hot nor cold, I will spit you out of My mouth." (Revelation 3: 15-16)

lust: 1) sin conceived in the heart, unnatural desires or cravings; 2) both the sinful desire and the acting out of the sin are equally wrong

"Beloved, I urge you as aliens and strangers to abstain from fleshly lusts, which wage war against the soul." (1 Peter 2:11)

"Therefore do not let sin reign in your mortal body that you should obey its lusts" (Romans 6:12)

lying: 1) a falsehood or distorted statement

"Lying lips are an abomination to the Lord" (Proverbs 12:22)

"Do not lie to one another, since you laid aside the old self with its evil practices" (Colossians 3:9)

"Therefore, laying aside falsehood, speak truth, each one of you, with his neighbor, for we are members of one another." (Ephesians 4:25)

"Deliver my soul, O Lord, from lying lips, from a deceitful tongue." (Psalm 120:2)

M PRAYER CARDS

man pleasers: 1) being motivated to action to please people instead of God; 2) our purpose must be to do the Lord's will

"... just as we have been approved by God to be entrusted with the gospel, so we speak, not as pleasing men but God, who examines our hearts . . . nor did we seek glory from men, either from you or from others..." (1 Thessalonians 2:4, 6)

"Beware of practicing your righteousness before men to be noticed by them; otherwise you have no reward with your Father who is in heaven." (Matthew 6:1)

"But they do all their deeds to be noticed by men; for they broaden their phylacteries, and lengthen the tassels of their garments. And they love the place of honor at banquets, and the chief seats in the synagogues." (Matthew 23:5-6)

marriage: 1) marriage is a gift from God in which a man and a woman join together in a covenant union and take responsibility for one another's welfare, and to love one another exclusively in a committed sexual relationship

"... For this cause a man shall leave his father and mother, and shall cleave to his wife; and the two shall become one flesh'? "Consequently they are no longer two, but one flesh. What therefore God has joined together, let no man separate." (Matthew 19:5-6)

"… Take heed then, to your spirit, and let no one deal treacherously against the wife of your youth. "For I hate divorce," says the Lord, the God of Israel, "and him who covers his garment with wrong," says the Lord of hosts." (Malachi 2:15-16)

"Husbands, love your wives, just as Christ also loved the church and gave Himself up for her." (Ephesians 5:25)

"Wives, be subject to your own husbands, as to the Lord. For the husband is the head of the wife, as Christ also is the head of the church…" (Ephesians 5:22-23)

'Mary': 1) figuratively, one who sits at the feet of Jesus, listening to His every Word and not letting the distractions of this world prevent her from serving the Lord wholeheartedly

"And she (Martha) had a sister called Mary, who moreover was listening to the Lord's word, seated at His feet… but only a few things are necessary, really only one, for Mary has chosen the good part, which shall not be taken away from her." (Luke 10:39, 42)

"But seek for His kingdom, and these things shall be added to you." (Luke 12:31)

meat: 1) the deeper spiritual truths available to the believer; 2) if Christians don't grow spiritually past basic doctrine, they are in danger of drifting back to their carnal ways

"I gave you milk to drink, not solid food; for you were not yet able to receive it. Indeed, even now you are not yet able, for you are still fleshly." (1 Corinthians 3:2-3)

"For though by this time you ought to be teachers, you have need again for someone to teach you the elementary principles of the oracles of

God, and you have come to need milk and not solid food." (Hebrew 5:12)

"But solid food is for the mature, who because of practice have their senses trained to discern good and evil." (Hebrews 5:14)

meditation: 1) serious reflection; 2) allowing the Word of God to linger in your mind and spirit, with a goal of understanding and application

"This book of the law shall not depart from your mouth, but you shall meditate on it day and night, so that you may be careful to do according to all that is written in it; for then you will make your way prosperous, and then you will have success." (Joshua 1:8)

"O how I love Thy law! It is my meditation all the day." (Psalms 119:97)

"Set your mind on the things above, not on the things that are on earth." (Colossians 3:2)

"Tremble, and do not sin; meditate in your heart upon your bed, and be still." (Psalm 4:4)

meekness: 1) having the quality of patience, submission, humbleness; 2) tenderness, gentleness, lovingkindness toward others

"Blessed are the meek: for they shall inherit the earth." (Matthew 5:5) (KJV)

"Seek the Lord, all you humble of the earth who have carried out His ordinances; seek righteousness, seek humility..." (Zephaniah 2:3)

"Gird Thy sword on Thy thigh, O Mighty One, in Thy splendor and Thy majesty! And in Thy majesty ride on victoriously, for the cause of truth and meekness and righteousness; let Thy right hand teach Thee awesome things." (Psalm 45:3-4)

meets needs: 1) God will take care of our needs, He delights in answering our prayers; 2) the proper order is to seek His will and then pray for our needs

"Therefore do not be like them; for your Father knows what you need, before you ask Him." (Matthew 6:8)

"But seek first His kingdom and His righteousness; and all these things shall be added to you." (Matthew 6:33)

"Ask, and it shall be given to you; seek, and you shall find; knock, and it shall be opened to you... "If you then, being evil, know how to give good gifts to your children, how much more shall your Father who is in heaven give what is good to those who ask Him!" (Matthew 7:7, 11)

mercy; 1) the desire to show generosity, compassion and forgiveness; 2) the desire to alleviate suffering

"Blessed are the merciful, for they shall receive mercy." (Matthew 5:7)

"And be kind to one another, tender-hearted, forgiving each other, just as God in Christ also has forgiven you." (Ephesians 4:32)

"But love your enemies, and do good, and lend, expecting nothing in return; and your reward will be great, and you will be sons of the Most High; for He Himself is kind to ungrateful and evil men. Be merciful, just as your Father is merciful." (Luke 6:35-36)

mind of Christ: 1) the ability to understand spiritual truths through the indwelling Holy Spirit, especially regarding salvation and the message of the Cross

"But he who is spiritual appraises all things, yet he himself is appraised by no man. For who has known the mind of the Lord, that he should instruct Him? But we have the mind of Christ." (1 Corinthians 2:15-16)

"And do not be conformed to this world, but be transformed by the renewing of your mind, that you may prove what the will of God is, that which is good and acceptable and perfect." (Romans 12:2)

"Search me, O God, and know my heart; try me and know my anxious thoughts; and see if there be any hurtful way in me, and lead me in the everlasting way." (Psalm 139:23-24)

"For My thoughts are not your thoughts, neither are your ways My ways," declares the Lord... So shall My word be which goes forth from My mouth; it shall not return to Me empty, without accomplishing what I desire, and without succeeding in the matter for which I sent it." (Isaiah 55:8, 11)

minister: 1) using your spiritual gifts to serve others especially in the Church, having a servant's heart

"Now there are varieties of gifts, but the same Spirit. And there are varieties of ministries, and the same Lord... But now God has placed the members, each one of them, in the body, just as He desired." (1 Corinthians 12:4-5,18)

"For you were called to freedom, brethren; only do not turn your freedom into an opportunity for the flesh, but through love serve one another. For the whole Law is fulfilled in one word, in the statement, 'You shall love your neighbor as yourself.'" (Galatians 5:13-14)

"And while they were ministering to the Lord and fasting, the Holy Spirit said, "Set apart for Me Barnabas and Saul for the work to which I have called them." (Acts 13:2)

miracles: 1) a supernatural event performed by the power of God

"He delivers and rescues and performs signs and wonders In heaven and on earth, Who has also delivered Daniel from the power of the lions." (Daniel 6:27)

"And God was performing extraordinary miracles by the hands of Paul." (Acts 19:11)

"Does He then, who provides you with the Spirit and works miracles among you, do it by the works of the Law, or by hearing with faith?" (Galatians 3:5)

"And as He was now approaching, near the descent of the Mount of Olives, the whole multitude of the disciples began to praise God joyfully with a loud voice for all the miracles which they had seen." (Luke 19:37)

"But to each one is given the manifestation of the Spirit... to another the effecting of miracles..." (1 Corinthians 12:7,10)

(lack of) moderation: 1) allowing the temptations of the world to distract us from following God, gratifying our passions to excess; i.e. materialism, gluttony, alcoholism

"Be on guard, that your hearts may not be weighted down with dissipation and drunkenness and the worries of life" (Luke 21:34)

"And do not get drunk with wine, for that is dissipation, but be filled with the Spirit" (Ephesians 5:18)

(love of) money: 1) greed, trying to gain contentment through the accumulation of wealth

"But those who want to get rich fall into temptation and a snare and many foolish and harmful desires which plunge men into ruin and destruction. For the love of money is a root of all sorts of evil, and some by longing for it have wandered away from the faith, and pierced themselves with many a pang." (1 Timothy 6:9-10)

"for where your treasure is, there will your heart be also." (Matthew 6:21)

moral impurity: 1) sexual immorality including prostitution, adultery and homosexuality

"For God has not called us for the purpose of impurity, but in sanctification." (1 Thessalonians 4:7)

"For this is the will of God, your sanctification; that is, that you abstain from sexual immorality; that each of you know how to possess his own vessel in sanctification and honor." (1 Thessalonians 4:3-4)

motive: 1) the cause, reason for a choice or action; 2) the guiding or controlling idea which compels you to act in a certain way

"… pursue righteousness, faith, love and peace, with those who call on the Lord from a pure heart." (2 Timothy 2:22)

"For the word of God is living and active and sharper than any two-edged sword, and piercing as far as the division of soul and spirit, of both joints and marrow, and able to judge the thoughts and intentions of the heart." (Hebrews 4:12)

"let us consider how to stimulate one another to love and good deeds." (Hebrews 10:24)

"But if you have bitter jealousy and selfish ambition in your heart, do not be arrogant and so lie against the truth." (James 3:14)

"Since you have in obedience to the truth purified your souls for a sincere love of the brethren, fervently love one another from the heart." (1 Peter 1:22)

(wrong) motives: 1) doing good works to be praised by man; 2) rather, everything we do should glorify God

"Beware of practicing your righteousness before men to be noticed by them; otherwise you have no reward with your Father who is in heaven." (Matthew 6:1)

"Whether, then, you eat or drink or whatever you do, do all to the glory of God." (1 Corinthians 10:31)

mourn: 1) grief over personal sin; 2) to have sorrow or grief over the death of a loved one

"Martha therefore said to Jesus, "Lord, if You had been here, my brother would not have died . . . Jesus said to her (Martha), "I am the resurrection and the life; he who believes in Me shall live even if he dies, and everyone who lives and believes in Me shall never die..." (John 11: 21, 25-26)

"Blessed are those who mourn, for they shall be comforted." (Matthew 5:4)

"Even though I walk through the valley of the shadow of death, I fear no evil; for Thou art with me; Thy rod and Thy staff, they comfort me." (Psalm 23:4)

murder: 1) killing someone in anger, especially since we are all made in the image of God

"You shall not murder." (Exodus 20:13)

"Everyone who hates his brother is a murderer; and you know that no murderer has eternal life abiding in him." (1 John 3:15)

"But I say to you who hear, love your enemies, do good to those who hate you, bless those who curse you, pray for those who mistreat you." (Luke 6:27-28)

murmuring: 1) a discontented complaint made under one's breath; 2) murmuring against God or His leaders can result in divine punishment

"Do all things without grumbling or disputing, that you may prove yourselves to be blameless and innocent, children of God above reproach in the midst of a crooked and perverse generation, among whom you appear as lights in the world." (Philippians 2:14-15)

"Nor grumble, as some of them did, and were destroyed by the destroyer." (1 Corinthians 10:10)

"And the Lord spoke to Moses and Aaron, saying, "How long shall I bear with this evil congregation who are grumbling against Me?... As I live,' says the Lord, 'just as you have spoken in My hearing, so I will surely do to you; your corpses shall fall in this wilderness..." (Numbers 14:26-29)

"And when they (the crowd) saw it (Zaccheus receive Jesus gladly) they all murmured, saying, That He has gone to be guest of a sinner... the Son of man is come to seek and to save that which was lost." (Luke 19:7, 10)

(fleshly) music: 1) being desensitized to sin through lyrics which are carnal or even profane

"Let no unwholesome word proceed from your mouth, but only such a word as is good for edification according to the need of the moment, that it may give grace to those who hear." (Ephesians 4:29)

"be filled with the Spirit, speaking to one another in Psalms and hymns and spiritual songs, singing and making melody with your heart to the Lord" (Ephesians 5:18-19)

N PRAYER CARDS

national repentance: 1) corporate sin as a nation, God requires a repentance in the heart and changed behavior in order to receive forgiveness and restoration

"If… My people who are called by My name humble themselves and pray, and seek My face and turn from their wicked ways, then I will hear from heaven, will forgive their sin, and will heal their land." (2 Chronicles 7:14)

O PRAYER CARDS

obedience: 1) to follow God's teachings, serve others and share our faith, complete self-surrender to God

"But this is what I commanded them, saying, 'Obey My voice, and I will be your God, and you will be My people; and you will walk in all the way which I command you, that it may be well with you.'" (Jeremiah 7:23)

"But prove yourselves doers of the word, and not merely hearers who delude themselves." (James1:22)

"If you keep My commandments, you will abide in My love; just as I have kept My Father's commandments, and abide in His love." These things I have spoken to you, that My joy may be in you, and that your joy may be made full." (John 15:10-11)

"... blessed are those who hear the word of God, and observe it." (Luke 11:28)

offensive: 1) causing pain or displeasure by our words or actions, deliberately harsh

"A brother offended is harder to be won than a strong city... " (Proverbs 18:19)

"Do not tear down the work of God for the sake of food. All things indeed are clean, but they are evil for the man who eats and gives offense." (Romans 14:20)

oil of gladness: 1) God's promise of guidance and protection to believers, He fills our heart with His joy and strengthens us

"Thou hast loved righteousness, and hated wickedness; therefore God, Thy God, has anointed Thee with the oil of joy above Thy fellows." (Psalm 45:7)

The Spirit of the Lord God is upon me… To grant those who mourn in Zion, Giving them a garland instead of ashes, the oil of gladness instead of mourning, the mantle of praise instead of a spirit of fainting…" (Isaiah 61:1, 3)

"Thou dost prepare a table before me in the presence of my enemies; Thou hast anointed my head with oil; my cup overflows. Surely goodness and lovingkindness will follow me all the days of my life, and I will dwell in the house of the Lord forever." (Psalm 23:5-6)

open my eyes: 1) the wisdom and revelation the Father makes available to believers through the Holy Spirit and His Word; 2) spiritual illumination which results in hope

"I too… do not cease giving thanks for you, while making mention of you in my prayers; that the God of our Lord Jesus Christ, the Father of glory, may give to you a spirit of wisdom and of revelation in the knowledge of Him. I pray that the eyes of your heart may be enlightened, so that you may know what is the hope of His calling, what are the riches of the glory of His inheritance in the saints." (Ephesians 1:15-18)

"Behold, a king will reign righteously... Then the eyes of those who see will not be blinded, and the ears of those who hear will listen." (Isaiah 32: 1, 3)

"Then Elisha prayed and said, "O Lord, I pray, open his eyes that he may see." And the Lord opened the servant's eyes, and he saw; and behold, the mountain was full of horses and chariots of fire all around Elisha." (2 Kings 6:17)

opinionated: 1) firmly adhering to one's own preconceived notions; 2) making decisions or forming conclusions without consulting God or His will

"For My thoughts are not your thoughts, neither are your ways My ways," declares the Lord." (Isaiah 55:8)

"The Lord knows the thoughts of man, that they are a mere breath." (Psalm 94:11)

"The heart of the righteous ponders how to answer, but the mouth of the wicked pours out evil things." (Proverbs 15:28)

"But He (Jesus) turned and said to Peter, "Get behind Me, Satan! You are a stumbling block to Me; for you are not setting your mind on God's interests, but man's." (Matthew 16:23)

opportunities: 1) a suitable occasion or convenient time for action; 2) sensing the urgency of sharing the Gospel in season and out, taking advantage of one's circumstances to glorify God

"Conduct yourselves with wisdom toward outsiders, making the most of the opportunity." (Colossians 4:5)

"For if you remain silent at this time, relief and deliverance will arise for the Jews from another place and you and your father's house will perish. And who knows whether you have not attained royalty for such a time as this?" (Esther 4:14)

"... Come, you who are blessed of My Father, inherit the kingdom prepared for you from the foundation of the world. 'For I was hungry, and you gave Me something to eat; I was thirsty, and you gave Me drink; I was a stranger, and you invited Me in." (Matthew 25:34-35)

order: 1) regular, harmonious procedure, correct deportment

"But let all things be done properly and in an orderly manner." (1 Corinthians 14:40)

"for God is not a God of confusion but of peace, as in all the churches of the saints." (1 Corinthians 14:33)

"For even though I am absent in body, nevertheless I am with you in spirit, rejoicing to see your good discipline and the stability of your faith in Christ." (Colossians 2:5)

'order my steps': 1) asking God to point out wrong motives and guide us in His path

"Order my steps in Thy word: and let not any iniquity have dominion over me." (Psalm 119:133 KJV)

"Search me, O God, and know my heart; try me, and know my thoughts; and see if there be any hurtful way in me, and lead me in the way everlasting." (Psalm 139:23-24)

overcome: 1) to conquer or subdue; 2) to resist temptation, in Christ we have victory over sin and evil in the world

"These things I have spoken to you, that in Me you may have peace. In the world you have tribulation, but take courage; I have overcome the world." (John 16:33)

"But in all these things we overwhelmingly conquer through Him who loved us." (Romans 8:37)

"For whatever is born of God overcomes the world; and this is the victory that has overcome the world— our faith. And who is the one who overcomes the world, but he who believes that Jesus is the Son of God?" (1 John 5:4-5)

"To him who overcomes, I will grant to eat of the tree of life, which is in the Paradise of God." (Revelation 2:7)

P PRAYER CARDS

parenting: 1) patiently raising your children in a loving, Christ-honoring manner, teaching them respect and obedience to God and parents with gentleness

"And, fathers, do not provoke your children to anger; but bring them up in the discipline and instruction of the Lord." (Ephesians 6:4)

"And these words, which I am commanding you today, shall be on your heart; and you shall teach them diligently to your sons and shall talk of them when you sit in your house and when you walk by the way and when you lie down and when you rise up." (Deuteronomy 6:6-7)

"You, however, continue in the things you have learned and become convinced of, knowing from whom you have learned them; and that from childhood you have known the sacred writings which are able to give you the wisdom that leads to salvation through faith which is in Christ Jesus." (2 Timothy 3:14-15)

passion: 1) fervor, conviction, spiritual enthusiasm, joyful exuberance

"My zeal has consumed me, because my adversaries have forgotten Thy words." (Psalm 119:139)

"For zeal for Thy house has consumed me..." (Psalms 69:9)

"Be devoted to one another in brotherly love; give preference to one another in honor; not lagging behind in diligence, fervent in spirit, serving the Lord." (Romans 12:10-11)

"looking for the blessed hope and the appearing of the glory of our great God and Savior, Christ Jesus; who gave Himself for us, that He might redeem us from every lawless deed and purify for Himself a people for His own possession, zealous for good deeds." (Titus 2:13-14)

pastors: 1) spirit-led leaders of local congregations, who keep watch over their flock to protect them from Satan's attack; 2) responsible for teaching right doctrine, preaching the Word and equipping believers to serve Christ

"Let the elders who rule well be considered worthy of double honor, especially those who work hard at preaching and teaching... Do not receive an accusation against an elder except on the basis of two or three witnesses." (1 Timothy 5:17, 19)

"... appoint elders in every city as I directed you, namely, if any man be above reproach, the husband of one wife, having children who believe, not accused of dissipation or rebellion. For the overseer must be above reproach as God's steward, not self-willed, not quick-tempered, not addicted to wine . . . but hospitable, loving what is good, sensible, just, devout, self-controlled, holding fast the faithful word which is in accordance with the teaching, that he may be able both to exhort in sound doctrine and to refute those who contradict." (Titus 1:5-9)

patience: 1) suffering without complaining, waiting calmly with hope, perseverance; 2) an attribute of God, long-suffering, slow to anger; 3) a fruit of the Spirit, endurance, putting up with people who irritate us with grace

"Knowing this, that the trying of your faith worketh patience. But let patience have her perfect work, that ye may be perfect and entire, wanting nothing." (James 1:3-4 KJV)

"And we urge you, brethren, admonish the unruly, encourage the fainthearted, help the weak, be patient with all men." (1 Thessalonians 5:14)

"Love is patient..." (1 Corinthians 13:4)

"Rest in the Lord and wait patiently for Him..." (Psalm 37:7)

peace: 1) a fruit of the Spirit, inner quietness, trusting God to bring harmony in difficult circumstances; 2) to bring about reconciliation, to end strife

"For He Himself is our peace..." (Ephesians 2:14)

"... the mind set on the Spirit is life and peace." (Romans 8:6)

"Therefore having been justified by faith, we have peace with God through our Lord Jesus Christ." (Romans 5:1)

"Be anxious for nothing, but in everything by prayer and supplication with thanksgiving let your requests be made known to God. And the peace of God, which surpasses all comprehension, shall guard your hearts and your minds in Christ Jesus." (Philippians 4:6-7)

"Now may the Lord of peace Himself continually grant you peace in every circumstance..." (2 Thessalonians 3:16)

"But the wisdom from above is first pure, then peaceable, gentle, reasonable, full of mercy and good fruits, unwavering, without hypocrisy. And the seed whose fruit is righteousness is sown in peace by those who make peace." (James 3:17-18)

peace of Jerusalem: 1) shalom, absence of conflict, health, justice, prosperity, protection

"Pray for the peace of Jerusalem: "May they prosper who love you. May peace be within your walls, and prosperity within your palaces." (Psalm 122:6-7)

"(If) My people who are called by My name humble themselves and pray, and seek My face and turn from their wicked ways, then I will hear from heaven, will forgive their sin, and will heal their land." (2 Chronicles 7:14)

"Also concerning the foreigner who is not from Thy people Israel, when he comes from a far country for Thy great name's sake and Thy mighty hand and Thine outstretched arm, when they come and pray toward this house, then hear Thou from heaven... and do according to all for which the foreigner calls to Thee, in order that all the peoples of the earth may know Thy name, and fear Thee, as do Thy people Israel, and that they may know that this house which I have built is called by Thy name." (2 Chronicles 6:32-33)

performance: 1) human achievement, works, rather than heart attitude which is what God is looking for

"And when you pray, you are not to be as the hypocrites; for they love to stand and pray in the synagogues and on the street corners, in order to be seen by men. Truly I say to you, they have their reward in full." (Matthew 6:5)

"This people honors Me with their lips, but their heart is far away from me. 'But in vain do they worship Me, teaching as doctrines the precepts of men.'" (Matthew 15:8-9)

perseverance: 1) staying strong until the end, enduring daily trials through trust and obedience "not lagging behind in diligence, fervent in spirit, serving the Lord; rejoicing in hope, persevering in tribulation, devoted to prayer." (Romans 12:11-12)

"... He has now reconciled you in His fleshly body through death, in order to present you before Him holy and blameless and beyond reproach- - if indeed you continue in the faith firmly established and steadfast, and not moved away from the hope of the gospel that you have heard..." (Colossians 1:22-3)

"And the seed in the good soil, these are the ones who have heard the word in an honest and good heart, and hold it fast, and bear fruit with perseverance." (Luke 8:15)

perspective: 1) that which we focus on, Jesus calls us to a divine perspective – seeking God's kingdom; 2) determining our values and making decisions with eternity in view

"For My thoughts are not your thoughts, neither are your ways My ways," declares the Lord. For as the heavens are higher than the earth, so are My ways higher than your ways, and My thoughts than your thoughts." (Isaiah 55:8-9)

"Remember the former things long past, for I am God, and there is no other; I am God, and there is no one like Me, declaring the end from the beginning and from ancient times things which have not been done, saying, My purpose will be established, and I will accomplish all My good pleasure." (Isaiah 46:9-10)

"But I say, walk by the Spirit, and you will not carry out the desire of the flesh." (Galatians 5:16-17)

"And we know that God causes all things to work together for good to those who love God, to those who are called according to His purpose." (Romans 8:28)

"Consider it all joy, my brethren, when you encounter various trials, knowing that the testing of your faith produces endurance. And let endurance have its perfect result, that you may be perfect and complete, lacking in nothing." (James 1:2-4)

"Blessed be the God and Father of our Lord Jesus Christ . . . (who) has caused us to be born again... to obtain an inheritance which is imperishable and undefiled... reserved in heaven for you... even though now for a little while, if necessary, you have been distressed by various trials, that the proof of your faith... even though tested by fire, may be found to result in praise and glory and honor at the revelation of Jesus Christ." (1 Peter 1:3-7)

petition: 1) a prayer or a formal written request to someone with the power to grant the request; 2) praying for the Lord to meet an urgent need

"With all prayer and petition pray at all times in the Spirit, and with this in view, be on the alert with all perseverance and petition for all the saints" (Ephesians 6:18)

"May the Lord answer you in the day of trouble!... May the Lord fulfill all your petitions." (Psalm 20:1, 5)

"First of all, then, I urge that entreaties and prayers, petitions and thanksgivings, be made on behalf of all men, for kings and all who are in authority, in order that we may lead a tranquil and quiet life in all godliness and dignity." (1 Timothy 2:1-2)

pity: 1) feeling another's distress, compassion, sympathy

"And be kind to one another, tender-hearted, forgiving each other, just as God in Christ also has forgiven you." (Ephesians 4:32)

"Little children, let us not love with word or with tongue, but in deed and truth." (1 John 3:18)

"To sum up, let all be harmonious, sympathetic, brotherly, kindhearted, and humble in spirit; not returning evil for evil, or insult for insult, but giving a blessing instead; for you were called for the very purpose that you might inherit a blessing... For the eyes of the Lord are upon the righteous and His ears attend to their prayer." (1 Peter 3: 8-9, 12)

please God: 1) a desire to live for God, dying to self and becoming a humble servant, exercising faith

"... the prayer of the upright is His delight." (Proverbs 15:8)

"And this is His commandment, that we believe in the name of His Son Jesus Christ, and love one another, just as He commanded us." (1 John 3:23)

"... we have not ceased to pray for you and to ask that you may be filled with the knowledge of His will in all spiritual wisdom and understanding, so that you may walk in a manner worthy of the Lord, to please Him in all respects, bearing fruit in every good work and increasing in the knowledge of God." (Colossians 1: 9-10)

pornography: 1) unrestrained, provocative literature or pictures

"I will set no worthless thing before my eyes; I hate the work of those who fall away; it shall not fasten its grip on me." (Psalm 101:3)

"The lamp of the body is the eye; if therefore your eye is clear, your whole body will be full of light." (Matthew 6:22)

power: 1) capable of action, ability, strength, potency; 2) omniscience – attribute of God, supernatural power to perform miracles

"... Not by might nor by power, but by My Spirit,' says the Lord of hosts." (Zechariah 4:6)

"in the power of signs and wonders, in the power of the Spirit... I (Paul) have fully preached the gospel of Christ." (Romans 15:19)

"For God has not given us a spirit of timidity, but of power and love and discipline." (2 Timothy 1:7)

praise: 1) heartfelt expressions of thanksgiving and awe to God; glorifying Him through worship and prayer

"For it is written, As I live, says the Lord, every knee shall bow to Me, and every tongue shall give praise to God." (Romans 14:11)

"Great is the Lord, and highly to be praised and His greatness is unsearchable." (Psalm 145:3)

"Shout joyfully to God, all the earth; Sing the glory of His name; Make His praise glorious. Say to God, 'How awesome are Thy works! . . . "All the earth will worship Thee, and will sing praises to Thee; They will sing praises to Thy name." (Psalm 66:1-4)

"It is good to give thanks to the Lord, and to sing praises to Thy name, O Most High" (Psalm 92:1)

prayerlessness: 1) the sin of failing to pray for others, indicates independence from God

"And there is no one who calls on Thy name, who arouses himself to take hold of Thee..." (Isaiah 64:7)

"As it is written in the law of Moses, all this calamity has come on us; yet we have not sought the favor of the Lord our God by turning from our iniquity and giving attention to Thy truth." (Daniel 9:13)

"… You do not have because you do not ask." (James 4:2)

"And those who have turned back from following the Lord, and those who have not sought the Lord or inquired of Him." (Zephaniah 1:6)

"(If) My people who are called by My name humble themselves and pray, and seek My face and turn from their wicked ways, then I will hear from heaven, will forgive their sin, and will heal their land." (2 Chronicles 7:14)

"Now He was telling them a parable to show that at all times they ought to pray and not to lose heart." (Luke 18:1)

"… far be it from me that I should sin against the Lord by ceasing to pray for you… " (1 Samuel 12:23)

prayer warrior: 1) praying in the Spirit at all times; 2) Prayer is the oil which keeps the Church running; 3) keeping alert in prayer against the schemes of Satan

"Therefore, confess your sins to one another, and pray for one another, so that you may be healed. The effective prayer of a righteous man can accomplish much." (James 5:16)

"Devote yourselves to prayer, keeping alert in it with an attitude of thanksgiving." (Colossians 4:2)

"For our struggle is not against flesh and blood, but against the rulers, against the powers, against the world forces of this darkness, against the spiritual forces of wickedness in the heavenly places… and take the helmet of salvation, and the sword of the Spirit, which is the word of God. With all prayer and petition pray at all times in the Spirit, and with this in view, be on the alert with all perseverance and petition for all the saints." (Ephesians 6: 12, 17-18)

"Keep watching and praying, that you may not enter into temptation; the spirit is willing, but the flesh is weak." (Matthew 26:41)

preferential treatment: 1) playing favorites while ignoring others; 2) being partial to someone because of riches, intelligence or beauty

"My brethren, do not hold your faith in our glorious Lord Jesus Christ with an attitude of personal favoritism. For if a man comes into your assembly with a gold ring and dressed in fine clothes, and there also comes in a poor man in dirty clothes, and you pay special attention to the one who is wearing the fine clothes, and say, "You sit here in a good place," and you say to the poor man, "You stand over there, or sit down by my footstool," have you not made distinctions among yourselves, and become judges with evil motives?" (James 2:1-4)

prejudice: 1) forming an opinion without careful examination, bias; 2) to damage another by an act of bias or an unfair notion; 3) treating someone as an outcast, social stigma

"but glory and honor and peace to every man who does good, to the Jew first and also to the Greek. For there is no partiality with God." (Romans 2:10-11)

"… To show partiality in judgment is not good." (Proverbs 24:23)

"You shall not distort justice; you shall not be partial, and you shall not take a bribe, for a bribe blinds the eyes of the wise and perverts the words of the righteous." (Deuteronomy 16:19)

"My brethren, do not hold your faith in our glorious Lord Jesus Christ with an attitude of personal favoritism. For if a man comes into your assembly with a gold ring and dressed in fine clothes, and there also comes in a poor man in dirty clothes, and you pay special attention to the one who is wearing the fine clothes, and say, "You sit here in a good place," and you say to the poor man, "You stand over there, or sit down by my footstool," have you not made distinctions among yourselves, and become judges with evil motives?" (James 2:1-4)

presence: 1) the awe and reverence we feel at God's nearness, His influence within us through the Holy Spirit; 2) coming before His throne in prayer and worship

"Thou hast made known to me the ways of life; Thou wilt make me full of gladness with Thy presence" (Acts 2:28)

"Humble yourselves in the presence of the Lord, and He will exalt you." (James 4:10)

"Where can I go from Thy Spirit? Or where can I flee from Thy presence? If I ascend to heaven, Thou art there; If I make my bed in Sheol, behold, Thou art there." (Psalm 139:7-8)

"Thou wilt make known to me the path of life; in Thy presence is fulness of joy; in Thy right hand there are pleasures forever." (Psalm 16:11)

presence of the Lord: 1) God is omnipresent, present everywhere, we cannot escape His notice, His Spirit is with us wherever we are

"And the Lord was going before them in a pillar of cloud by day to lead them on the way, and in a pillar of fire by night to give them light, that they might travel by day and by night." (Exodus 13:21)

"And I will ask the Father, and He will give you another Helper, that He may be with you forever." (John 14:16)

"And there shall no longer be any night; and they shall not have need of the light of a lamp nor the light of the sun, because the Lord God shall illumine them; and they shall reign forever and ever." (Revelation 22:5)

"Thou wilt make known to me the path of life; in Thy presence is fulness of joy; in Thy right hand there are pleasures forever." (Psalm 16:11)

preservation: 1) to keep safe from destruction; 2) God's protection and care, He watches over us

"He will not allow your foot to slip; He who keeps you will not slumber… The Lord is your keeper; the Lord is your shade on your right hand." (Psalm 121:3, 5)

"The Lord will protect you from all evil; He will keep your soul. The Lord will guard your going out and your coming in from this time forth and forever." (Psalms 121:7-8)

"He stores up sound wisdom for the upright; He is a shield to those who walk in integrity, guarding the paths of justice, and He preserves the way of His godly ones." (Proverbs 2:7-8)

presumption of the future: 1) planning for the future without consulting God, He alone knows the number of our days

"Do not boast about tomorrow, for you do not know what a day may bring forth." (Proverbs 27:1)

"Come now, you who say, "Today or tomorrow, we shall go to such and such a city, and spend a year there and engage in business and make a profit." Yet you do not know what your life will be like tomorrow. You are just a vapor that appears for a little while and then vanishes away. Instead, you ought to say, "If the Lord wills, we shall live and also do this or that." (James 4:13-15)

presumptuous sin: 1) assuming we can use God's power for our own ends, prideful self-confidence, assuming God's grace in the absence of repentance; 2) overconfident, taking undue liberties

"Also keep back Thy servant from presumptuous sins; let them not rule over me; then I shall be blameless, and I shall be acquitted of great transgression." (Psalm 19:13)

"Thou dost rebuke the arrogant, the cursed, who wander from Thy commandments." (Psalm 119:21)

"'Proud,' 'Haughty,' 'Scoffer,' are his names, who acts with insolent pride." (Proverbs 21:24)

"When pride comes, then comes dishonor, but with the humble is wisdom." (Proverbs 11:2)

"Through presumption comes nothing but strife, but with those who receive counsel is wisdom." (Proverbs 13:10)

pride: 1) attempting to gain wisdom to be equal to God; 2) taking credit for what God has done; unmerited self-esteem

"… He is able to humble those who walk in pride." (Daniel 4:37)

"For through the grace given to me I say to every man among you not to think more highly of himself than he ought to think; but to think so as to have sound judgment, as God has allotted to each a measure of faith." (Romans 12:3)

"God is opposed to the proud, but gives grace to the humble." (James 4:6)

"Pride goes before destruction, and a haughty spirit before stumbling." (Proverbs 16:18)

"Everyone who is proud in heart is an abomination to the Lord; assuredly, he will not be unpunished." (Proverbs 16:5)

priorities: 1) those projects and purposes which we devote the most time to; 2) God's kingdom principles such as righteous, submission, obedience should always come first.

"But the Lord answered and said to her, Martha, Martha, you are worried and bothered about so many things; but only a few things are necessary, really only one, for Mary has chosen the good part, which shall not be taken away from her. . . Mary, who moreover was listening to the Lord's word, seated at His feet." (Luke 10: 41-42, 39)

"But seek first His kingdom and His righteousness; and all these things shall be added to you." (Matthew 6:33)

"And they were continually devoting themselves to the apostles' teaching and to fellowship, to the breaking of bread and to prayer." (Acts 2:42)

"… make it your ambition to lead a quiet life and attend to your own business and work with your hands, just as we commanded you; so that you may behave properly toward outsiders and not be in any need." (1 Thessalonians 4:11-12)

procrastination: 1) knowing our spiritual duty but failing to perform it

"Therefore be careful how you walk, not as unwise men, but as wise, making the most of your time, because the days are evil." (Ephesians 5:15-16)

"for He says, "At the acceptable time I listened to you, and on the day of salvation I helped you"; behold, now is "the acceptable time," behold, now is "the day of salvation." (2 Corinthians 6:2)

"For this reason you be ready too; for the Son of Man is coming at an hour when you do not think He will." (Matthew 24:44)

"He who gathers in summer is a son who acts wisely, but he who sleeps in harvest is a son who acts shamefully." (Proverbs 10:5)

"And another also said, "I will follow You, Lord; but first permit me to say good-bye to those at home." But Jesus said to him, "No one, after putting his hand to the plow and looking back, is fit for the kingdom of God." (Luke 9:61-62)

"She (an excellent wife) looks well to the ways of her household, and does not eat the bread of idleness." (Proverbs 31:27)

profanity: 1) unholy, coarse language, impure, blasphemy, swearing

"You shall not take the name of the Lord your God in vain, for the Lord will not leave him unpunished who takes His name in vain." (Exodus 20:7)

"Better is a poor man who walks in his integrity than he who is perverse in speech and is a fool." (Proverbs 19:1)

"The mouth of the righteous is a fountain of life, but the mouth of the wicked conceals violence." (Proverbs 10:11)

promises: 1) a declaration to either perform or not perform a certain act; 2) every promise of God, every statement of intent either was or will be fulfilled

"Not one of the good promises which the Lord had made to the house of Israel failed; all came to pass." (Joshua 21:45)

"For as many as may be the promises of God, in Him they are yes; wherefore also by Him is our Amen to the glory of God through us." (2 Corinthians 1:20)

"… His divine power has granted to us everything pertaining to life and godliness, through the true knowledge of Him who called us by His own glory and excellence. For by these He has granted to us His precious and magnificent promises, in order that by them you might become partakers of the divine nature, having escaped the corruption that is in the world by lust." (2 Peter 1:3-4)

protection: 1) to defend, shield, rescue, keep safe; 2) God promises to guard and keep those who trust in Him and obey His commands

"Keep me as the apple of the eye; hide me in the shadow of Thy wings." (Psalm 17:8)

"I call upon the Lord, who is worthy to be praised, and I am saved from my enemies." (Psalm 18:3)

"and you will be hated by all on account of My name. Yet not a hair of your head will perish." (Luke 21:17-18)

"He will cover you with His pinions, and under His wings you may seek refuge; His faithfulness is a shield and bulwark." (Psalm 91:4)

"Put on the full armor of God, that you may be able to stand firm against the schemes of the devil. For our struggle is not against flesh and blood, but against the rulers, against the powers, against the world forces of this darkness, against the spiritual forces of wickedness in the heavenly places. Therefore, take up the full armor of God, that you may be able to resist in the evil day, and having done everything, to stand firm." (Ephesians 6:11-13)

prudence: 1) wisdom, caution, circumspect, not rash

"A fool's vexation is known at once, but a prudent man conceals dishonor." (Proverbs 12:16)

"A prudent man conceals knowledge, but the heart of fools proclaims folly." (Proverbs 12:23)

"Every prudent man acts with knowledge, but a fool displays folly." (Proverbs 13:16)

"A fool rejects his father's discipline, but he who regards reproof is prudent" (Proverbs 15:5)

purify: 1) to make clean, especially from sin and guilt; 2) only Christ's sacrifice has the power to remove the sin and guilt from our lives

"Create in me a clean heart, O God, and renew a steadfast spirit within me." (Psalm 51:10)

"Purify me with hyssop, and I shall be clean; wash me, and I shall be whiter than snow." (Psalms 51:7)

"Draw near to God and He will draw near to you. Cleanse your hands, you sinners; and purify your hearts, you double-minded... Humble yourselves in the presence of the Lord, and He will exalt you." (James 4: 8, 10)

purity: 1) honesty, sincerity, morally clean, through commitment to God

"Blessed are the pure in heart, for they shall see God." (Matthew 5:8)

"Finally, brethren, whatever is true, whatever is honorable, whatever is right, whatever is pure, whatever is lovely, whatever is of good repute, if there is any excellence and if anything worthy of praise, let your mind dwell on these things." (Philippians 4:8)

purpose: 1) one's aim or objective; 2) God's purpose for believers is becoming sanctified, loving, trusting and serving Him

"For we are His workmanship, created in Christ Jesus for good works, which God prepared beforehand, that we should walk in them." (Ephesians 2:10)

"And we proclaim Him, admonishing every man and teaching every man with all wisdom, that we may present every man complete in Christ." (Colossians 1:28)

"And we know that God causes all things to work together for good to those who love God, to those who are called according to His purpose. For whom He foreknew, He also predestined to become conformed to the image of His Son, that He might be the first-born among many brethren; and whom He predestined, these He also called; and whom He called, these He also justified; and whom He justified, these He also glorified." (Romans 8:28-30)

Q PRAYER CARDS

quench the Spirit: 1) to stifle or restrain the work of the Holy Spirit through unconfessed sin or forbidding the exercise of the gifts of the Spirit

"Do not quench the Spirit" (1 Thessalonians 5:19)

"And do not grieve the Holy Spirit of God, by whom you were sealed for the day of redemption." (Ephesians 4:30)

"But they rebelled and grieved His Holy Spirit; Therefore, He turned Himself to become their enemy, He fought against them." (Isaiah 63:10)

quicken: 1) to make alive, to restore; 2) to be made alive in Christ, saved by His blood and indwelt by the Holy Spirit

"So will not we go back from thee: quicken us, and we will call upon Thy name. Turn us again, O Lord God of hosts, cause Thy face to shine; and we shall be saved." (Psalm 80:18-19 KJV)

"Even when we were dead in sins, hath quickened us together with Christ, (by grace ye are saved)." (Ephesians 2:5 KJV)

"For as the Father raiseth up the dead, and quickeneth them; even so the Son quickeneth whom He will." (John 5:21 KJV)

quiet spirit: 1) gentle, not causing dissensions, having a humble state of mind when coming before the Lord, allowing the Holy Spirit to fill your heart

"In the same way, you wives, be submissive to your own husbands so that even if any of them are disobedient to the word, they may be won without a word by the behavior of their wives... but let it (your adornment) be the hidden person of the heart, with the imperishable quality of a gentle and quiet spirit, which is precious in the sight of God." (1 Peter 3:1, 4)

"... What credit is there if, when you sin and are harshly treated, you endure it with patience? But if when you do what is right and suffer for it you patiently endure it, this finds favor with God... "and while being reviled, He did not revile in return; while suffering, He uttered no threats, but kept entrusting Himself to Him who judges righteously." (1 Peter 2:20, 23)

"My soul, wait in silence for God only, for my hope is from Him. He only is my rock and my salvation, my stronghold; I shall not be shaken." (Psalm 62:5-6)

R PRAYER CARDS

rebellion: 1) rejecting God's authority over us; 2) refusing to acknowledge our sin and our need for a Savior

"For rebellion is as the sin of divination, and insubordination is as iniquity and idolatry..." (1 Samuel 15:23)

"And if you will not listen to the voice of the Lord, but rebel against the command of the Lord, then the hand of the Lord will be against you, as it was against your fathers." (1 Samuel 12:15)

"But they rebelled and grieved His Holy Spirit; therefore, He turned Himself to become their enemy, He fought against them." (Isaiah 63:10)

reckon: 1) to calculate or conclude, to examine and determine

"Likewise reckon ye also yourselves to be dead indeed unto sin, but alive unto God through Jesus Christ our Lord. Let not sin therefore reign in your mortal body, that ye should obey it in the lusts thereof." (Romans 6:11-12 KJV)

"Therefore also it (Abraham's faith) was reckoned to him as righteousness. Now not for his sake only was it written, that it was reckoned to him, but for our sake also, to whom it will be reckoned, as those who believe in Him who raised Jesus our Lord from the dead." (Romans 4:22-24)

reconciliation: 1) to restore a relationship, bring peace out of conflict; 2) Christ reconciles us to God through His atonement

"For it was the Father's good pleasure for all the fullness to dwell in Him, and through Him to reconcile all things to Himself, having made peace through the blood of His cross…" (Colossians 1: 19-20)

"But let everyone be quick to hear, slow to speak and slow to anger." (James 1:19)

"But I say to you that everyone who is angry with his brother shall be guilty before the court; and whoever shall say to his brother, 'Raca,' shall be guilty before the supreme court; and whoever shall say, 'You fool,' shall be guilty enough to go into the fiery hell. "If therefore you are presenting your offering at the altar, and there remember that your brother has something against you, leave your offering there before the altar, and go your way; first be reconciled to your brother, and then come and present your offering." (Matthew 5:22-24)

redeem the time: 1) make the most of every God-given opportunity to do good

"Therefore be careful how you walk, not as unwise men, but as wise, making the most of your time, because the days are evil." (Ephesians 5:15-16)

"There is an appointed time for everything. And there is a time for every event under heaven." (Ecclesiastes 3:1)

"So then, while we have opportunity, let us do good to all men, and especially to those who are of the household of the faith." (Galatians 6:10)

"So teach us to number our days, that we may present to Thee a heart of wisdom." (Psalm 90:12)

redemption: 1) the power of God to provide salvation to those who have faith; 2) to purchase back; 3) Christ paid our debt so we can become free from the power and penalty of sin

"O Israel, hope in the Lord; for with the Lord there is lovingkindness, And with Him is abundant redemption. And He will redeem Israel from all his iniquities." (Psalm 130:7-8)

"But now having been freed from sin and enslaved to God, you derive your benefit, resulting in sanctification, and the outcome, eternal life." (Romans 6:22)

"… Christ Jesus; who gave Himself for us, that He might redeem us from every lawless deed and purify for Himself a people for His own possession, zealous for good deeds." (Titus 2:13-14)

refine: 1) to make pure, make us more like Jesus

"I will also turn My hand against you, and will smelt away your dross as with lye, and will remove all your alloy." (Isaiah 1:25)

"The words of the Lord are pure words; as silver tried in a furnace on the earth, refined seven times. Thou, O Lord, wilt keep them; Thou wilt preserve him from this generation forever." (Psalm 12: 6-7)

"And I will bring the third part through the fire, refine them as silver is refined, and test them as gold is tested. They will call on My name, and I will answer them; I will say, 'They are My people,' and they will say, 'The Lord is my God.'" (Zechariah 13:9)

"Behold, I have refined you, but not as silver; I have tested you in the furnace of affliction." (Isaiah 48:10)

reflection: 1) to ponder in the heart, meditate

"I passed by the field of the sluggard, and by the vineyard of the man lacking sense; and behold, it was completely overgrown with thistles, its surface was covered with nettles, and its stone wall was broken down. When I saw, I reflected upon it; I looked, and received instruction." (Proverbs 24:30-32)

"And all they that heard it wondered at those things which were told them by the shepherds. But Mary kept all these things, and pondered them in her heart." (Luke 2:18-19 KJV)

refreshment: 1) to restore the spirit, new life

"Trust in the Lord with all your heart, and do not lean on your own understanding. In all your ways acknowledge Him... It will be healing to your body, and refreshment to your bones." (Proverbs 3:5-6, 8)

refuge: 1) a place where people find help; 2) God is our Spiritual refuge who protects us from Satan

"Trust in Him at all times, O people; pour out your heart before Him; God is a refuge for us." (Psalm 62:8)

"... How blessed are all who take refuge in Him!" (Psalm 2:12)

regeneration: 1) becoming a child of God; 2) spiritual rebirth, receiving God's eternal life

"And I will give them a heart to know Me, for I am the Lord; and they will be My people, and I will be their God, for they will return to Me with their whole heart." (Jeremiah 24:7)

"Therefore if any man is in Christ, he is a new creature; the old things passed away; behold, new things have come." (2 Corinthians 5:17)

"… in reference to your former manner of life, you lay aside the old self, which is being corrupted in accordance with the lusts of deceit, and that you be renewed in the spirit of your mind, and put on the new self, which in the likeness of God has been created in righteousness and holiness of the truth." (Ephesians 4:22-24)

rejoice: 1) to experience joy, to be glad because we belong to God

"Rejoice always." (1 Thessalonians 5:16)

"Rejoice with those who rejoice, and weep with those who weep." (Romans 12:15)

"… And as the bridegroom rejoices over the bride, so your God will rejoice over you." (Isaiah 62:5)

"Thou hast loved righteousness, and hated wickedness; therefore God, Thy God, has anointed Thee with the oil of joy above Thy fellows." (Psalm 45:7)

"Be glad in the Lord and rejoice, you righteous ones, and shout for joy, all you who are upright in heart." (Psalm 32:11)

"Rejoice in the Lord always; again I will say, rejoice! Let your forbearing spirit be known to all men. The Lord is near." (Philippians 4:4-5)

relationships: 1) a spiritual family, an eternal bond between believers and the Godhead

"what we have seen and heard we proclaim to you also, that you also may have fellowship with us; and indeed our fellowship is with the Father, and with His Son Jesus Christ." (1 John 1:3)

"Do not be bound together with unbelievers; for what partnership have righteousness and lawlessness, or what fellowship has light with darkness?... or what has a believer in common with an unbeliever?" (2 Corinthians 6:14-15)

"For whoever does the will of My Father who is in heaven, he is My brother and sister and mother." (Matthew 12:50)

"So then you are no longer strangers and aliens, but you are fellow citizens with the saints, and are of God's household." (Ephesians 2:19)

"So then, while we have opportunity, let us do good to all men, and especially to those who are of the household of the faith." (Galatians 6:10)

religion: 1) the outward form of worship and service to a deity, including profession of belief and conduct of life

"Not everyone who says to Me, 'Lord, Lord,' will enter the kingdom of heaven; but he who does the will of My Father who is in heaven." (Matthew 7:21)

"And when you are praying, do not use meaningless repetition, as the Gentiles do, for they suppose that they will be heard for their many words."(Matthew 6:7)

"For I bear them witness that they have a zeal for God, but not in accordance with knowledge... For Christ is the end of the law for righteousness to everyone who believes." (Romans 10:2, 4)

rely: 1) to rest with confidence on the integrity of another; God is trustworthy in all circumstances

"Trust in Him at all times, O people; pour out your heart before Him; God is a refuge for us." (Psalm 62:8)

"For the Scripture says, "Whoever believes in Him will not be disappointed." (Romans 10:11)

"The steadfast of mind Thou wilt keep in perfect peace, because he trusts in Thee." (Isaiah 26:3)

"Now it will come about in that day that the remnant of Israel, and those of the house of Jacob who have escaped, will never again rely on the one who struck them, but will truly rely on the Lord, the Holy One of Israel." (Isaiah 10:20)

"And we know that God causes all things to work together for good to those who love God, to those who are called according to His purpose." (Romans 8:28)

remember: 1) to recall, to bring to mind again

"But the Helper, the Holy Spirit, whom the Father will send in My name, He will teach you all things, and bring to your remembrance all that I said to you." (John 14:26)

"And when He had taken some bread and given thanks, He broke it, and gave it to them, saying, "This is My body which is given for you; do this in remembrance of Me." (Luke 22:19)

"I thank God… as I constantly remember you in my prayers night and day." (2 Timothy 1:3)

"… I am stirring up your sincere mind by way of reminder, that you should remember the words spoken beforehand by the holy prophets and the commandment of the Lord and Savior spoken by your apostles." (2 Peter 3:1-2)

"Thou dost meet him who rejoices in doing righteousness, who remembers Thee in Thy ways..." (Isaiah 64:5)

remnant: 1) those faithful believers who never abandon God or His Word, especially in the nation of Israel

"In the same way then, there has also come to be at the present time a remnant according to God's gracious choice." (Romans 11:5)

"But you have a few people in Sardis who have not soiled their garments; and they will walk with Me in white; for they are worthy." (Revelation 3:4)

renew: 1) to restore, to make new again, especially spiritually; 2) the Holy Spirit can make all things new, your mind, your faith, your body

"Create in me a clean heart, O God, and renew a steadfast spirit within me." (Psalm 51:10)

"Restore us to Thee, O Lord, that we may be restored; renew our days as of old" (Lamentations 5:21)

"And do not be conformed to this world, but be transformed by the renewing of your mind, that you may prove what the will of God is, that which is good and acceptable and perfect." (Romans 12:2)

"... put on the new self who is being renewed to a true knowledge according to the image of the One who created him a renewal in which there is no distinction between Greek and Jew... but Christ is all, and in all." (Colossians 3:10-11)

repentance: 1) to turn away from sin, toward God, involves both a change of attitude and action

"Or do you think lightly of the riches of His kindness and forbearance and patience, not knowing that the kindness of God leads you to repentance?" (Romans 2:4)

"Therefore bring forth fruit in keeping with repentance." (Matthew 3:8)

"The Lord is not slow about His promise, as some count slowness, but is patient toward you, not wishing for any to perish but for all to come to repentance." (2 Peter 3:9)

"You shall fear the Lord your God; you shall serve Him and cling to Him, and you shall swear by His name." (Deuteronomy 10:20)

reputation: 1) how the public views your hidden character; 2) for a Christian, the actions must match the words

"And he (an overseer) must have a good reputation with those outside the church, so that he may not fall into reproach and the snare of the devil." (1 Timothy 3:7)

"A good name is to be more desired than great riches, favor is better than silver and gold." (Proverbs 22:1)

"And all those who had believed were together, and had all things in common; and they began selling their property and possessions, and were sharing them with all, as anyone might have need. And day by day continuing with one mind in the temple, and breaking bread from house to house, they were taking their meals together with gladness and sincerity of heart, praising God, and having favor with all the people..." (Acts 2:44-47)

respect: 1) to consider worthy of esteem; 2) to care for all people regardless of theological or ethnic differences; (We are all made in the image of God.) 3) Greatness in the kingdom of God requires humility and a servant's heart.

"But the greatest among you shall be your servant. And whoever exalts himself shall be humbled; and whoever humbles himself shall be exalted." (Matthew 23:11-12)

"Whoever then annuls one of the least of these commandments, and so teaches others, shall be called least in the kingdom of heaven; but whoever keeps and teaches them, he shall be called great in the kingdom of heaven." (Matthew 5:19)

"Honor all men; love the brotherhood, fear God, honor the king." (1 Peter 2:17)

responsible: 1) being accountable or answerable for our conduct; 2) Christians are responsible for how they use the enlightenment they have received from the Holy Spirit

"He who rejects Me, and does not receive My sayings, has one who judges him; the word I spoke is what will judge him at the last day." (John 12:48)

"Therefore, to one who knows the right thing to do, and does not do it, to him it is sin." (James 4:17)

"each man's work will become evident; for the day will show it, because it is to be revealed with fire; and the fire itself will test the quality of each man's work." (1 Corinthians 3:13)

rest: 1) to find relief from the labor of obeying the Law; 2) refreshment through a new relationship with Jesus Christ and the promise of eternal rest with Him

"Let us therefore be diligent to enter that rest… Let us therefore draw near with confidence to the throne of grace, that we may receive mercy and may find grace to help in time of need." (Hebrews 4:11, 16)

"Come to Me, all who are weary and heavy-laden, and I will give you rest. "Take My yoke upon you, and learn from Me, for I am gentle and humble in heart; and you shall find rest for your souls." (Matthew 11:28-29)

"But the Lord answered and said to her, "Martha, Martha, you are worried and bothered about so many things; but only a few things are necessary, really only one, for Mary has chosen the good part, which shall not be taken away from her." (Luke 10:41-42)

restore: 1) to bring back to original condition, to renew; 2) Jesus came to restore Israel and all sinners to a right relationship with God

"O God, restore us, and cause Thy face to shine upon us, and we will be saved." (Psalm 80:3)

"The law of the Lord is perfect, restoring the soul…" (Psalm 19:7)

"Brethren, even if a man is caught in any trespass, you who are spiritual, restore such a one in a spirit of gentleness; each one looking to yourself, lest you too be tempted." (Galatians 6:1)

"Restore to me the joy of Thy salvation, and sustain me with a willing spirit." (Psalm 51:12)

restraint: 1) absence of total freedom, submission to the Holy Spirit to guide us in our walk, teaching us self-control

"If anyone thinks himself to be religious, and yet does not bridle his tongue but deceives his own heart, this man's religion is worthless." (James 1:26)

"Take My yoke upon you, and learn from Me, for I am gentle and humble in heart and you shall find rest for your souls." (Matthew 11:29)

retaliation: 1) a desire to get even with those who have hurt us

"Do not say, "Thus I shall do to him as he has done to me; I will render to the man according to his work." (Proverbs 24:29)

"Vengeance is Mine, and retribution, in due time their foot will slip; for the day of their calamity is near, and the impending things are hastening upon them." (Deuteronomy 32:35)

reveal: 1) to make known that which is hidden; 2) God chooses to reveal His character and His will to His children

"Then a man of God came to Eli and said to him, Thus says the Lord, "Did I not indeed reveal Myself to the house of your father when they were in Egypt in bondage to Pharaoh's house?" (1 Samuel 2:27)

"However, there is a God in heaven who reveals mysteries, and He has made known to King Nebuchadnezzar what will take place in the latter days..." (Daniel 2:28)

"He made known to us the mystery of His will, according to His kind intention which He purposed in Him" (Ephesians 1:9)

"And Simon Peter answered and said, "Thou art the Christ, the Son of the living God." And Jesus answered and said to him, "Blessed are you, Simon Barjona, because flesh and blood did not reveal this to you, but My Father who is in heaven." (Matthew 16:16-17)

reverence: 1) profound respect and esteem, to show honor especially to the Lord

"Establish Thy word to Thy servant, as that which produces reverence for Thee." (Psalm 119:38)

"Worship the Lord with reverence, and rejoice with trembling." (Psalm 2:11)

"... sanctify Christ as Lord in your hearts, always being ready to make a defense to everyone who asks you to give an account for the hope that is in you, yet with gentleness and reverence." (1 Peter 3:15)

revival: 1) spiritual renewal characterized by confession of sins, reading the Bible, commitment to obedience, removal of idols, and tithing

"Wilt Thou not Thyself revive us again, that Thy people may rejoice in Thee?" (Psalm 85:6)

"Lord, I have heard the report about Thee and I fear. O Lord, revive Thy work in the midst of the years, In the midst of the years make it known; in wrath remember mercy." (Habakkuk 3:2)

"... I dwell on a high and holy place, and also with the contrite and lowly of spirit in order to revive the spirit of the lowly and to revive the heart of the contrite." (Isaiah 57:15)

rhema: 1) the part of a sentence which expresses an essential idea; especially Scripture which the Holy Spirit brings to a person's mind

"Thy word I have treasured in my heart, that I may not sin against Thee." (Psalm 119:11)

"Establish Thy word to Thy servant, as that which produces reverence for Thee." (Psalm 119:38)

"Thy word is a lamp to my feet, and a light to my path." (Psalm 119:105)

"But the Helper, the Holy Spirit, whom the Father will send in My name, He will teach you all things, and bring to your remembrance all that I said to you." (John 14:26)

"Now these (Bereans) were more noble-minded than those in Thessalonica, for they received the word with great eagerness, examining the Scriptures daily, to see whether these things were so." (Acts 17:11)

"And as for Me, this is My covenant with them," says the Lord: "My Spirit which is upon you, and My words which I have put in your mouth, shall not depart from your mouth, nor from the mouth of your offspring, nor from the mouth of your offspring's offspring," says the Lord, "from now and forever." (Isaiah 59:21)

"So shall My word be which goes forth from My mouth; it shall not return to Me empty, without accomplishing what I desire, and without succeeding in the matter for which I sent it." (Isaiah 55:11)

righteousness: 1) obeying God in every aspect of our lives; 2) conforming to the revealed will of God

"that, in reference to your former manner of life, you lay aside the old self, which is being corrupted in accordance with the lusts of deceit, and that you be renewed in the spirit of your mind, and put on the new self, which in the likeness of God has been created in righteousness and holiness of the truth." (Ephesians 4:22-24)

"And this I pray, that your love may abound still more and more in real knowledge and all discernment, so that you may approve the things that are excellent, in order to be sincere and blameless until the day of Christ; having been filled with the fruit of righteousness which comes through Jesus Christ, to the glory and praise of God." (Philippians 1:9-11)

run: 1) to move rapidly; 2) the way in which we live out our Christian lives, especially through trials

"And they heard the sound of the Lord God walking in the garden in the cool of the day, and the man and his wife hid themselves from the presence of the Lord God among the trees of the garden. Then the Lord God called to the man, and said to him, "Where are you?" And he said, "I heard the sound of Thee in the garden, and I was afraid because I was naked; so I hid myself." (Genesis 3:8-10)

"I shall run the way of Thy commandments, for Thou wilt enlarge my heart." (Psalm 119:32)

"… let us also lay aside every encumbrance, and the sin which so easily entangles us, and let us run with endurance the race that is set before us, fixing our eyes on Jesus the author and perfecter of faith…" (Hebrews 12:1-2)

"Do you not know that those who run in a race all run, but only one receives the prize? Run in such a way that you may win." (1 Corinthians 9:24)

"I have directed you in the way of wisdom; I have led you in upright paths. When you walk, your steps will not be impeded; and if you run, you will not stumble." (Proverbs 4:11-12)

S PRAYER CARDS

Sabbath: 1) a day set aside by the Jews for rest and worship in the Old Testament; 2) traditionally, Christians celebrate the Lord's Day on Sunday, Jesus is Lord of the Sabbath, and teaches that faith and not the keeping of the Law is paramount

"One man regards one day above another, another regards every day alike. Let each man be fully convinced in his own mind. He who observes the day, observes it for the Lord, and he who eats, does so for the Lord, for he gives thanks to God; and he who eats not, for the Lord he does not eat, and gives thanks to God..." (Romans 14:5-6)

sacrifice: 1) God prefers life-long obedience rather than sacrifices; 2) He desires a contrite heart and a teachable spirit; 3) God desires a daily submission to Him as our living-sacrifice.

"I urge you therefore, brethren, by the mercies of God, to present your bodies a living and holy sacrifice, acceptable to God, which is your spiritual service of worship." (Romans 12:1)

"To Thee I shall offer a sacrifice of thanksgiving, and call upon the name of the Lord." (Psalm 116:17)

"Through Him then, let us continually offer up a sacrifice of praise to God, that is, the fruit of lips that give thanks to His name." (Hebrews 13:15)

"Then Jesus said to His disciples, "If anyone wishes to come after Me, let him deny himself, and take up his cross, and follow Me." (Matthew 16:24)

"And the smoke of the incense, with the prayers of the saints, went up before God out of the angel's hand." (Revelation 8:4)

salt: 1) believers are to live in such a way that they preserve and affect other's lives with the Gospel; 2) discipleship to a perishing world; 3) making a difference in the world because of our sanctification

"You are the salt of the earth; but if the salt has become tasteless, how will it be made salty again? It is good for nothing anymore, except to be thrown out and trampled underfoot by men." (Matthew 5:13)

"Conduct yourselves with wisdom toward outsiders, making the most of the opportunity. Let your speech always be with grace, seasoned, as it were, with salt, so that you may know how you should respond to each person." (Colossians 4:5-6)

salvation: 1) accepting the free gift of eternal life by placing one's trust in Jesus as the Lamb of God who was slain for our sins

"For God so loved the world, that He gave His only begotten Son, that whoever believes in Him should not perish, but have eternal life. "For God did not send the Son into the world to judge the world, but that the world should be saved through Him." (John 3:16-17)

"All that the Father gives Me shall come to Me, and the one who comes to Me I will certainly not cast out... "For this is the will of My Father, that everyone who beholds the Son and believes in Him, may have eternal life; and I Myself will raise him up on the last day." (John 6:37, 40)

sanctification: 1) set apart for holy use; 2) the purifying effect of the Word of God, through the Holy Spirit within a believer's heart to bring about our desire to share and live out the Gospel message

"But to each one of us grace was given according to the measure of Christ's gift… until we all attain to the unity of the faith, and of the knowledge of the Son of God, to a mature man, to the measure of the stature which belongs to the fullness of Christ. As a result… speaking the truth in love, we are to grow up in all aspects into Him, who is the head, even Christ" (Ephesians 4:7, 13-15)

"Now may the God of peace Himself sanctify you entirely; and may your spirit and soul and body be preserved complete, without blame at the coming of our Lord Jesus Christ." (1 Thessalonians 5:23)

"… but you were washed, but you were sanctified, but you were justified in the name of the Lord Jesus Christ, and in the Spirit of our God." (1 Corinthians 6:11)

"Sanctify them in the truth; Thy word is truth." (John 17:17)

Scripture: 1) the Word inspired by God, written by men, without error, revealing the character and heart of God; teaching teach men and guiding their lives

"All Scripture is inspired by God and profitable for teaching, for reproof, for correction, for training in righteousness; that the man of God may be adequate, equipped for every good work." (2 Timothy 3:16-17)

"But know this first of all, that no prophecy of Scripture is a matter of one's own interpretation, for no prophecy was ever made by an act of human will, but men moved by the Holy Spirit spoke from God." (2 Peter 1:20-21)

"Or do you think that the Scripture speaks to no purpose: "He jealously desires the Spirit which He has made to dwell in us?" (James 4:5)

seek: 1) to go in search of, to strive to discover; 2) Christians are to seek God and His wisdom and opportunities to serve others

"Seek the Lord while He may be found; call upon Him while He is near." (Isaiah 55:6)

"Seek the Lord, all you humble of the earth who have carried out His ordinances; seek righteousness, seek humility." (Zephaniah 2:3)

"If then you have been raised up with Christ, keep seeking the things above, where Christ is, seated at the right hand of God. Set your mind on the things above, not on the things that are on earth." (Colossians 3:1-2)

"(If) My people who are called by My name humble themselves and pray, and seek My face and turn from their wicked ways, then I will hear from heaven, will forgive their sin, and will heal their land." (2 Chronicles 7:14)

"But seek first His kingdom and His righteousness; and all these things shall be added to you." (Matthew 6:33)

"And without faith it is impossible to please Him, for he who comes to God must believe that He is, and that He is a rewarder of those who seek Him." (Hebrews 11:6)

"Seek the Lord and His strength; seek His face continually." (Psalm 105:4)

self: 1) man's nature is to be self-centered and self-satisfied rather than God-centered and humble

"… our old self was crucified with Him, that our body of sin might be done away with, that we should no longer be slaves to sin; for he who has died is freed from sin." (Romans 6:6-7)

"… in reference to your former manner of life, you lay aside the old self, which is being corrupted in accordance with the lusts of deceit, and that you be renewed in the spirit of your mind." (Ephesians 4:22-23)

"…put on the new self who is being renewed to a true knowledge according to the image of the One who created him… And so, as those who have been chosen of God, holy and beloved, put on a heart of compassion, kindness, humility, gentleness and patience; bearing with one another, and forgiving each other, whoever has a complaint against anyone; just as the Lord forgave you, so also should you." (Colossians 3:10, 12-13)

self-control: 1) a fruit of the Spirit, the gradual retraining of natural man's appetites toward God's purposes

"But the fruit of the Spirit is… self-control" (Galatians 5:22-23)

"And everyone who competes in the games exercises self-control in all things. They then do it to receive a perishable wreath, but we an imperishable." (1 Corinthians 9:25)

"Now for this very reason also, applying all diligence, in your faith supply moral excellence, and in your moral excellence, knowledge; and in your knowledge, self-control, and in your self-control, perseverance, and in your perseverance, godliness; and in your godliness, brotherly kindness, and in your brotherly kindness, love. For if these qualities are yours and are increasing, they render you neither useless nor unfruitful in the true knowledge of our Lord Jesus Christ." (2 Peter 1:5-8)

"Now the chief priests and the whole Council kept trying to obtain false testimony against Jesus, in order that they might put Him to death . . . But Jesus kept silent..." (Matthew 26:59, 63)

"He who restrains his words has knowledge, and he who has a cool spirit is a man of understanding. Even a fool, when he keeps silent, is considered wise; when he closes his lips, he is counted prudent." (Proverbs 17:27-28)

self-disciplined: 1) developing self-restraint, regular obedience; 2) learning to value wisdom and desiring the knowledge of Christ above all else

"I press on toward the goal for the prize of the upward call of God in Christ Jesus. Let us therefore, as many as are perfect, have this attitude; and if in anything you have a different attitude, God will reveal that also to you; however, let us keep living by that same standard to which we have attained." (Philippians 3:14-16)

"For you yourselves know how you ought to follow our example, because we did not act in an undisciplined manner among you, nor did we eat anyone's bread without paying for it, but with labor and hardship we kept working night and day so that we might not be a burden to any of you." (2 Thessalonians 3:7-8)

selfishness: 1) putting one's own interests before others, self-centered, desiring power and pleasure rather than loving and serving others

"For they all seek after their own interests, not those of Christ Jesus." (Philippians 2:21)

"For men will be lovers of self, lovers of money, boastful, arrogant, revilers, disobedient to parents, ungrateful, unholy" (2 Timothy 3:2)

"Then Jesus said to His disciples, "If anyone wishes to come after Me, let him deny himself, and take up his cross, and follow Me." (Matthew 16:24)

selfless: 1) a love that seeks to serve others in imitation of Christ

"A new commandment I give to you, that you love one another, even as I have loved you, that you also love one another." (John 13:34)

"We know love by this, that He laid down His life for us; and we ought to lay down our lives for the brethren." (1 John 3:16)

"Greater love has no one than this, that one lay down his life for his friends." (John 15:13)

self-opinionated: 1) firmly adhering to one's own opinions without considering others

"And do not be conformed to this world, but be transformed by the renewing of your mind, that you may prove what the will of God is, that which is good and acceptable and perfect. For through the grace given to me I say to every man among you not to think more highly of himself than he ought to think; but to think so as to have sound judgment, as God has allotted to each a measure of faith. For just as we have many members in one body and all the members do not have the same function, so we, who are many, are one body in Christ, and individually members one of another." (Romans 12:2-5)

self-righteousness: 1) egotistical, proud of one's morals, convinced of one's own goodness; 2) denying our desperate need for God's mercy

"The Pharisee stood and was praying thus to himself, 'God, I thank Thee that I am not like other people: swindlers, unjust, adulterers, or even like this tax-gatherer. 'I fast twice a week; I pay tithes of all that I get… "I tell you… everyone who exalts himself shall be humbled, but he who humbles himself shall be exalted." (Luke 18:11-12, 14)

"But he who boasts, let him boast in the Lord. For not he who commends himself is approved, but whom the Lord commends." (2 Corinthians 10:17-18)

self-will: 1) pride, disobedience, the lust of the eyes, boasting, leads to destruction; 2) obstinate

"You shall not put the Lord your God to the test." (Matthew 4:7)

"Do all things without grumbling or disputing." (Philippians 2:14)

"For this reason I say to you, do not be anxious for your life, as to what you shall eat, or what you shall drink; nor for your body, as to what you shall put on. Is not life more than food, and the body than clothing?… "But seek first His kingdom and His righteousness; and all these things shall be added to you." (Matthew 6:25, 33)

"And everyone who hears these words of Mine, and does not act upon them, will be like a foolish man, who built his house upon the sand." (Matthew 7:26)

"And his lord, moved with anger, handed him over to the torturers until he should repay all that was owed him. So shall My heavenly Father also do to you, if each of you does not forgive his brother from your heart." (Matthew 18:34-35)

separate: 1) to devote ourselves to God's desires, to distance ourselves from the sinful values of this world

"Therefore, come out from their midst and be separate," says the Lord. "and do not touch what is unclean; and I will welcome you." (2 Corinthians 6:17)

"But may it never be that I should boast, except in the cross of our Lord Jesus Christ, through which the world has been crucified to me, and I to the world." (Galatians 6:14)

servant's heart: 1) taking the initiative to help others without being asked, humbly serving others without looking for honor

"And Mary said, "Behold, the bondslave of the Lord; be it done to me according to your word..." (Luke 1:38)

"... through love serve one another." (Galatians 5:13)

"As each one has received a special gift, employ it in serving one another, as good stewards of the manifold grace of God." (1 Peter 4:10)

"and whoever wishes to be first among you shall be your slave; just as the Son of Man did not come to be served, but to serve, and to give His life a ransom for many." (Matthew 20:27-28)

sexual temptation: 1) the desire to fulfill sexual desires in immoral ways; 2) Christians need to avoid places and circumstances which might feed sexual temptation

"And the man and his wife were both naked and were not ashamed." (Genesis 2:25)

"... Do not be deceived; neither fornicators, nor idolaters, nor adulterers, nor effeminate, nor homosexuals, nor thieves, nor the covetous, nor drunkards, nor revilers, nor swindlers, shall inherit the kingdom of God." (1 Corinthians 6:9-10)

"It is actually reported that there is immorality among you, and immorality of such a kind as does not exist even among the Gentiles, that someone has his father's wife. And you have become arrogant, and have not mourned instead, in order that the one who had done this deed might be removed from your midst." (1 Corinthians 5:1-2)

Shekinah glory: 1) the divine splendor of the majesty of God, as depicted in the tabernacle in the wilderness, and the transfiguration of Christ

"And the Lord said to Moses, "Tell your brother Aaron that he shall not enter at any time into the holy place inside the veil, before the mercy seat which is on the ark, lest he die; for I will appear in the cloud over the mercy seat." (Leviticus 16:2)

"Immediately I was in the Spirit; and behold, a throne was standing in heaven, and One sitting on the throne. And He who was sitting was like a jasper stone and a sardius in appearance; and there was a rainbow around the throne, like an emerald in appearance." (Revelation 4:2-3)

shepherd: 1) one who protects his flock, provides for them, guides them, and looks for lost sheep; 2) figuratively, one who leads others, protects them and guides them, especially Jesus

"Then I will give you shepherds after My own heart, who will feed you on knowledge and understanding." (Jeremiah 3:15)

"He (Jesus) said to him again a second time, "Simon, son of John, do you love Me?" He said to Him, "Yes, Lord; You know that I love You." He said to him, "Shepherd My sheep." (John 21:16)

"shepherd the flock of God among you, exercising oversight not under compulsion, but voluntarily, according to the will of God; and not for sordid gain, but with eagerness; nor yet as lording it over those allotted to your charge, but proving to be examples to the flock." (1 Peter 5:2-3)

showing off: 1) displaying your 'good works' in order to receive the praise of man

"Beware of practicing your righteousness before men to be noticed by them; otherwise you have no reward with your Father who is in heaven." (Matthew 6:1)

"When you are invited by someone to a wedding feast, do not take the place of honor, lest someone more distinguished than you may have been invited by him, and he who invited you both shall come and say to you, 'Give place to this man,' and then in disgrace you proceed to occupy the last place." (Luke 14:8-9)

silence: 1) taking time to come before the Lord with a quiet spirit to exalt Him and wait upon Him with keen attention

"My soul waits in silence for God only; from Him is my salvation. He only is my rock and my salvation, my stronghold; I shall not be greatly shaken." (Psalm 62:1-2)

"Be silent before the Lord God! For the day of the Lord is near..." (Zephaniah 1:7)

"Do not be hasty in word or impulsive in thought to bring up a matter in the presence of God. For God is in heaven and you are on the earth; therefore let your words be few." (Ecclesiastes 5:2)

"Coastlands, listen to Me in silence, and let the peoples gain new strength; let them come forward, then let them speak; let us come together for judgment." (Isaiah 41:1)

"And when He broke the seventh seal, there was silence in heaven for about half an hour… And the smoke of the incense, with the prayers of the saints, went up before God out of the angel's hand." (Revelation 8:1, 4)

silly talk: 1) conversation which is foolish, unwise, and without purpose; 2) language which indicates a lack of a spiritual life

"and there must be no filthiness and silly talk, or coarse jesting, which are not fitting, but rather giving of thanks." (Ephesians 5:4)

simplicity: 1) free from guile, unpretentious, sincere

"Slaves, be obedient to those who are your masters according to the flesh, with fear and trembling, in the sincerity of your heart, as to Christ" (Ephesians 6:5)

"But I am afraid, lest as the serpent deceived Eve by his craftiness, your minds should be led astray from the simplicity and purity of devotion to Christ." (2 Corinthians 11:3)

"but only a few things are necessary, really only one, for Mary has chosen the good part, which shall not be taken away from her." (Luke 10:42)

"You shall love the Lord your God with all your heart, and with all your soul, and with all your mind. This is the great and foremost commandment. The second is like it, 'You shall love your neighbor as yourself. On these two commandments depend the whole Law and the Prophets." (Matthew 22:37-40)

sin: 1) disobeying God's Law; 2) violating God's will either through sins of commission or omission

"Wash me thoroughly from my iniquity, and cleanse me from my sin. For I know my transgressions, and my sin is ever before me." (Psalm 51:2-3)

"For our transgressions are multiplied before Thee, and our sins testify against us; for our transgressions are with us, and we know our iniquities: transgressing and denying the Lord, and turning away from our God..." (Isaiah 59:12-13)

"All of us like sheep have gone astray, each of us has turned to his own way; but the Lord has caused the iniquity of us all to fall on Him." (Isaiah 53:6)

sincere heart: 1) moral purity, honesty, integrity, genuine; 2) single-minded devotion to God

"And day by day continuing with one mind in the temple, and breaking bread from house to house, they were taking their meals together with gladness and sincerity of heart." (Acts 2:46)

"But the goal of our instruction is love from a pure heart and a good conscience and a sincere faith." (1 Timothy 1:5)

"let us draw near with a sincere heart in full assurance of faith, having our hearts sprinkled clean from an evil conscience and our bodies washed with pure water." (Hebrews 10:22)

"Since you have in obedience to the truth purified your souls for a sincere love of the brethren, fervently love one another from the heart." (1 Peter 1:22)

sit: 1) a position of rest; 2) to linger before another to receive instruction and listen intently

"And she (Martha) had a sister called Mary, who moreover was listening to the Lord's word, seated at His feet... But the Lord answered and said... only a few things are necessary, really only one, for Mary has chosen the good part, which shall not be taken away from her." (Luke 10:39, 41-42)

"And the people went out to see what had happened; and they came to Jesus, and found the man from whom the demons had gone out, sitting down at the feet of Jesus, clothed and in his right mind..." (Luke 8:35)

skill: 1) God' given expertise in a craft, He gives the opportunity and strength to perform that skill to His glory

"Now Bezalel and Oholiab, and every skillful person in whom the Lord has put skill and understanding to know how to perform all the work in the construction of the sanctuary, shall perform in accordance with all that the Lord has commanded." (Exodus 36:1)

"Do you see a man skilled in his work? He will stand before kings; He will not stand before obscure men." (Proverbs 22:29)

slacker: 1) one who does not practice diligence or care in their duties, to neglect or evade work

"He also who is slack in his work is brother to him who destroys." (Proverbs 18:9)

"The soul of the sluggard craves and gets nothing, but the soul of the diligent is made fat." (Proverbs 13:4)

sober-minded: 1) clear-minded, exercising self-restraint, leading a disciplined spiritual life, taking the Gospel seriously

"An overseer, then, must be above reproach, the husband of one wife, temperate, prudent, respectable, hospitable, able to teach." (1 Timothy 3:2)

"The end of all things is at hand; therefore, be of sound judgment and sober spirit for the purpose of prayer. Above all, keep fervent in your love for one another, because love covers a multitude of sins." (1 Peter 4:7-8)

sound doctrine: 1) the principles of the faith, accurate teaching of Christian truth found in Scripture

"For the overseer must be above reproach as God's steward... holding fast the faithful word which is in accordance with the teaching, that he may be able both to exhort in sound doctrine and to refute those who contradict." (Titus 1:7, 9)

"For everything created by God is good, and nothing is to be rejected, if it is received with gratitude; for it is sanctified by means of the word of God and prayer. In pointing out these things to the brethren, you will be a good servant of Christ Jesus, constantly nourished on the words of the faith and of the sound doctrine which you have been following." (1 Timothy 4:4-6)

"All Scripture is inspired by God and profitable for teaching, for reproof, for correction, for training in righteousness; that the man of God may be adequate, equipped for every good work." (2 Timothy 3:16-17)

sound mind: 1) self-control, self-discipline; a mind focused on Christ, able to understand and live by the truth found in the Bible

"For God has not given us a spirit of timidity, but of power and love and discipline." (2 Timothy 1:7 KJV)

"Set your mind on the things above, not on the things that are on earth." (Colossians 3:2)

"Finally, brethren, whatever is true, whatever is honorable, whatever is right, whatever is pure, whatever is lovely, whatever is of good repute, if there is any excellence and if anything worthy of praise, let your mind dwell on these things." (Philippians 4:8)

sovereignty: 1) God's supreme power over the universe He created; 2) we are the caretakers of this world, but He owns it; 3) It is God's desire to work through us to accomplish His good pleasure.

"But the Lord abides forever; He has established His throne for judgment, and He will judge the world in righteousness; He will execute judgment for the peoples with equity." (Psalm 9:7-8)

"He rules by His might forever; His eyes keep watch on the nations; let not the rebellious exalt themselves." (Psalm 66:7)

"Are not two sparrows sold for a cent? And yet not one of them will fall to the ground apart from your Father. But the very hairs of your head are all numbered." (Matthew 10:29-30)

"The earth is the Lord's, and all it contains, the world, and those who dwell in it." (Psalm 24:1)

"for it is God who is at work in you, both to will and to work for His good pleasure." (Philippians 2:13)

spirit of control: 1) either a satanic spirit or a worldly, carnal manipulating human spirit that battles against the Holy Spirit for the control of a man's soul and exercise ungodly authority over others

"And He answered and said to them, "And why do you yourselves transgress the commandment of God for the sake of your tradition? ... This people honors me with their lips, but their heart is far away from me. But in vain do they worship Me, teaching as doctrines the precepts of men." (Matthew 15:3, 8-9)

"And He put all things in subjection under His feet, and gave Him as head over all things to the church, which is His body, the fullness of Him who fills all in all." (Ephesians 1:22-23)

spirit of a Pharisee: 1) the hypocrisy of religious and political leaders whose evil teachings lead an entire nation astray; 2) studying the Word regularly prevent us from being misled by false teaching

"And Jesus said to them, "Watch out and beware of the leaven of the Pharisees and Sadducees." (Matthew 16:6)

"The scribes and the Pharisees have seated themselves in the chair of Moses; therefore all that they tell you, do and observe, but do not do according to their deeds; for they say things, and do not do them... But they do all their deeds to be noticed by men; for they broaden their phylacteries, and lengthen the tassels of their garments... But the greatest among you shall be your servant. And whoever exalts himself shall be humbled; and whoever humbles himself shall be exalted. But woe to you, scribes and Pharisees, hypocrites, because you shut off the kingdom of heaven from men; for you do not enter in yourselves, nor do you allow those who are entering to go in." (Matthew 23:2-3,5, 11-13)

spiritual gifts: 1) the measure of faith God gives every believer to serve Him; 2) the special abilities God gives us to use in building up the body of Christ

"Now concerning spiritual gifts, brethren, I do not want you to be unaware . . . Now there are varieties of gifts, but the same Spirit. And there are varieties of ministries, and the same Lord... But to each one is given the manifestation of the Spirit for the common good... But now God has placed the members, each one of them, in the body, just as He desired." (1 Corinthians 12:1, 4-5, 7, 18)

"And since we have gifts that differ according to the grace given to us, let each exercise them accordingly..." (Romans 12:6)

"As each one has received a special gift, employ it in serving one another, as good stewards of the manifold grace of God. Whoever speaks, let him speak, as it were, the utterances of God; whoever serves, let him do so as by the strength which God supplies; so that in all things God may be glorified through Jesus Christ..." (1 Peter 4:10-11)

spiritual maturity: 1) the gradual process of growing in Christ as He works in every believers heart; 2) submitting to the indwelling Holy Spirit for guidance and sanctification

"Yet we do speak wisdom among those who are mature; a wisdom, however, not of this age, nor of the rulers of this age, who are passing away; but we speak God's wisdom in a mystery, the hidden wisdom, which God predestined before the ages to our glory." (1 Corinthians 2:6-7)

"Brethren, do not be children in your thinking; yet in evil be babes, but in your thinking be mature." (1 Corinthians 14:20)

"until we all attain to the unity of the faith, and of the knowledge of the Son of God, to a mature man, to the measure of the stature which belongs to the fullness of Christ. As a result, we are no longer to be children, tossed here and there by waves, and carried about by every wind of doctrine, by the trickery of men, by craftiness in deceitful scheming; but speaking the truth in love, we are to grow up in all aspects into Him, who is the head, even Christ" (Ephesians 4:13-15)

"But solid food is for the mature, who because of practice have their senses trained to discern good and evil." (Hebrews 5:14)

spiritual strength: 1) the strength we obtain to withstand Satan's attacks through prayer, worship and studying God's Word for guidance; 2) the Holy Spirit provides the strength we need to overcome

"Yet those who wait for the Lord will gain new strength; they will mount up with wings like eagles, they will run and not get tired, they will walk and not become weary." (Isaiah 40:31)

"My flesh and my heart may fail, but God is the strength of my heart and my portion forever." (Psalm 73:26)

"I can do all things through Him who strengthens me." (Philippians 4:13)

"For this reason, I bow my knees before the Father... that He would grant you, according to the riches of His glory, to be strengthened with power through His Spirit in the inner man" (Ephesians 3:14, 16)

spiritual warfare: 1) Satan is the source of all the evil in this world, and he is the enemy of God and all believers; 2) his goal is to attack and defeat every Christian

"Be of sober spirit, be on the alert. Your adversary, the devil, prowls about like a roaring lion, seeking someone to devour." (1 Peter 5:8)

"for the weapons of our warfare are not of the flesh, but divinely powerful for the destruction of fortresses." (2 Corinthians 10:4)

"Put on the full armor of God, that you may be able to stand firm against the schemes of the devil. For our struggle is not against flesh and blood, but against the rulers, against the powers, against the world forces of this darkness, against the spiritual forces of wickedness in the heavenly places." (Ephesians 6:11-12)

"And even if our gospel is veiled, it is veiled to those who are perishing, in whose case the god of this world has blinded the minds of the unbelieving, that they might not see the light of the gospel of the glory of Christ, who is the image of God." (2 Corinthians 4:3-4)

"But the Lord is faithful, and He will strengthen and protect you from the evil one." (2 Thessalonians 3:3)

spring of the water of life: 1) the indwelling Holy Spirit which Christ promises to all who believe; 2) the Holy Spirit meets our every spiritual need and provides us with eternal life

"… Jesus stood and cried out, saying, "If any man is thirsty, let him come to Me and drink. He who believes in Me, as the Scripture said, 'From his innermost being shall flow rivers of living water.'" But this He spoke of the Spirit, whom those who believed in Him were to receive." (John 7:37-39)

"… I am the Alpha and the Omega, the beginning and the end. I will give to the one who thirsts from the spring of the water of life without cost." (Revelation 21:6)

"And he showed me a river of the water of life, clear as crystal, coming from the throne of God and of the Lamb, in the middle of its street. And on either side of the river was the tree of life." (Revelation 22:1-2)

stand firm: 1) continue to follow hard after Christ even during times of persecution; 2) the Holy Spirit created a unified Church which Satan will not conquer

"Be on the alert, stand firm in the faith, act like men, be strong. Let all that you do be done in love." (1 Corinthians 16:13-14)

"Only conduct yourselves in a manner worthy of the gospel of Christ; so that whether I come and see you or remain absent, I may hear of you that you are standing firm in one spirit, with one mind striving together for the faith of the gospel." (Philippians 1:27)

"Put on the full armor of God, that you may be able to stand firm against the schemes of the devil." (Ephesians 6:11)

steadfast: 1) remaining loyal to God's truth, to persevere in the faith without faltering

"The steadfast of mind Thou wilt keep in perfect peace, because he trusts in Thee." (Isaiah 26:3)

"Create in me a clean heart, O God, and renew a steadfast spirit within me." (Psalm 51:10)

"Therefore, my beloved brethren, be steadfast, immovable, always abounding in the work of the Lord, knowing that your toil is not in vain in the Lord." (1 Corinthians 15:58)

stealing: 1) to take something you do not own without permission

"You shall not steal." (Exodus 20:15)

"Will a man rob God? Yet you are robbing Me! But you say, 'How have we robbed Thee?' In tithes and offerings." (Malachi 3:8)

"Let him who steals steal no longer; but rather let him labor, performing with his own hands what is good, in order that he may have something to share with him who has need." (Ephesians 4:28)

stewardship: 1) managing that which God provides for us, to meet needs and glorify God and His kingdom

"As each one has received a special gift, employ it in serving one another, as good stewards of the manifold grace of God." (1 Peter 4:10)

"It is well with the man who is gracious and lends; He will maintain his cause in judgment." (Psalm 112:5)

"For where your treasure is, there will your heart be also." (Luke 12:34)

"Then God said, "Let Us make man in Our image, according to Our likeness; and let them rule over the fish of the sea and over the birds of the sky and over the cattle and over all the earth, and over every creeping thing that creeps on the earth." (Genesis 1:26)

"Therefore be careful how you walk, not as unwise men, but as wise, making the most of your time, because the days are evil." (Ephesians 5:15-16)

stillness: 1) quiet, calmness, tranquil; 2) being silent in the presence of the Lord, in order to hear from Him

"Be still, and know that I am God…" (Psalm 46:10 KJV)

"But Moses said to the people, "Do not fear! Stand by and see the salvation of the Lord which He will accomplish for you today; for the Egyptians whom you have seen today, you will never see them again forever." (Exodus 14:13)

"Tremble, and do not sin; meditate in your heart upon your bed, and be still." (Psalm 4:4)

"For David says of Him, 'I was always beholding the Lord in my presence; for He is at my right hand, that I may not be shaken." (Acts 2:25)

stinginess: 1) not generous, miserly; 2) not giving to those in need, holding back the tithe

"But whoever has the world's goods, and beholds his brother in need and closes his heart against him, how does the love of God abide in him?" (1 John 3:17)

"There is one who scatters, yet increases all the more, and there is one who withholds what is justly due, but it results only in want. The generous man will be prosperous, and he who waters will himself be watered." (Proverbs 11:24-25)

strength: 1) vigor, power to resist, firmness, confidence; 2) God is the source of our strength

"He gives strength to the weary, and to him who lacks might He increases power... Yet those who wait for the Lord will gain new strength; they will mount up with wings like eagles, they will run and not get tired, they will walk and not become weary." (Isaiah 40: 29, 31)

"For this reason, I bow my knees before the Father... that He would grant you, according to the riches of His glory, to be strengthened with power through His Spirit in the inner man; so that Christ may dwell in your hearts through faith; and that you, being rooted and grounded in love... know the love of Christ which surpasses knowledge, that you may be filled up to all the fullness of God." (Ephesians 3:14, 16-17, 19)

strife: 1) fight, contention, bitter conflict

"There are six things which the Lord hates... one who spreads strife among brothers." (Proverbs 6:16, 19)

"for you are still fleshly. For since there is jealousy and strife among you, are you not fleshly, and are you not walking like mere men?" (1 Corinthians 3:3)

"But shun foolish controversies and genealogies and strife and disputes about the Law; for they are unprofitable and worthless." (Titus 3:9)

"Through presumption comes nothing but strife, but with those who receive counsel is wisdom." (Proverbs 13:10)

strive: 1) to make great effort, to work toward with earnestness

"Cease striving and know that I am God." (Psalm 46:10)

"Know that the Lord Himself is God; it is He who has made us, and not we ourselves; we are His people and the sheep of His pasture." (Psalm 100:3)

"... do not fight against the Lord God of your fathers, for you will not succeed." (2 Chronicles 13:12)

"Wait for the Lord, and keep His way, and He will exalt you to inherit the land; When the wicked are cut off, you will see it." (Psalm 37:34)

"... we were afflicted on every side: conflicts without, fears within. But God, who comforts the depressed, comforted us by the coming of Titus... so that I rejoiced even more." (2 Corinthians 7:5-7)

stronghold: 1) rebellious ideas, proud arguments against Christianity, satanic influence; 2) the Holy Spirit and the truth of the Word of God protects believers from allowing evil strongholds to gain control of their lives

"for the weapons of our warfare are not of the flesh, but divinely powerful for the destruction of fortresses. We are destroying speculations and every lofty thing raised up against the knowledge of God, and we are taking every thought captive to the obedience of Christ." (2 Corinthians 10:4-5)

"And do not be conformed to this world, but be transformed by the renewing of your mind, that you may prove what the will of God is, that which is good and acceptable and perfect." (Romans 12:2)

"Establish my footsteps in Thy word, and do not let any iniquity have dominion over me." (Psalm 119:133)

stubbornness: 1) a heart that resists the influence of the Holy Spirit, human willfulness, steadfast refusal to submit to the Lord

"Therefore, just as the Holy Spirit says, "Today if you hear His voice, do not harden your hearts as when they provoked Me, as in the days of trial in the wilderness." (Hebrews 3:7-8)

"But because of your stubbornness and unrepentant heart you are storing up wrath for yourself in the day of wrath and revelation of the righteous judgment of God, who will render to every man according to his deeds" (Romans 2:5-6)

"And I shall give them one heart, and shall put a new spirit within them. And I shall take the heart of stone out of their flesh and give them a heart of flesh, that they may walk in My statutes and keep My ordinances, and do them. Then they will be My people, and I shall be their God." (Ezekiel 11:19-20)

"For rebellion is as the sin of divination, and insubordination is as iniquity and idolatry. Because you have rejected the word of the Lord, He has also rejected you from being king." (1 Samuel 15:23)

submission: 1) to be willing to place our lives and our will in the hands of our loving Lord

"Submit therefore to God. Resist the devil and he will flee from you." (James 4:7)

"… be filled with the Spirit, speaking to one another in Psalms and hymns and spiritual songs, singing and making melody with your heart to the Lord; always giving thanks for all things in the name of our Lord Jesus Christ to God, even the Father; and be subject to one another in the fear of Christ." (Ephesians 5:18-21)

"Obey your leaders, and submit to them; for they keep watch over your souls, as those who will give an account. Let them do this with joy and not with grief, for this would be unprofitable for you." (Hebrews 13:17)

sufficient: 1) attribute of God, He will provide all that is necessary for life

"For He has satisfied the thirsty soul, and the hungry soul He has filled with what is good." (Psalm 107:9)

"Thou dost open Thy hand, and dost satisfy the desire of every living thing." (Psalm 145:16)

"And my God shall supply all your needs according to His riches in glory in Christ Jesus." (Philippians 4:19)

"Bring the whole tithe into the storehouse, so that there may be food in My house, and test Me now in this," says the Lord of hosts, "if I will not open for you the windows of heaven, and pour out for you a blessing until it overflows." (Malachi 3:10)

"And He has said to me, "My grace is sufficient for you, for power is perfected in weakness..." (2 Corinthians 12:9)

"For I am confident of this very thing, that He who began a good work in you will perfect it until the day of Christ Jesus." (Philippians 1:6)

surrender: 1) radical discipleship, immediate obedience, to deny one's self in order to follow Christ

"Then Jesus said to His disciples, "If anyone wishes to come after Me, let him deny himself, and take up his cross, and follow Me. For whoever wishes to save his life shall lose it; but whoever loses his life for My sake shall find it." (Matthew 16:24-25)

"Now do not stiffen your neck like your fathers, but yield to the Lord and enter His sanctuary which He has consecrated forever, and serve the Lord your God, that His burning anger may turn away from you." (2 Chronicles 30:8)

"Nebuchadnezzar responded and said, "Blessed be the God of Shadrach, Meshach and Abed-nego, who has sent His angel and delivered His servants who put their trust in Him, violating the king's command, and yielded up their bodies so as not to serve or worship any god except their own God." (Daniel 3:28)

surround: 1) to encircle, to envelop

"As the mountains surround Jerusalem, so the Lord surrounds His people from this time forth and forever." (Psalm 125:2)

"For it is Thou who dost bless the righteous man, O Lord, Thou dost surround him with favor as with a shield." (Psalm 5:12)

Sword of the Lord: 1) the Bible, the Word of God, an offensive weapon with which to defeat Satan

"And take the... sword of the Spirit, which is the word of God." (Ephesians 6:17)

"For the word of God is living and active and sharper than any two-edged sword, and piercing as far as the division of soul and spirit, of both joints and marrow, and able to judge the thoughts and intentions of the heart." (Hebrews 4:12)

"All Scripture is inspired by God and profitable for teaching, for reproof, for correction, for training in righteousness; that the man of God may be adequate, equipped for every good work." (2 Timothy 3:16-17)

T PRAYER CARDS

tact: 1) perception, discernment regarding what is required under the circumstances, diplomacy

"A gentle answer turns away wrath, but a harsh word stirs up anger." (Proverbs 15:1)

"Brethren, even if a man is caught in any trespass, you who are spiritual, restore such a one in a spirit of gentleness; each one looking to yourself, lest you too be tempted." (Galatians 6:1)

"Who among you is wise and understanding? Let him show by his good behavior his deeds in the gentleness of wisdom." (James 3:13)

teachable spirit: 1) the opposite of dogmatism, being receptive, eager to hear from God and do His will

"Incline your ear and hear the words of the wise, and apply your mind to my knowledge; for it will be pleasant if you keep them within you, that they may be ready on your lips. So that your trust may be in the Lord." (Proverbs 22:17-19)

"Now we have received… the Spirit who is from God, that we might know the things freely given to us by God, which things we also speak, not in words taught by human wisdom, but in those taught by the Spirit, combining spiritual thoughts with spiritual words. But a natural man does not accept the things of the Spirit of God; for they are foolishness to him, and he cannot understand them, because they are spiritually appraised." (1 Corinthians 2: 12-14)

"Turn to my reproof, behold, I will pour out my spirit on you; I will make my words known to you." (Proverbs 1:23)

teaching: 1) instructing others by word and deed, about the Bible, and how to achieve spiritual maturity in obedience to Christ

"Older men are to be temperate, dignified, sensible, sound in faith, in love, in perseverance. Older women likewise are to be reverent in their behavior, not malicious gossips, nor enslaved to much wine, teaching what is good, that they may encourage the young women to love their husbands, to love their children, to be sensible, pure, workers at home, kind, being subject to their own husbands, that the word of God may not be dishonored. Likewise urge the young men to be sensible; in all things show yourself to be an example of good deeds, with purity in doctrine, dignified." (Titus 2:2-7)

"She (an excellent wife) opens her mouth in wisdom, and the teaching of kindness is on her tongue." (Proverbs 31:26)

"then teach them (the people) the statutes and the laws, and make known to them the way in which they are to walk, and the work they are to do." (Exodus 18:20)

temper: 1) acting out in anger, saying or doing things you will later regret

"A quick-tempered man acts foolishly, and a man of evil devices is hated." (Proverbs 14:17)

"Let all bitterness and wrath and anger and clamor and slander be put away from you, along with all malice." (Ephesians 4:31)

"(Love) does not act unbecomingly; it does not seek its own, is not provoked, does not take into account a wrong suffered." (1 Corinthians 13:5)

"… But let everyone be quick to hear, slow to speak and slow to anger; for the anger of man does not achieve the righteousness of God." (James 1:19-20)

"A fool always loses his temper, but a wise man holds it back." (Proverbs 29:11)

"He who is slow to anger is better than the mighty, and he who rules his spirit, than he who captures a city." (Proverbs 16:32)

temple: 1) every believer is a temple for the indwelling Holy Spirit

"Do you not know that you are a temple of God, and that the Spirit of God dwells in you? If any man destroys the temple of God, God will destroy him, for the temple of God is holy, and that is what you are." (1 Corinthians 3:16-17)

"Or do you not know that your body is a temple of the Holy Spirit who is in you, whom you have from God, and that you are not your own? For you have been bought with a price: therefore glorify God in your body." (1 Corinthians 6:19-20)

temporal values: 1) the world's present values which change over time, rather than eternal values based on Christ and His kingdom

"Do not lay up for yourselves treasures upon earth, where moth and rust destroy, and where thieves break in and steal." (Matthew 6:19)

"But those who want to get rich fall into temptation and a snare and many foolish and harmful desires which plunge men into ruin and destruction. For the love of money is a root of all sorts of evil, and some by longing for it have wandered away from the faith, and pierced themselves with many a pang." (1 Timothy 6:9-10)

"But lay up for yourselves treasures in heaven, where neither moth nor rust destroys, and where thieves do not break in or steal; for where your treasure is, there will your heart be also." (Matthew 6:20-21)

temptation: 1) the enticement to meet real needs in ways that violate Scripture; 2) Satan exploits our desires by offering sinful solutions to our needs

"And do not lead us into temptation, but deliver us from evil..." (Matthew 6:13)

"Keep watching and praying, that you may not enter into temptation; the spirit is willing, but the flesh is weak." (Matthew 26:41)

"No temptation has overtaken you but such as is common to man; and God is faithful, who will not allow you to be tempted beyond what you are able, but with the temptation will provide the way of escape also, that you may be able to endure it." (1 Corinthians 10:13)

thankful: 1) praising God for all His grace and benefits; 2) acknowledging God's lovingkindness

"I will give thanks to the Lord with all my heart; I will tell of all Thy wonders." (Psalm 9:1)

"Enter His gates with thanksgiving, and His courts with praise. Give thanks to Him; bless His name. For the Lord is good; His lovingkindness is everlasting, and His faithfulness to all generations." (Psalm 100:4-5)

"speaking to one another in Psalms and hymns and spiritual songs, singing and making melody with your heart to the Lord; always giving thanks for all things in the name of our Lord Jesus Christ to God, even the Father." (Ephesians 5:19-20)

(spiritual) thirst: 1) a soul which yearns for the living God, who seeks personal righteousness so that they might follow Him in complete obedience

"My soul thirsts for God, for the living God..." (Psalm 42:2)

"O God, Thou art my God; I shall seek Thee earnestly; my soul thirsts for Thee, my flesh yearns for Thee, in a dry and weary land where there is no water... Because Thy lovingkindness is better than life, my lips will praise Thee." (Psalm 63:1, 3)

"Jesus answered and said to her, "Everyone who drinks of this water shall thirst again; but whoever drinks of the water that I shall give him shall never thirst; but the water that I shall give him shall become in him a well of water springing up to eternal life." (John 4:13-14)

(taking) thoughts captive: 1) battling rebellious ideas with the knowledge of God; 2) equipping believers with the Word of God to withstand Satan's lies

"We are destroying speculations and every lofty thing raised up against the knowledge of God, and we are taking every thought captive to the obedience of Christ." (2 Corinthians 10:5)

timing: 1) God ordains when to fulfill His plans. We are to wait for His will and the right circumstances to be revealed.

"There is an appointed time for everything. And there is a time for every event under Heaven... He has made everything appropriate in its time.

He has also set eternity in their heart, yet so that man will not find out the work which God has done from the beginning even to the end." (Ecclesiastes 3:1, 11)

"It is time for the Lord to act, for they have broken Thy law." (Psalm 119:126)

"But when the fullness of the time came, God sent forth His Son, born of a woman, born under the Law" (Galatians 4:4)

tithe: 1) returning a portion of our possessions (10% according to Genesis 14:20) to the Lord as an act of obedience and in gratitude for His blessings; 2) financial stewardship which equips the Church to carry out ministry and meet the needs of the poor

"Thus all the tithe of the land, of the seed of the land or of the fruit of the tree, is the Lord's; it is holy to the Lord... 'And for every tenth part of herd or flock, whatever passes under the rod, the tenth one shall be holy to the Lord." (Leviticus 27:30, 32)

"Bring the whole tithe into the storehouse, so that there may be food in My house, and test Me now in this," says the Lord of hosts, "if I will not open for you the windows of heaven, and pour out for you a blessing until it overflows." (Malachi 3:10)

"But lay up for yourselves treasures in heaven, where neither moth nor rust destroys, and where thieves do not break in or steal; for where your treasure is, there will your heart be also." (Matthew 6:20-21)

tongue: 1) the instrument of speech, with which we either glorify the Lord and share the Gospel, or allow Satan to use to divide people and commit sin

"The good man out of the good treasure of his heart brings forth what is good; and the evil man out of the evil treasure brings forth what is evil; for his mouth speaks from that which fills his heart." (Luke 6:45)

"And the tongue is a fire, the very world of iniquity; the tongue is set among our members as that which defiles the entire body, and sets on fire the course of our life, and is set on fire by hell... With it we bless our Lord and Father; and with it we curse men, who have been made in the likeness of God." (James 3:6, 9)

"Let no unwholesome word proceed from your mouth, but only such a word as is good for edification according to the need of the moment, that it may give grace to those who hear." (Ephesians 4:29)

"Let the words of my mouth and the meditation of my heart be acceptable in Thy sight, O Lord, my rock and my Redeemer." (Psalm 19:14)

"If anyone thinks himself to be religious, and yet does not bridle his tongue but deceives his own heart, this man's religion is worthless." (James 1:26)

"Set a guard, O Lord, over my mouth; keep watch over the door of my lips." (Psalm 141:3)

"The heart of the wise teaches his mouth, and adds persuasiveness to his lips. Pleasant words are a honeycomb, sweet to the soul and healing to the bones." (Proverbs 16:23-24)

traditions of men: 1) following the authority of man's teaching rather than honoring God with obedience to His Word; indicates a heart which is far from God

"Why do Your disciples transgress the tradition of the elders? For they do not wash their hands when they eat bread." And He answered and said to them, "And why do you yourselves transgress the commandment of God for the sake of your tradition?" (Matthew 15:2-3)

"But in vain do they worship Me, teaching as doctrines the precepts of men." (Matthew 15:9)

"See to it that no one takes you captive through philosophy and empty deception, according to the tradition of men, according to the elementary principles of the world, rather than according to Christ." (Colossians 2:8)

transparent: 1) honest, without guile, without hidden motives, frank

"How blessed is the man to whom the Lord does not impute iniquity, and in whose spirit there is no deceit!" (Psalm 32:2)

"Keep your tongue from evil, and your lips from speaking deceit." (Psalm 34:13)

"Therefore, putting aside all malice and all guile and hypocrisy and envy and all slander, like newborn babes, long for the pure milk of the word..." (1 Peter 2:1-2)

"And do not participate in the unfruitful deeds of darkness, but instead even expose them; for it is disgraceful even to speak of the things which are done by them in secret. But all things become visible when they are exposed by the light, for everything that becomes visible is light." (Ephesians 5:11-13)

tranquil heart: 1) having a heart that is calm, quiet, peaceful; 2) trusting in God, spiritually equipped to meet life's trials

"A tranquil heart is life to the body, but passion is rottenness to the bones." (Proverbs 14:30)

"First of all, then, I urge that entreaties and prayers, petitions and thanksgivings, be made on behalf of all men... all who are in authority, in order that we may lead a tranquil and quiet life in all godliness and dignity." (1 Timothy 2:1-2)

"Search me, O God, and know my heart; try me and know my anxious thoughts; and see if there be any hurtful way in me, and lead me in the everlasting way." (Psalm 139:23-24)

transformed: 1) submitting to the Holy Spirit and God's Word to effect His sanctification in every area of our lives

"I urge you therefore, brethren, by the mercies of God, to present your bodies a living and holy sacrifice, acceptable to God, which is your spiritual service of worship. And do not be conformed to this world, but be transformed by the renewing of your mind, that you may prove what the will of God is, that which is good and acceptable and perfect." (Romans 12:1-2)

"But we all, with unveiled face beholding as in a mirror the glory of the Lord, are being transformed into the same image from glory to glory, just as from the Lord, the Spirit." (2 Corinthians 3:18)

"This book of the law shall not depart from your mouth, but you shall meditate on it day and night, so that you may be careful to do according to all that is written in it; for then you will make your way prosperous, and then you will have success." (Joshua 1:8)

travel mercies: 1) God's divine protection of His children, providing assurance and controlling circumstances, away from 'home'

"And the Lord was going before them in a pillar of cloud by day to lead them on the way, and in a pillar of fire by night to give them light, that they might travel by day and by night." (Exodus 13:21)

"Behold, I am going to send an angel before you to guard you along the way, and to bring you into the place which I have prepared." (Exodus 23:20)

"And behold, I am with you, and will keep you wherever you go…" (Genesis 28:15)

trials: 1) being tested or tempted, suffering; 2) God uses these trials to test our faith and produce endurance and build Christian character

"Consider it all joy, my brethren, when you encounter various trials, knowing that the testing of your faith produces endurance. And let endurance have its perfect result, that you may be perfect and complete, lacking in nothing." (James 1:2-4)

"In this you greatly rejoice, even though now for a little while, if necessary, you have been distressed by various trials, that the proof of your faith, being more precious than gold which is perishable, even though tested by fire, may be found to result in praise and glory and honor at the revelation of Jesus Christ." (1 Peter 1:6-7)

"Beloved, do not be surprised at the fiery ordeal among you, which comes upon you for your testing, as though some strange thing were happening to you; but to the degree that you share the sufferings of Christ, keep on rejoicing; so that also at the revelation of His glory, you may rejoice with exultation." (1 Peter 4:12-13)

tribulation: 1) persecution, times of severe affliction; 2) God uses these occasions to teach us perseverance and reconfirm His love

"... Through many tribulations we must enter the kingdom of God." (Acts 14:22)

"And not only this, but we also exult in our tribulations, knowing that tribulation brings about perseverance; and perseverance, proven character; and proven character, hope; and hope does not disappoint, because the love of God has been poured out within our hearts through the Holy Spirit who was given to us." (Romans 5: 3-5)

trouble: 1) the daily burdens of living in a fallen world; 2) believers should respond with trust in God and seeking His guidance

"God is our refuge and strength, a very present help in trouble." (Psalm 46:1)

"Because he who is blessed in the earth shall be blessed by the God of truth; and he who swears in the earth shall swear by the God of truth; because the former troubles are forgotten, and because they are hidden from My sight!" (Isaiah 65:16)

"How blessed is he who considers the helpless; The Lord will deliver him in a day of trouble." (Psalm 41:1)

"He will call upon Me, and I will answer him; I will be with him in trouble; I will rescue him, and honor him." (Psalm 91:15)

"Therefore do not be anxious for tomorrow; for tomorrow will care for itself. Each day has enough trouble of its own." (Matthew 6:34)

trust: 1) assurance of God's integrity, power and love; 2) We must exercise our faith to have the power to walk in His will and to overcome life's storms.

"Commit your way to the Lord, trust also in Him, and He will do it." (Psalm 37:5)

"Trust in the Lord with all your heart, and do not lean on your own understanding. In all your ways acknowledge Him, and He will make your paths straight." (Proverbs 3:5-6)

"Behold, God is my salvation, I will trust and not be afraid; for the Lord God is my strength and song, and He has become my salvation." (Isaiah 12:2)

trustworthy: 1) worthy of our trust or confidence; 2) God is worthy of all our praise because of the integrity of His holy character

"In this case, moreover, it is required of stewards that one be found trustworthy." (1 Corinthians 4:2)

"He who goes about as a talebearer reveals secrets, but he who is trustworthy conceals a matter." (Proverbs 11:13)

"Many a man proclaims his own loyalty, but who can find a trustworthy man?" (Proverbs 20:6)

"And he said unto him, Well, thou good servant: because thou hast been faithful in a very little, have thou authority over ten cities." (Luke 19:17 KJV)

truth: 1) God's Word, the eternal presentation of the Gospel, all that He reveals to His children

"Jesus therefore was saying to those Jews who had believed Him, "If you abide in My word, then you are truly disciples of Mine; and you shall know the truth, and the truth shall make you free." (John 8:31-32)

"But when He, the Spirit of truth, comes, He will guide you into all the truth; for He will not speak on His own initiative, but whatever He hears, He will speak; and He will disclose to you what is to come." (John 16:13)

"For the wrath of God is revealed from heaven against all ungodliness and righteousness of men, who suppress the truth in unrighteousness, because that which is known about God is evident within them; for God made it evident to them." (Romans 1:18-19)

U PRAYER CARDS

unbelief: 1) those who reject the Word of God and Jesus because of the hardness of their heart

"Take care, brethren, lest there should be in any one of you an evil, unbelieving heart, in falling away from the living God." (Hebrews 3:12)

"And even if our gospel is veiled, it is veiled to those who are perishing, in whose case the god of this world has blinded the minds of the unbelieving, that they might not see the light of the gospel of the glory of Christ, who is the image of God." (2 Corinthians 4:3-4)

unconditional love: 1) God's love for us even though we are sinners; 2) believers are called to the same kind of love, which is only possible because of the change He made in our hearts

"But God demonstrates His own love toward us, in that while we were yet sinners, Christ died for us." (Romans 5:8)

"(Love) bears all things, believes all things, hopes all things, endures all things." (1 Corinthians 13:7)

"But I say to you, love your enemies, and pray for those who persecute you..." (Matthew 5:44)

"(Love) does not act unbecomingly; it does not seek its own, is not provoked, does not take into account a wrong suffered" (1 Corinthians 13:5)

under His wings: 1) Jesus' description of how He desires to love and protect all people; 2) The Ark of the Covenant is a picture of God's love. It was placed in the Holy of Holies in the Temple and surrounded by cherubim wings, and the presence of the Lord was manifested by His Shekinah glory.

"May the Lord reward your work, and your wages be full from the lord, the God of Israel, under whose wings you have come to seek refuge." (Ruth 2:12)

"Let me dwell in Thy tent forever; let me take refuge in the shelter of Thy wings." (Psalm 61:4)

"O Jerusalem, Jerusalem, who kills the prophets and stones those who are sent to her! How often I wanted to gather your children together, the way a hen gathers her chicks under her wings, and you were unwilling." (Matthew 23:37)

understanding: 1) to discern the deep truths of God's Word and apply them accurately in our lives

"The unfolding of Thy words gives light; it gives understanding to the simple." (Psalm 119:130)

"Consider what I say, for the Lord will give you understanding in everything." (2 Timothy 2:7)

"For if you cry for discernment, lift your voice for understanding; if you seek her as silver, and search for her as for hidden treasures... the Lord gives wisdom; from His mouth come knowledge and understanding." (Proverbs 2:3-4, 6)

"Then He opened their minds to understand the Scriptures." (Luke 24:45)

unfaithful: 1) violating a trust or a promise; 2) rejecting God's Truth, scorning God's gift of forgiveness and eternal life

"Listen to the word of the Lord, O sons of Israel, for the Lord has a case against the inhabitants of the land, because there is no faithfulness or kindness or knowledge of God in the land." (Hosea 4:1)

"Thus I will make the land desolate, because they have acted unfaithfully,'" declares the Lord God." (Ezekiel 15:8)

"If they confess their iniquity and the iniquity of their forefathers, in their unfaithfulness which they committed against Me, and also in their acting with hostility against Me... then I will remember My covenant with Jacob, and I will remember also My covenant with Isaac, and My covenant with Abraham as well, and I will remember the land." (Leviticus 26:40, 42)

unforgiveness: 1) showing no mercy, not allowing for mistakes; 2) if we do not forgive others, God will not forgive us

"For if you forgive men for their transgressions, your heavenly Father will also forgive you. But if you do not forgive men, then your Father will not forgive your transgressions." (Matthew 6: 14-15)

"Be on your guard! If your brother sins, rebuke him; and if he repents, forgive him. And if he sins against you seven times a day, and returns to you seven times, saying, 'I repent,' forgive him." (Luke 17:3-4)

ungratefulness: 1) not appreciating the favors and blessings you receive, especially from God

"But realize this, in the last days difficult times will come. For men will be lovers of self, lovers of money, boastful, arrogant, revilers, disobedient to parents, ungrateful, unholy, unloving... treacherous, reckless, conceited, lovers of pleasure rather than lovers of God; holding to a form of godliness, although they have denied its power; and avoid such men as these." (2 Timothy 3:1-2, 4-5)

"And if we have food and covering, with these we shall be content." (1 Timothy 6:8)

"For even though they knew God, they did not honor Him as God, or give thanks; but they became futile in their speculations, and their foolish heart was darkened... Therefore God gave them over in the lusts of their hearts to impurity, that their bodies might be dishonored among them." (Romans 1:21, 24)

"Now one of them (the ten lepers) when he saw that he had been healed, turned back, glorifying God with a loud voice, and he fell on his face at His feet, giving thanks to Him, And he was a Samaritan. And Jesus answered and said, "Were there not ten cleansed? But the nine-- where are they? Was no one found who turned back to give glory to God, except this foreigner?" And He said to him, "Rise, and go your way; your faith has made you well." (Luke 17:15-19)

unity: 1) there is one faith, one God, one Church, and all believers are part of the same kingdom, eternally

"But the one who joins himself to the Lord is one spirit with Him." (1 Corinthians 6:17)

"but speaking the truth in love, we are to grow up in all aspects into Him, who is the head, even Christ, from whom the whole body, being fitted and held together by that which every joint supplies, according to the proper working of each individual part, causes the growth of the body for the building up of itself in love." (Ephesians 4:15-16)

"… walk in a manner worthy of the calling with which you have been called, with all humility and gentleness, with patience, showing forbearance to one another in love, being diligent to preserve the unity of the Spirit in the bond of peace." (Ephesians 4:1-3)

"And the congregation of those who believed were of one heart and soul; and not one of them claimed that anything belonging to him was his own; but all things were common property to them." (Acts 4:32)

"So then you are no longer strangers and aliens, but you are fellow citizens with the saints, and are of God's household, having been built upon the foundation of the apostles and prophets, Christ Jesus Himself being the corner stone, in whom the whole building, being fitted together is growing into a holy temple in the Lord; in whom you also are being built together into a dwelling of God in the Spirit." (Ephesians 2:19-22)

unrest: 1) trouble, discord, which can lead to strife, rebellion and spiritual corruption

"Hatred stirs up strife, but love covers all transgressions." (Proverbs 10:12)

"Through presumption comes nothing but strife, but with those who receive counsel is wisdom." (Proverbs 13:10)

"Drive out the scoffer, and contention will go out, even strife and dishonor will cease." (Proverbs 22:10)

"I rise before dawn and cry for help; I wait for Thy words. My eyes anticipate the night watches, that I may meditate on Thy word. Hear my voice according to Thy lovingkindness; revive me, O Lord, according to Thine ordinances." (Psalm 119:147-149)

upright: 1) honest, moral, Christ honoring, just

"For the Lord will not abandon His people, nor will He forsake His inheritance. For judgment will again be righteous; and all the upright in heart will follow it." (Psalm 94:14-15)

"For the Lord God is a sun and shield; The Lord gives grace and glory; no good thing does He withhold from those who walk uprightly." (Psalm 84:11)

"Guard my soul and deliver me; do not let me be ashamed, for I take refuge in Thee. Let integrity and uprightness preserve me, for I wait for Thee." (Psalm 25:20-21)

"He who walks in his uprightness fears the Lord, but he who is crooked in his ways despises Him." (Proverbs 14:2)

V PRAYER CARDS

vanity: 1) conceit over one's accomplishments; 2) pride, looking for human approval and craving respect in public; 3) self-sufficiency rather than dependence on God

"Vanity of vanities," says the Preacher, "Vanity of vanities! All is vanity." (Ecclesiastes 1:2)

"I have seen all the works which have been done under the sun, and behold, all is vanity and striving after wind." (Ecclesiastes 1:14)

"But they are altogether stupid and foolish in their discipline of delusion-- their idol is wood!" (Jeremiah 10:8)

"This I say therefore, and affirm together with the Lord, that you walk no longer just as the Gentiles also walk, in the futility of their mind, being darkened in their understanding, excluded from the life of God, because of the ignorance that is in them, because of the hardness of their heart." (Ephesians 4:17-18)

vessel: 1) possessing moral purity so that we can fulfill the role God has for us; 2) believers who are the recipients of God's mercy selected by Him to demonstrate His glory with their lives

"Therefore, if a man cleanses himself from these things, he will be a vessel for honor, sanctified, useful to the Master, prepared for every good work." (2 Timothy 2:21)

"What if God, although willing to demonstrate His wrath and to make His power known, endured with much patience vessels of wrath prepared for destruction? And He did so in order that He might make known the riches of His glory upon vessels of mercy, which He prepared beforehand for glory, even us, whom He also called, not from among Jews only, but also from among Gentiles." (Romans 9:22-24)

"For God, who said, "Light shall shine out of darkness," is the One who has shone in our hearts to give the light of the knowledge of the glory of God in the face of Christ. But we have this treasure in earthen vessels, that the surpassing greatness of the power may be of God and not from ourselves." (2 Corinthians 4:6-7)

"For this is the will of God, your sanctification; that is, that you abstain from sexual immorality; that each of you know how to possess his own vessel in sanctification and honor." (1 Thessalonians 4:3-4)

victory: 1) conquest, triumph, winning; 2) God has defeated Satan, sin, death, and hopelessness

"Submit therefore to God. Resist the devil and he will flee from you." (James 4:7)

"Where there is no guidance, the people fall, but in abundance of counselors there is victory." (Proverbs 11:14)

"Who shall separate us from the love of Christ? Shall tribulation, or distress, or persecution, or famine, or nakedness, or peril, or sword?... But in all these things we overwhelmingly conquer through Him who loved us." (Romans 8:35, 37)

"For whatever is born of God overcomes the world; and this is the victory that has overcome the world— our faith. And who is the one who overcomes the world, but he who believes that Jesus is the Son of God?" (1 John 5:4-5)

vindicate: 1) an attribute of God; to bring about justice; 2) to support, to defend, to avenge

"Let them shout for joy and rejoice, who favor my vindication; and let them say continually, "The Lord be magnified, Who delights in the prosperity of His servant." (Psalm 35:27)

"Vindicate me, O God, and plead my case against an ungodly nation; O deliver me from the deceitful and unjust man!" (Psalm 43:1)

"He who vindicates Me is near; who will contend with Me? Let us stand up to each other; who has a case against Me? Let him draw near to Me. Behold, the Lord God helps Me." (Isaiah 50:8-9)

virtue: 1) a quality, power, or capacity; excellence, merit

"Finally, brethren, whatever is true, whatever is honorable, whatever is right, whatever is pure, whatever is lovely, whatever is of good repute, if there is any excellence and if anything worthy of praise, let your mind dwell on these things." (Philippians 4:8)

"Now for this very reason also, applying all diligence, in your faith supply moral excellence, and in your moral excellence, knowledge; and in your knowledge, self-control, and in your self-control, perseverance, and in your perseverance, godliness; and in your godliness, brotherly kindness, and in your brotherly kindness, love." (2 Peter 1:5-7)

vision: 1) a dream from God; 2) spiritual sight or revelation of God's Truth; 3) miraculous perception of a future event

"Then Moses went up with Aaron, Nadab and Abihu, and seventy of the elders of Israel, and they saw the God of Israel; and under His feet there appeared to be a pavement of sapphire, as clear as the sky itself… Now the Lord said to Moses, "Come up to Me on the mountain and remain there, and I will give you the stone tablets with the law and the commandment which I have written for their instruction." (Exodus 24:9-10, 12)

"About the ninth hour of the day he clearly saw in a vision an angel of God who had just come in to him, and said to him, "Cornelius!" And fixing his gaze upon him and being much alarmed, he said, "What is it, Lord?" And he said to him, "Your prayers and alms have ascended as a memorial before God." And now dispatch some men to Joppa, and send for a man named Simon, who is also called Peter; he is staying with a certain tanner named Simon, whose house is by the sea." (Acts 10:3-6)

"I know a man in Christ who fourteen years ago-- whether in the body I do not know, or out of the body I do not know, God knows-- such a man was caught up to the third heaven. And… was caught up into Paradise, and heard inexpressible words, which a man is not permitted to speak." (2 Corinthians 12:2, 4)

W PRAYER CARDS

wait: 1) to rest in the Lord, trusting that the Lord will answer prayer and keep His promises in His perfect time

"For we through the Spirit, by faith, are waiting for the hope of righteousness." (Galatians 5:5)

"For our citizenship is in heaven, from which also we eagerly wait for a Savior, the Lord Jesus Christ." (Philippians 3:20)

"… walk in a manner worthy of the calling with which you have been called, with all humility and gentleness, with patience, showing forbearance to one another in love, being diligent to preserve the unity of the Spirit in the bond of peace… until we all attain to the unity of the faith, and of the knowledge of the Son of God, to a mature man, to the measure of the stature which belongs to the fullness of Christ." (Ephesians 4:1-3, 13)

walk: 1) practicing obedience, demonstrating a living faith

"Trust in the Lord with all your heart, and do not lean on your own understanding. In all your ways acknowledge Him, and He will make your paths straight." (Proverbs 3:5-6)

"And Enoch walked with God; and he was not, for God took him." (Genesis 5:24)

"If we say that we have fellowship with Him and yet walk in the darkness, we lie and do not practice the truth; but if we walk in the light as He Himself is in the light, we have fellowship with one another, and the blood of Jesus His Son cleanses us from all sin." (1 John 1:6-7)

walk by the Spirit: 1) believers following the guidance of the indwelling Holy Spirit rather than carrying out the deeds of the flesh

"If we live by the Spirit, let us also walk by the Spirit." (Galatians 5:25)

"But I say, walk by the Spirit, and you will not carry out the desire of the flesh." (Galatians 5:16)

"As you therefore have received Christ Jesus the Lord, so walk in Him, having been firmly rooted and now being built up in Him and established in your faith, just as you were instructed, and overflowing with gratitude." (Colossians 2:6-7)

walking in the light: 1) following the beacon of Christ's example, reflecting the Gospel to a dark world

"If we say that we have fellowship with Him and yet walk in the darkness, we lie and do not practice the truth; but if we walk in the light as He Himself is in the light, we have fellowship with one another, and the blood of Jesus His Son cleanses us from all sin." (1 John 1:6-7)

"The night is almost gone, and the day is at hand. Let us therefore lay aside the deeds of darkness and put on the armor of light." (Romans 13:12)

watchman: 1) warns others of coming judgment; 2) preaches a message of hope; 3) praying for spiritual protection from Satan's schemes for the saints

"With all prayer and petition pray at all times in the Spirit, and with this in view, be on the alert with all perseverance and petition for all the saints." (Ephesians 6:18)

"Be of sober spirit, be on the alert. Your adversary, the devil, prowls about like a roaring lion, seeking someone to devour." (1 Peter 5:8)

"And the word of the Lord came to me saying, Son of man, speak to the sons of your people, and say to them, 'If I bring a sword upon a land, and the people of the land take one man from among them and make him their watchman; and he sees the sword coming upon the land, and he blows on the trumpet and warns the people, then he who hears the sound of the trumpet and does not take warning, and a sword comes and takes him away, his blood will be on his own head." (Ezekiel 33:1-4)

weakness: 1) physical infirmity; 2) lack of moral strength; 3) teaches us to depend on God

"And because of the surpassing greatness of the revelations, for this reason, to keep me from exalting myself, there was given me a thorn in the flesh, a messenger of Satan to buffet me-- to keep me from exalting myself! Concerning this I entreated the Lord three times that it might depart from me. And He has said to me, "My grace is sufficient for you, for power is perfected in weakness." Most gladly, therefore, I will rather boast about my weaknesses, that the power of Christ may dwell in me. Therefore I am well content with weaknesses, with insults, with distresses, with persecutions, with difficulties, for Christ's sake; for when I am weak, then I am strong." (2 Corinthians 12:7-10)

"I can do all things through Him who strengthens me." (Philippians 4:13)

"For we do not have a high priest who cannot sympathize with our weaknesses, but One who has been tempted in all things as we are, yet without sin. Let us therefore draw near with confidence to the throne of grace, that we may receive mercy and may find grace to help in time of need." (Hebrews 4:15-16)

wholeness: 1) physical health; 2) spiritual maturity; 3) God has the power to provide both

"For in Him all the fulness of Deity dwells in bodily form, and in Him you have been made complete, and He is the head over all rule and authority." (Colossians 2:9-10)

"Now may the God of peace Himself sanctify you entirely; and may your spirit and soul and body be preserved complete, without blame at the coming of our Lord Jesus Christ." (1 Thessalonians 5:23)

"Therefore you are to be perfect, as your heavenly Father is perfect." (Matthew 5:48)

(godly) wife: 1) helper; 2) virtuous, God-fearing; 3) a wife who shows her husband the same self-giving love that Christ shows the Church

"An excellent wife, who can find? For her worth is far above jewels. The heart of her husband trusts in her, and he will have no lack of gain." (Proverbs 31:10-11)

"In the same way, you wives, be submissive to your own husbands so that even if any of them are disobedient to the word, they may be won without a word by the behavior of their wives, as they observe your chaste and respectful behavior... but let it be the hidden person of the heart, with the imperishable quality of a gentle and quiet spirit, which is precious in the sight of God." (1 Peter 3:1-2, 4)

willfulness: 1) refusal to repent and follow Christ; 2) obstinate, stubborn, determined to have one's own way

"A man who hardens his neck after much reproof will suddenly be broken beyond remedy." (Proverbs 29:1)

"But because of your stubbornness and unrepentant heart you are storing up wrath for yourself in the day of wrath and revelation of the righteous judgment of God." (Romans 2:5)

will of God: 1) that which conforms to God's perfect purpose; 2) the fulfillment of all His prophecies

"And (Jesus) went a little beyond them, and fell on His face and prayed, saying, "My Father, if it is possible, let this cup pass from Me; yet not as I will, but as Thou wilt." (Matthew 26:39)

"for it is God who is at work in you, both to will and to work for His good pleasure." (Philippians 2:13)

"Teach me to do Thy will, for Thou art my God; let Thy good Spirit lead me on level ground." (Psalm 143:10)

"Thy kingdom come. Thy will be done, on earth as it is in heaven." (Matthew 6:10)

"And do not be conformed to this world, but be transformed by the renewing of your mind, that you may prove what the will of God is, that which is good and acceptable and perfect." (Romans 12:2)

willing: 1) following God's guidance with a cheerful obedient heart

"As for you, my son Solomon, know the God of your father, and serve Him with a whole heart and a willing mind; for the Lord searches all hearts, and understands every intent of the thoughts. If you seek Him, He will let you find Him; but if you forsake Him, He will reject you forever." (1 Chronicles 28:9)

"Restore to me the joy of Thy salvation, and sustain me with a willing spirit." (Psalm 51:12)

"Keep watching and praying, that you may not enter into temptation; the spirit is willing, but the flesh is weak." (Matthew 26:41)

winking: 1) to close and open the eye quickly; 2) implies scorn, taking some serious lightly

"He who winks the eye causes trouble… " (Proverbs 10:10)

"Do not let those who are wrongfully my enemies rejoice over me; either let those who hate me without cause wink maliciously." (Psalm 35:19)

"A worthless person, a wicked man, is the one who walks with a false mouth, who winks with his eyes, who signals with his feet, who points with his fingers; who with perversity in his heart devises evil continually, who spreads strife." (Proverbs 6:12-14)

wisdom: 1) acquired knowledge, discernment; 2) accurately applying Scriptural truth to your situation; 3) access to the mind of God through prayer and Bible Study

"For the Lord gives wisdom; from His mouth come knowledge and understanding. He stores up sound wisdom for the upright; He is a shield to those who walk in integrity." (Proverbs 2:6-7)

"that the God of our Lord Jesus Christ, the Father of glory, may give to you a spirit of wisdom and of revelation in the knowledge of Him." (Ephesians 1:17)

"But if any of you lacks wisdom, let him ask of God, who gives to all men generously and without reproach, and it will be given to him." (James 1:5)

"But the wisdom from above is first pure, then peaceable, gentle, reasonable, full of mercy and good fruits, unwavering, without hypocrisy." (James 3:17)

"My son, let them not depart from your sight; keep sound wisdom and discretion, so they will be life to your soul, and adornment to your neck." (Proverbs 3:21-22)

witchcraft: 1) practicing the powers of evil, including the occult and fortune telling, satanic form of rebellion; 2) strictly forbidden by God, worthy of death

"There shall not be found among you anyone who makes his son or his daughter pass through the fire, one who uses divination, one who practices witchcraft, or one who interprets omens, or a sorcerer, or one who casts a spell, or a medium, or a spiritist, or one who calls up the dead. For whoever does these things is detestable to the Lord; and because of these detestable things the Lord your God will drive them out before you. You shall be blameless before the Lord your God." (Deuteronomy 18:10-13)

witness: 1) testifying to a fact or an event, furnishing evidence; 2) Christians are called to testify to the reality of the kingdom of God and the Gospel, according to power of God in their own lives

"but you shall receive power when the Holy Spirit has come upon you; and you shall be My witnesses both in Jerusalem, and in all Judea and Samaria, and even to the remotest part of the earth." (Acts 1:8)

"For the promise is for you and your children, and for all who are far off, as many as the Lord our God shall call to Himself. And with many other words he solemnly testified and kept on exhorting them, saying, "Be saved from this perverse generation!" (Acts 2:39-40)

"... Paul began devoting himself completely to the word, solemnly testifying to the Jews that Jesus was the Christ." (Acts 18:5)

"In the same way, you wives, be submissive to your own husbands so that even if any of them are disobedient to the word, they may be won without a word by the behavior of their wives" (1 Peter 3:1)

wolves: 1) false prophets and teachers who attempt to sow Satan's lies among believers, trying to destroy the Church from within; 2) masquerade as sheep, as fellow believers

"Beware of the false prophets, who come to you in sheep's clothing, but inwardly are ravenous wolves. You will know them by their fruits... " (Matthew 7:15-16)

"Behold, I send you out as sheep in the midst of wolves; therefore be shrewd as serpents, and innocent as doves." (Matthew 10:16)

"Be on guard for yourselves and for all the flock . . . I know that after my departure savage wolves will come in among you, not sparing the flock; and from among your own selves men will arise, speaking perverse things, to draw away the disciples after them. Therefore be on the alert... " (Acts 20:28-31)

Word: 1) God's message to His children, the mind of God revealed; 2) also Christ, the Logos, the Scriptures come in the flesh to communicate the will of God to us; 3) powerful, without error, living, and life-transforming

"With all my heart I have sought Thee; do not let me wander from Thy commandments. Thy word I have treasured in my heart, that I may not sin against Thee." (Psalm 119:10-11)

"And the Word became flesh, and dwelt among us, and we beheld His glory, glory as of the only begotten from the Father, full of grace and truth." (John 1:14)

"Open my eyes, that I may behold wonderful things from Thy law." (Psalm 119:18)

"Teach me good discernment and knowledge, for I believe in Thy commandments." (Psalm 119:66)

"All Scripture is inspired by God and profitable for teaching, for reproof, for correction, for training in righteousness; that the man of God may be adequate, equipped for every good work." (2 Timothy 3:16-17)

"For the word of God is living and active and sharper than any two-edged sword, and piercing as far as the division of soul and spirit, of both joints and marrow, and able to judge the thoughts and intentions of the heart." (Hebrews 4:12)

"So shall My word be which goes forth from My mouth; it shall not return to Me empty, without accomplishing what I desire, and without succeeding in the matter for which I sent it." (Isaiah 55:11)

(handling the) Word: 1) proclaiming, explaining and applying the Word of God accurately

"Be diligent to present yourself approved to God as a workman who does not need to be ashamed, handling accurately the word of truth." (2 Timothy 2:15)

"In the exercise of His will He brought us forth by the word of truth, so that we might be, as it were, the first fruits among His creatures." (James 1:18)

(idle words): 1) using many words which have no importance and do not glorify God

"And I say to you, that every careless word that men shall speak, they shall render account for it in the day of judgment. For by your words you shall be justified, and by your words you shall be condemned." (Matthew 12:36-37)

"But avoid worldly and empty chatter, for it will lead to further ungodliness, and their talk will spread like gangrene... (2 Timothy 2:16-17)

"Let no unwholesome word proceed from your mouth, but only such a word as is good for edification according to the need of the moment, that it may give grace to those who hear." (Ephesians 4:29)

word of knowledge: 1) a supernatural revelation from God about the future, a present circumstance, or as a warning against Satan's deceptions; a spiritual gift

"For to one is given the word of wisdom through the Spirit, and to another the word of knowledge according to the same Spirit." (1 Corinthians 12:8)

word of wisdom: 1) a special message of wisdom from the Holy Spirit especially to those facing adversaries or persecution, a spiritual gift

"For to one is given the word of wisdom through the Spirit, and to another the word of knowledge according to the same Spirit." (1 Corinthians 12:8)

workers: 1) disciples of Christ who warn the people of coming judgment and call them to repentance

"Then He said to His disciples, "The harvest is plentiful, but the workers are few. Therefore beseech the Lord of the harvest to send out workers into His harvest." (Matthew 9:37-38)

works: 1) deeds performed to glorify God and advance the Gospel and as a witness to others

"Truly, truly, I say to you, he who believes in Me, the works that I do shall he do also; and greater works than these shall he do; because I go to the Father." (John 14:12)

"Let your light shine before men in such a way that they may see your good works, and glorify your Father who is in heaven." (Matthew 5:16)

"For we are His workmanship, created in Christ Jesus for good works, which God prepared beforehand, that we should walk in them." (Ephesians 2:10)

"For this reason also, since the day we heard of it, we have not ceased to pray for you and to ask that you may be filled with the knowledge of His will in all spiritual wisdom and understanding, so that you may walk in a manner worthy of the Lord, to please Him in all respects, bearing fruit in every good work and increasing in the knowledge of God." (Colossians 1:9-10)

"Whatever you do, do your work heartily, as for the Lord rather than for men; knowing that from the Lord you will receive the reward of the inheritance. It is the Lord Christ whom you serve." (Colossians 3:23-24)

"For just as the body without the spirit is dead, so also faith without works is dead." (James 2:26)

works of the flesh: 1) sinful acts, thoughts and behavior of non-believers or carnal Christians; 2) deeds performed to bring glory to ourselves, or to try to earn our way into heaven

"nevertheless knowing that a man is not justified by the works of the Law but through faith in Christ Jesus, even we have believed in Christ Jesus, that we may be justified by faith in Christ, and not by the works of the Law; since by the works of the Law shall no flesh be justified." (Galatians 2:16)

"Therefore leaving the elementary teaching about the Christ, let us press on to maturity, not laying again a foundation of repentance from dead works and of faith toward God." (Hebrews 6:1)

"For if the blood of goats and bulls and the ashes of a heifer sprinkling those who have been defiled, sanctify for the cleansing of the flesh, how much more will the blood of Christ, who through the eternal Spirit offered Himself without blemish to God, cleanse your conscience from dead works to serve the living God?" (Hebrews 9:13-14)

"When therefore you give alms, do not sound a trumpet before you, as the hypocrites do in the synagogues and in the streets, that they may be honored by men. Truly I say to you, they have their reward in full." (Matthew 6:2)

"and those who are in the flesh cannot please God. However, you are not in the flesh but in the Spirit, if indeed the Spirit of God dwells in you. But if anyone does not have the Spirit of Christ, he does not belong to Him." (Romans 8:8-9)

worldliness: 1) attitudes of the heart, sinful desires such as pride and lust; 2) focusing on the world and not on the will of God; 3) trying to live with one foot in the world and one foot in the kingdom of heaven

"Do not love the world, nor the things in the world. If anyone loves the world, the love of the Father is not in him. For all that is in the world, the lust of the flesh and the lust of the eyes and the boastful pride of life, is not from the Father, but is from the world. And the world is passing away, and also its lusts; but the one who does the will of God abides forever" (1 John 2:15-17)

"You adulteresses, do you not know that friendship with the world is hostility toward God? Therefore whoever wishes to be a friend of the world makes himself an enemy of God." (James 4:4)

worry: 1) lack of faith, not trusting God to answer prayer and meet needs; 2) fear of the unknown, forgetting that our God is in control

"For this reason I say to you, do not be anxious for your life, as to what you shall eat, or what you shall drink; nor for your body, as to what you shall put on. Is not life more than food, and the body than clothing? Look at the birds of the air, that they do not sow, neither do they reap, nor gather into barns, and yet your heavenly Father feeds them. Are you not worth much more than they?" (Matthew 6:25-26)

"Do not be anxious then, saying, 'What shall we eat?' or 'What shall we drink?' or 'With what shall we clothe ourselves?' For all these things the Gentiles eagerly seek; for your heavenly Father knows that you need all these things. But seek first His kingdom and His righteousness; and all these things shall be added to you. Therefore do not be anxious for tomorrow; for tomorrow will care for itself. Each day has enough trouble of its own." (Matthew 6:31-34)

worship: 1) giving God glory for His holy attributes; 2) recognizing God's power and giving Him all the honor; 3) the personal response to a loving relationship with our Father, an attitude of joy and devotion, bowing down before Him in awe

"But an hour is coming, and now is, when the true worshipers shall worship the Father in spirit and truth; for such people the Father seeks to be His worshipers. God is spirit, and those who worship Him must worship in spirit and truth." (John 4:23-24)

"Worship the Lord in holy attire; tremble before Him, all the earth." (Psalm 96:9)

"Be glad in the Lord, you righteous ones; and give thanks to His holy name." (Psalm 97:12)

"and he said with a loud voice, "Fear God, and give Him glory, because the hour of His judgment has come; and worship Him who made the heaven and the earth and sea and springs of waters." (Revelation 14:7)

wounded spirit: 1) experiencing hate, rejection and conflict for following Jesus; 2) persecution within the church for radical obedience

"Blessed are the poor in spirit, for theirs is the kingdom of heaven." (Matthew 5:3)

"Blessed are you when men hate you, and ostracize you, and cast insults at you, and spurn your name as evil, for the sake of the Son of Man. Be glad in that day, and leap for joy, for behold, your reward is great in heaven; for in the same way their fathers used to treat the prophets." (Luke 6:22-23)

wrath: 1) violent anger, personal indignation; 2) God's terrible judgment of sin and rebellion, including earthquakes, fire, and eternal damnation; 3) Christians will not face God's destructive wrath

"A jealous and avenging God is the Lord; The Lord is avenging and wrathful. The Lord takes vengeance on His adversaries, and He reserves wrath for His enemies." (Nahum 1:2).

"Never take your own revenge, beloved, but leave room for the wrath of God, for it is written, "Vengeance is Mine, I will repay," says the Lord" (Romans 12:19).

"Wherefore, my beloved brethren, let every man be swift to hear, slow to speak, slow to wrath: for the wrath of man worketh not the righteousness of God." (James 1:19-20 KJV)

"A gentle answer turns away wrath, but a harsh word stirs up anger." (Proverbs 15:1)

Y PRAYER CARDS

yield: 1) submitting to the leading of the Holy Spirit; 2) giving up personal control

"Therefore putting aside all filthiness and all that remains of wickedness, in humility receive the word implanted, which is able to save your souls." (James 1:21)

"All discipline for the moment seems not to be joyful, but sorrowful; yet to those who have been trained by it, afterwards it yields the peaceful fruit of righteousness." (Hebrews 12:11)

"Neither yield ye your members as instruments of unrighteousness unto sin: but yield yourselves unto God, as those that are alive from the dead, and your members as instruments of righteousness unto God." (Romans 6:13 KJV)

"I speak after the manner of men because of the infirmity of your flesh: for as ye have yielded your members servants to uncleanness and to iniquity unto iniquity; even so now yield your members servants to righteousness unto holiness." (Romans 6:19 KJV)

Z PRAYER CARDS

zeal: 1) passion, enthusiasm, eagerness

"For the eyes of the Lord are upon the righteous, and His ears attend to their prayer, but the face of the Lord is against those who do evil. And who is there to harm you if you prove zealous for what is good?" (1 Peter 3:12-13)

"And He made a scourge of cords, and drove them all out of the temple, with the sheep and the oxen; and He poured out the coins of the moneychangers, and overturned their tables; and to those who were selling the doves He said, "Take these things away; stop making My Father's house a house of merchandise." His disciples remembered that it was written, "Zeal for Thy house will consume me." (John 2:15-17)

"… Christ Jesus; who gave Himself for us, that He might redeem us from every lawless deed and purify for Himself a people for His own possession, zealous for good deeds." (Titus 2:13-14)

ABOUT THE AUTHOR

Gail Appel resides in Chattanooga, Tennessee with her husband Buddy. They traded the snow of upstate New York for retirement in the Bible Belt in 1994, where both have been active in church life ever since. Gail is a former Christian Preschool owner and Emergency Medical Technician who became a born-again Christian in August of 1978.

Using her research skills developed while obtaining her B.S. in Anthropology at the State University of New York at Brockport in 1974, she quickly became an avid Bible student. She identifies herself as a Berean (Acts 17:11) and believes that Christianity is meant to be Radical.

Gail has been blessed with the opportunity to serve the Lord in many capacities since her retirement, as a Children's Sunday School Teacher, short-term missionary, tutor, mentor, choir and orchestra member, Women's Group facilitator, and currently co-teaches the Silver Saints Senior Bible Study Class with her husband at Silverdale Baptist Church in Chattanooga.

She has a passion for Bible Study, prayer, praise and learning to walk in obedience and believes that Christians are meant to be bond-servants of the Lord Jesus Christ as long as they have breath. The Prayer Warrior project is a labor of love spanning 20 years of creating Prayer Cards. This is her first attempt at writing a book, but with God's help and your support may not be the last!

Gail's email address is gailappel@epbfi.com

She would love to hear your comments and suggestions.

ENDNOTES

Preface

1 Tada, Joni Eareckson. *Joni.* 1976.

Chapter 1 Praying Without Ceasing

2 Bounds, E. M. "Christian Classics Ethereal Library" Website. *Purpose in Prayer.* June 11, 2013.

Chapter 3 Effective Prayer

3 Murray, Andrew. *With Christ in the School of Prayer.* Andrew Murray on Prayer. Whitaker House, New Kensington, PA. 1998.

Chapter 5

4 Muller, George. *George Muller Man of Faith and Miracles.* Bethany House Publishers. Ada, MI. 1972.

Chapter 7 God's Creativity

5 ten Boom, Corrie. *Tramp for the Lord.* Jove. New York, NY. 1982.

6 Ibid.

7 *365-Day Reading Plan Key Selections from the Bible.* encounterparents.files.wordpress.com. June 12, 2013.

Chapter 9 Praying For Myself

8   Walvoord, John F. and Roy B. Zuck. *The Bible Knowledge Commentary.* Chariot Victor Publishing. Colorado Springs, CO. 1983.

Chapter 10 Family Matters

9   *National Association of Marriage Enhancement.* The Couple That Prays Together. drstoop.com. June 12, 2013.

Chapter 13 Praying For Our Nation

10   Rushnell, Squire. *When God Winks.* Pocket Books. New York, NY. 2002.
11   Cline, Austin. *In God We Trust- Trusting in God as a National Motto.*atheism.about.com. June 13, 2013.
12   *One Nation Under God.* nytimes.com. 2002/06/27.
13   de Tocqueville, Alex. Thinkexist.com. June 13, 2013.
14   Ibid.
15   Nee, Watchman. *Spiritual Man.* Living Stream Ministry. Anaheim, CA. 1992.
16   Fogel, Robert. *The Phases of the Four Great Awakenings.*press. uchicago.edu. June 13, 2013.
17   Berlin, Irving. *God Bless America.* Irving Berlin Music. A Division of Williamson Music. 1918. Revised in 1938.

Chapter 14 Praying For the World

18   Walesa, Lech. *Mothers of Influence.* p. 35 Honor Books. Cook Communications Ministries. Colorado Springs, CO. 2005.
19   Ibid. p. 36.
20   Reagan, Ronald. *Brandenburg Gate Speech.* Berlin, Germany. June 12, 1987.

Chapter 15 Spiritual Warfare and Prayer

21   *1 & 2 Corinthians, Life Application Bible Commentary.* The Livingstone Corporation. Tyndale House Publishers, Inc. Wheaton, IL. 1999.

22   Ibid.

Chapter 16 Why Does Jesus Pray?

23   Cole, Steven, *The Kind of Priest You Need,* Bible.org, May 20, 2013.

24   Ibid.

Chapter 17 Writing Prayer Cards

25   Dictionary.com. June 17, 2013.

26   Google.com. June 17, 2013.

27   E-Sword.net. June 17, 2013.

28   the Word.net. June 17, 2013.

29   WordsearchBibleBasic.com. June 17, 2013.

30   QuickVerse 10. Wordsearchbible.com. January 17, 2014.

31   Brand, Chad, Charles Draper, Archie England, eds. *Holman Illustrated Bible Dictionary.* Holman Reference. Nashville, TN. 2003.

32   Unger, Merrill. *New Unger's Bible Dictionary.* WORDsearch Corp. 2003.

33   Easton, Matthew George. *Easton's Illustrated Dictionary.* WORDsearch Corp. 2008.

34   Fleming, Don. *Easton's Concise Bible Dictionary.* WORDsearch Corp. 2007.

35   *Holman Illustrated Bible Dictionary.* Holman Reference. Nashville, TN. 2003.

36   *Life Application Bible Notes.* Tyndale House Publishers. Carol Stream, IL. 1988.

37 VanDruff, Dean and Laura VanDruff. *God's Wrath*. Acts 17-11 Bible Studies.com. June 17, 2013.

38 Ibid.

39 *NASB Topical*. WORDsearch Corp. 2007.

40 Nave, Orville. *Nave's Topics*. WORDsearch Corp. 2008.

41 *New American Standard Bible*. 1977. (see Copyright Page)

42 *Zondervan NASB Exhaustive Concordance*. Zondervan Publishing. Grand Rapids, MI. 2000.

43 Strong, James. *Strong's Comprehensive Concordance of the Bible*. World Publishing. Grand Rapids. MI.

44 Day, A. Colin. *Roget's Thesaurus of the Bible*. Harper. San Francisco. CA. 1992.

45 Ibid. p. 926.

46 Ibid. p. 622.

47 Ibid. p. 625.

48 Taylor, Howard. *Borden of Yale*. Men of Faith. Mountain Twilight Book.

49 Garrison, David. *Church Planting Movements: The Next Wave*. Fall, 2004.

50 The Prayer Card definitions are paraphrased by the author using the following sources:

> *Life Application Bible Commentary*, Tyndale House Publishers, Inc., Wheaton, Illinois, 1999.
> *Life Application Bible Notes*, Tyndale House Publishers, Inc., Wheaton, Illinois, 1991.
> *Webster's Revised Unabridged Dictionary*, 1913.mshaffer. com.Public Domain.

CPSIA information can be obtained at www.ICGtesting.com
Printed in the USA
LVOW13s0009030414

380041LV00003B/4/P

9 781462 735563